"Wallis offers us a prophetic call to remember more truthfully. Tracing how race has been an integral part of America's history, its 'original sin,' he names the ways white supremacy was present in America's birth and continues to be present in the realities of police brutality, the criminal justice system, and educational inequality. This truthful telling is essential to our calling as Christians. . . . Wallis's book offers a beautiful starting point for white people who are beginning the journey, who do not yet understand the historical realities of race in America and their relationship to contemporary injustices. . . . [It is a call] to conversion, to actions that begin with the individual, move into the world, and stand in the face of systems that oppress."

—**Brian Bantum**, *The Christian Century*

"*America's Original Sin* addresses topics that have been central to [Wallis's] life and work for the past forty years. These same issues of race and racism are also central to our contemporary national story; that combination makes this one of Wallis's best efforts. . . . This book is a concise and focused primer for all Christians, but especially for white evangelicals who are reading the signs of the times and struggling to discern how to respond."

—**Ric Hudgens**, *Englewood Review of Books*

"In the face of the implicit and often unconscious structures of racism, 'it's time for white Christians to be more Christian than white,' says Jim Wallis. If you don't understand this quote—or if you do—read *America's Original Sin*. Wallis unpacks for white Americans how we lost our souls, and he maps out the road of repentance to systemic and personal racial healing."

—**Sharon E. Watkins**, general minister and president, Christian Church (Disciples of Christ)

"Jim Wallis has grasped with amazing clarity and insight the persistent pain and sin of racism in America. In *America's Original Sin* we have not only a recounting of the pain of racism and xenophobia but also a hope-filled cartography for a new, reconciled reality. As a Latino evangelical, I have found in Jim Wallis a key ally and fellow visionary for a racially reconciled America."

—**Rev. Dr. Gabriel Salguero**, president, National Latino Evangelical Coalition; pastor, Lamb's Church

"Jim Wallis is a clarion voice our nation desperately needs right now, especially the parents and grandparents raising our next generation of children. *Only the truth will set us free.*"

—**Marian Wright Edelman**, president, Children's Defense Fund

"Jim Wallis is a visionary veteran in the struggle against white supremacy. In this powerful book, he calls for a new conversation and action on the ground—in our

homes, churches, sports arenas, and schools—in order to be true to the best of who we are!"

—**Cornel West**, Union Theological Seminary; author of *Race Matters*

"Every so often a leader addresses the pressing crisis of his or her day with the clarity, passion, and conviction that offers not only critique but hope that can only be forged in the trenches of faithful struggle and engagement. Jim Wallis has done just that by confronting the injustice of racism in our nation."

—**Noel Castellanos**, CEO and president, Christian Community Development Association (CCDA)

"We will not get better as a country until we face the sin we've inherited, the sin that continues to wound our brothers and sisters. This book can help us build a better nation by facing the terrible truth of our self-centeredness and the wonderful truth of God's ongoing, redeeming love."

—**Joel C. Hunter**, senior pastor, Northland—A Church Distributed

"I am so grateful for Jim Wallis's new book. Racism is a sickness that is as old as America itself. *America's Original Sin* helps us see how this sickness creates patterns and systems that perpetuate national tragedies such as the one at Mother Emanuel AME Church. Jim gently and passionately invites us to look inside ourselves and acknowledge the ways that pride, privilege, and resentment affect our actions and words, and then he courageously extends a hand for us to walk together into a new future. As an African American man and a fellow brother in Christ, I trust Jim's offer in this powerful book, and extend my hand in return."

—**Joshua DuBois**, author of *The President's Devotional*; former director of the White House Office of Faith-Based and Neighborhood Partnerships under President Barack Obama

"Can we calculate the heartbreak, the destroyed families, the broken lives, the jobs denied, the inferior educations, the anger and hatred, the division, the laws meant to segregate or incarcerate, the lengths people go to avoid one another, or the number of deaths due to racism? The pain created by racism is huge, it's massive, and it needs to end—now. In this powerful book, Jim Wallis outlines the path forward, a path of true repentance and one that moves us in a new direction, as a new people. In the land of opportunity and hope, it can be done. With clarity and wisdom, this book shows us how."

—**Michael O. Emerson**, provost, North Park University; coauthor of *Transcending Racial Barriers*

"Jim Wallis takes on the defining challenge not only of our current cultural moment but also of our entire American history. By laying out a bold, prophetic message of hope, Jim calls for the change we need in a society suffering from the deep and open wounds of white supremacy."

—**Serene Jones**, president, Union Theological Seminary

"*America's Original Sin* confirms Jim Wallis's standing as one of America's foremost prophets and greatest truth tellers. This brilliantly argued, eloquently written, and passionately delivered analysis of the most stubborn feature of our national existence—the yawning chasm of race and the bitter divide of racism—forces us to confront both systemic inequities and individual habits that mock our claim to be the greatest democracy in the world. This book echoes the Old Testament prophet Amos and the American prophet Martin Luther King Jr. in calling for justice and righteousness to cleanse our country from the sin of racism that to this day stains our collective soul."

—**Michael Eric Dyson**, author of *The Black Presidency: Barack Obama and the Politics of Race in America*

"Jim Wallis is calling America to sincerely address the potholes of injustice that have damaged the undercarriage of justice in America. Civil and human rights are once again caught up in a traffic jam with racial profiling, police brutality, 'stand your ground' laws, poor public education, the lack of a living wage, and the school-to-prison pipeline. Wallis helps us see that this is more than a discussion of polity and praxis; this is a critical issue for people of faith in the sanctuary, the synagogue, and the temple."

—**Bishop Vashti Murphy McKenzie**, 10th Episcopal District, African Methodist Episcopal Church (AME)

"Jim Wallis loves Jesus and hates racial injustice. This gifted gospel preacher has written *America's Original Sin* with prophetic courage and pastoral care. In the tradition of Harriet Beecher Stowe, he uses his remarkable literary skills and searing analysis to force our not-yet-United States to look into the mirror of reality and confront the ugly wound of racism and white supremacy. This book may be the match that lights the fire of a redemptive revolution that makes America truly 'one nation under God, with liberty and justice for *all*.'"

—**Frederick Douglass Haynes III**, senior pastor, Friendship-West Baptist Church, Dallas, Texas; board chairman, Samuel DeWitt Proctor Conference

"*America's Original Sin* is both unsparing and sympathetic in its brilliant analysis of how racism and white privilege have shaped and disabled American society throughout history—and how they do so today. But Jim Wallis goes much further than tracing how the scourge of racism harms citizens and immigrants of color. This book is a call to action packed with practical and powerful lessons and solutions that individuals, churches, and community organizations can follow to create a new and just social contract for the country we love."

—**Eliseo V. Medina**, labor activist and immigration reform advocate

"Jim Wallis has a fire in his bones and cannot be silenced. In this landmark book, he takes on one of the most important issues of our age, America's original sin—racism. But this isn't a rant. It is a thoughtful, heartfelt, compassionate plea for us to heal the wounds of racial injustice and build a new America, and a new world, together."

—**Shane Claiborne**, author, activist, and founder of The Simple Way and
Red Letter Christians, www.redletterchristians.org

"We stand at a critical juncture in our nation's history, as the United States becomes a nation with no clear ethnic majority. Our future could be characterized by great unity or by great discord. Jim Wallis engages in the kind of truth telling that is necessary to move toward a more hopeful future. Revealing the depth of sin endemic in our racialized history, Wallis names not only the symptoms but also the disease. The book is difficult to read at times. But truth does not come easily. Please embrace the truths that are found in this text so that our conversations on race may begin to move us forward."

—**Soong-Chan Rah**, North Park Theological Seminary; author of
Prophetic Lament: A Call for Justice in Troubled Times

"Jim Wallis makes a convincing argument that honestly confronting the sins of our past does not paralyze us but rather compels us to act with moral urgency. His book is simultaneously a sermon of hope and repentance and a practical guide for making real and positive change, based in the gospel lessons of empathy and social responsibility. A work of both splendid critical analysis and profound faith."

—**Darren Walker**, president, Ford Foundation

"Jim Wallis has been a fighter for economic and racial justice for decades. Now this activist par excellence has written a brilliant, passionate exploration of racism and the surprisingly pervasive reality of white supremacist sensibilities in America and how they keep our nation divided. Wallis's purpose is not to indict but to chart a path to true community. This is a book that all Americans should read and ponder deeply, both those who acknowledge the reality of white privilege and those who do not."

—**Obery M. Hendricks Jr.**, The Institute for Research in African American
Studies (IRAAS), Columbia University

"In 1903, in *The Souls of Black Folk*, W. E. B. Du Bois engaged the questions of race, racial domination, and racial exploitation with the well-known proposition that 'the problem of the twentieth century is the problem of the color-line.' In *America's Original Sin*, Jim Wallis affirms that racism remains a primary problem in the twenty-first century. As a white, male Christian, Wallis lovingly but persuasively appeals to fellow white Americans of all faiths to reflect on this painful truth, repent of white privilege, and help build a bridge to a new America. It is a must-read for all who seek the healing of the soul of America."

—**Barbara Williams-Skinner**, president, Skinner Leadership Institute;
cochair, National African American Clergy Network

"Jim Wallis's latest book is a masterpiece that pulls readers into a conversation that the church and society have needed for decades. Jim has committed his life to correcting and eradicating ignorance, stereotypes, and biases, and he speaks with prophetic power and authority. He has witnessed countless examples of the double standards that exist in America and the world. He has questioned the church's silence on the evil acts of the racial divide. This book calls us to acknowledge, identify, and put away our prejudices, and challenges us to have honest discussions to end the biases and crimes against people of color."

—**Bishop Carroll A. Baltimore**, president emeritus,
Progressive National Baptist Convention, Inc. (PNBC)

"Jim Wallis continues to write, build, lead, and serve for common ground that leads to higher ground. Everyone who reads this book will grow wiser and stronger."

—**Rev. Otis Moss Jr.**, theologian, pastor, and civic leader

"Part theological treatise, part policy paper, *America's Original Sin* critically assesses and proposes solutions to some of our country's most pressing issues while offering tools for racial healing to every citizen of faith and good conscience. Jim Wallis calls our nation to a time of truth telling, storytelling, and action as faithful responses to a dark past and challenging present. While the book will be controversial to some, by treating racism as sin—not merely a social or political problem—Wallis opens the door of hope and redemption that is unlocked by true repentance, renunciation (of Whiteness), and restorative practices."

—**Rev. Starsky D. Wilson**, cochair, The Ferguson Commission; pastor,
Saint John's Church; president and CEO, Deaconess Foundation

"In classic Jim Wallis style, he speaks a powerful prophetic word about one of the most critical issues at this moment in time. Jim not only provides biblical insights but also calls for an action plan that requires transformative leadership. This book should be read and used as a road map for change. Its insightful biblical principles are applicable both in the USA and around the world."

—**Geoff Tunnicliffe**, chairman, Christian Media Corporation;
former secretary general, World Evangelical Alliance

"Jim Wallis's life and message have resonated with me for years because of his undying desire to overturn racial injustice in America. Read this book not because you must. Read it because together we are compelled to set right the path toward our country's promise of greatness as a diverse people who must treat one another in a gracist manner, not a racist one. I commend to you Wallis's message of hard truth with practical help toward a better future."

—**David Anderson**, talk show host and author of *Gracism: The Art of Inclusion*

"With prophetic vision, incisive analysis, and moral grounding in a paradigm of sin and repentance, Jim Wallis's deconstruction of racism and white privilege is a clarion call to twenty-first-century America. This book is a special charge to people of faith who have the power to change the course of the nation and cross the bridge of redemption and transformation."

—**Iva E. Carruthers**, social justice advocate and general secretary,
Samuel DeWitt Proctor Conference

"The word 'conversion' jumped out at me as I read Jim Wallis's important new book. If Christians—especially white Christians—read this book, they will experience a real conversion, and the fruit of that conversion could bring healing to deep wounds in the soul of our nation. Such a conversion could also save lives . . . lives that truly matter."

—**Brian D. McLaren**, author/speaker (brianmclaren.net)

AMERICA'S ORIGINAL SIN

Racism, White Privilege,
and the
Bridge to a New America

JIM WALLIS

BrazosPress
a division of Baker Publishing Group
Grand Rapids, Michigan

© 2016 by Jim Wallis

Published by Brazos Press
a division of Baker Publishing Group
P.O. Box 6287, Grand Rapids, MI 49516-6287
www.brazospress.com

Paperback edition published 2017
ISBN 978-1-58743-400-6

Printed in the United States of America

The Library of Congress has cataloged the hardcover edition as follows:
Wallis, Jim.
    America's original sin : racism, white privilege, and the bridge to a new America / Jim Wallis.
        pages cm
    Includes index.
    ISBN 978-1-58743-342-9 (cloth)
    1. United States—Race relations. 2. Racism—United States. I. Title.
E185.615.W3125 2016
305.800973—dc23   2015030263

Unless otherwise indicated, Scripture quotations are from the New Revised Standard Version of the Bible, copyright © 1989, by the Division of Christian Education of the National Council of the Churches of Christ in the United States of America. Used by permission. All rights reserved.

Scripture quotations labeled ESV are from The Holy Bible, English Standard Version® (ESV®), copyright © 2001 by Crossway, a publishing ministry of Good News Publishers. Used by permission. All rights reserved. ESV Text Edition: 2011

Scripture quotations labeled GW are from GOD'S WORD®. © 1995 God's Word to the Nations. Used by permission of Baker Publishing Group.

Scripture quotations labeled NIV are from the Holy Bible, New International Version®. NIV®. Copyright © 1973, 1978, 1984, 2011 by Biblica, Inc.™ Used by permission of Zondervan. All rights reserved worldwide. www.zondervan.com

Scripture quotations labeled NKJV are from the New King James Version®. Copyright © 1982 by Thomas Nelson, Inc. Used by permission. All rights reserved.

Scripture quotations labeled RSV are from the Revised Standard Version of the Bible, copyright 1952 [2nd edition, 1971] by the Division of Christian Education of the National Council of the Churches of Christ in the United States of America. Used by permission. All rights reserved.

Scripture quotations labeled TLB are from The Living Bible, copyright © 1971. Used by permission of Tyndale House Publishers, Inc., Carol Stream, Illinois 60188. All rights reserved.

"You've Got to Be Carefully Taught" by Richard Rodgers and Oscar Hammerstein II, copyright © 1949 by Richard Rodgers and Oscar Hammerstein II. Copyright renewed WILLIAMSON MUSIC owner of publication and allied rights throughout the World. International copyright secured. All rights reserved. Used by permission.

To Vincent Harding
Elder, Mentor, and Friend

Contents

Foreword

BRYAN STEVENSON

Late one night several years ago, I was getting out of my car on an empty midtown Atlanta street when a man standing fifteen feet away pointed a gun at me and threatened to "blow my head off." I had just moved to the neighborhood, which I didn't consider to be a high-crime area. Panicked thoughts raced through my mind as the threat was repeated. I quickly realized that my first instinct to run was misguided and dangerous, so I fearfully raised my hands in helpless, terrifying submission to the barrel of a handgun. I tried to stay calm and begged the man not to shoot me, repeating over and over again, "It's alright, it's okay."

As a young attorney working on criminal cases, I knew that my survival required careful, strategic thinking. I had to stay calm. I'd just returned home from my office with a car filled with legal papers, but I knew the man holding the gun wasn't targeting me because he thought I was a

Bryan Stevenson is a widely acclaimed public interest lawyer, the founder and executive director of the Equal Justice Initiative in Montgomery, Alabama, and the author of *Just Mercy*. He has spent his career advocating for the poor, the incarcerated, and the condemned, including successfully arguing several cases before the United States Supreme Court. Stevenson and his staff have won reversals, relief, or release for over 115 wrongly condemned prisoners on death row. He is also a member of the President's Task Force on 21st Century Policing.

young professional. A young, bearded black man dressed casually in jeans, I didn't look like a lawyer with a Harvard Law School degree to most people; I just looked like a black man in America. I had spent much of my life in the church. I graduated from a Christian college and was steeped in Dr. King's teachings of nonviolence, but none of that mattered to the Atlanta police officer threatening to kill me. To that officer, I looked like a criminal, dangerous and guilty.

People of color in the United States, particularly young black men, are burdened with a presumption of guilt and dangerousness. Some version of what happened to me has been unfairly experienced by hundreds of thousands of black and brown people throughout this country. As a consequence of our nation's historical failure to address the legacy of racial inequality, the presumption of guilt and the racial narrative that created it have significantly shaped every institution in American society, especially our criminal justice system.

While the mainstream church has been largely silent or worse, our nation has rationalized racial injustice ever since we first ignored the claims and rights of Native people, who were subjected to genocide and forced displacement.

Millions of African people were brought to America in chains, enslaved by a narrative of racial difference that was crafted to justify captivity and domination. Involuntary servitude was banned by the Thirteenth Amendment to the US Constitution, but nothing was done to confront the ideology of white supremacy. Slavery didn't end in 1865; it just evolved. Until the 1950s, thousands of black people were routinely lynched in acts of racial terror, often while many in the white community stood by and cheered. Throughout much of the twentieth century, African Americans were marginalized by racial segregation and silenced by humiliating Jim Crow laws that denied basic economic, social, and political rights.

The country made progress dismantling the most obvious forms of racial bigotry in the 1960s, but we refused to commit ourselves to a process of truth and reconciliation. Consequently, new forms of racial subordination have emerged. The complicity of the church continues to haunt us and undermine the credibility of too many faith leaders.

We are currently in an era of mass incarceration and excessive punishment in which the politics of fear and anger reinforce the narrative of racial difference. We imprison people of color at record levels by making up new crimes, which are disproportionately enforced against those who are black or brown. We are the nation with the highest rate of incarceration in the world, a phenomenon that is inexorably linked to our history of racial inequality.

The Justice Department projects that one in three black males born in the twenty-first century is expected to go to jail or prison at some point during his lifetime. Only in a country where we have learned to tolerate evidence of racial injustice would this be seen as something other than a national crisis.

That night in Atlanta, I was sitting in front of my apartment, in my parked, beat-up Honda Civic for ten or fifteen minutes listening to music after a long day of work. I had apparently attracted someone's attention simply by sitting in the car too long, and the police were summoned. Getting out of my car to explain to the police officer that this was my home and that everything was okay is what prompted him to pull his weapon and threaten to shoot me. Having drawn his weapon, the officer and his partner justified their overreaction by dramatizing their fears and suspicions about me. They threw me on the back of the vehicle, searched my car illegally, and kept me on the street for nearly fifteen humiliating minutes while neighbors got a look at the dangerous black man in their midst. When no crime could be discovered, I was told by the police officers to consider myself lucky. Although it was said as a taunt and threat, they were right: I was lucky; I survived. Sometimes the presumption of guilt results in young black men being killed.

From Ferguson, Missouri, to Charleston, South Carolina, communities are suffering the lethal consequences of our collective silence about racial injustice. The church should be a source of truth in a nation that has lost its way. As the dominant religion in the United States, Christianity is directly implicated when we Christians fail to speak more honestly about the legacy of racial inequality. Evangelicals, in particular, have much to overcome, given our tolerance of racial bias over the years.

This is a critically important time, when leaders of faith need to address issues of race more thoughtfully, prayerfully, and courageously. As the visionary and prophetic leader of Sojourners, Jim Wallis has been speaking truth to power for decades. This new work is timely, urgent, and necessary.

We expect too little of law enforcement officials when we fail to hold them accountable for the misjudgments represented by the shooting deaths of so many unarmed people of color. We expect too little of the church when we accept its silence in the face of these tragedies.

We expect too much of the poor and people of color, who have carried the burden of presumptive dangerousness for far too long. We expect too much of the marginalized and menaced when we ask them to stay calm and quiet in the face of persistent threats and abuse created by our history of racial inequality.

No historic presidential election, no athlete or entertainer's success, no silent tolerance of one another is enough to create the truth and reconciliation needed to eliminate racial inequality or the presumption of guilt. We're going to have to collectively acknowledge our failures at dealing with racial bias. People of faith are going to have to raise their voices and take action. Reading this extraordinary new work by Jim Wallis is a very good place to start.

Preface

I always knew I would write *America's Original Sin*, but I never could have imagined the circumstances under which it would be released. The 2012 murder of Trayvon Martin pushed me to write, but that act of violence was soon followed by yet more killings of young black men and women, one after another—something that had been ongoing before but was never as visible or as exposed in the larger society as it has now become. Then, just before the book was published, Dylann Roof murdered nine African Americans during their weekly prayer meeting at Mother Emanuel AME church in Charleston, South Carolina. Despite these devout Christians inviting Roof into their Bible study—which clearly moved him for a while—he acted on his white supremacist ideology and shot them anyway.

And now this paperback edition of *America's Original Sin* is being released in the wake of the most vitriolic American presidential campaign in modern history.

Many are still reeling from the election results. I can't count the legion of phone calls and conversations I've had in the days since. I've heard from young immigrants who fear a mass deportation that would break up their families. I've heard from black pastors and parents who fear for the safety of their young people, who could be subject to racialized "law and order" and "stop and frisk" policing without any accountability from

Washington.[1] I've heard from Muslim friends who don't know if they belong in America and fear recent talk of being monitored and even having
to register as Muslims.

Those fears were quickly compounded by a dramatic escalation of
hateful speech and behavior aimed at Hispanics, African Americans, and
Muslims, at coffee shops and restaurants, at shopping malls, and even in
subways and on airplanes. Saddest of all was that directed against children
in their schools and on playgrounds, who were told by others that they
would be sent away from America and put on the other side of "the wall,"
or that they might be "sent back to slavery." Some Muslim children were
told that theirs is a religion of hate, while some Muslim girls had their
hijabs ripped off their heads.

Especially painful to me as a white Christian and evangelical is that white
Christians—especially white evangelicals—made up the core of Donald
Trump's support. The racism that has often been implicit in American
politics was made explicit in this election campaign; the rhetoric that is
usually covert was shamefully and painfully overt this time. And the election results made clear that Trump's *use of racial bigotry was not a deal
breaker for a majority of white Christians.*

Trump successfully channeled genuine economic grievances among
white working-class and rural voters into racial resentment, which helped
make his movement so explosive. But instead of building a bigger-tent
Republican party, as some others were suggesting should be done, Trump
chose to galvanize and mobilize white voters, including manipulating their
racial fear and anger at cultural changes—and it worked. He won. No one
can truly know what is in the heart of the man who claims to be the "least
racist person there is,"[2] but the new resident of the Oval Office undeni-
ably used, fueled, and stoked bigotry in this election for his own political
ends, revealing an astonishing racial divide in America. A majority of

1. "Law and order" has historically been used as a racially coded appeal to white people
during elections dating back to 1968, while "stop and frisk" was declared unconstitutional
when its use in New York City disproportionately affected people of color. It was also shown
to be ineffective at actually reducing violent crime. The only thing that "stop and frisk" ac-
complishes is to continually terrorize many innocent people of color. Late on election night, a
friend's teenage son, who played sports with my sons, threw himself across his mother's bed,
sobbing and saying, "How can I live in this country as a black man? When they say 'stop and
frisk,' they mean me!"

2. Donald Trump, Twitter, June 11, 2016, 4:18 a.m., https://twitter.com/realDonaldTrump
/status/741590381503086592?ref_src=twsrc%5Etfw.

white voters—of all economic levels, ages, and genders—went for Donald Trump, while the vast majority of all people of color—of every economic background, gender, and even religion—voted against him.[3]

That racial divide is nothing new, of course, as the book will discuss. But in the aftermath of the election, many people of color are losing hope for an America that values diversity—and them—and losing trust in white Christians who loudly claim not to be racist but who clearly decided that Trump's racial bigotry was not enough to dissuade them from voting for him. These voters ultimately set aside his statements, which even other Republicans called "textbook racism," in favor of their other concerns or deep dislike of his opponent; but they did so with no seeming understanding of or empathy toward families of color. Further, when white people dismiss the real fears that parents of color have for their children after this election, it painfully reveals the distance of the white majority from people of color in America and the realities of their daily lives.

Later in the book, we'll talk about the "racial geography" that has so divided us and kept us from hearing and knowing one another's stories. In researching this book, I found that 75 percent of white people have no significant relationship with individuals or families of color. When mothers and fathers engage other parents in deep conversations about their hopes, dreams, and fears for their children, real bonding can happen—including across racial lines. But that isn't happening much at all, even in most of our churches. Not surprisingly, the voters who ultimately chose Donald Trump were the most racially isolated white people in America. When you don't have any dear friends or close fellow believers across racial lines, it's impossible to know their feelings about the potential outcome of an election—particularly if they're fearful of that outcome.

3. As Robert Jones of the Public Religion Research Institute explained right after the election, it's striking to look at a map of the states with the highest percentage of white Christians next to a map of the states Trump won and note how well they match up—especially states like Pennsylvania, Wisconsin, and Michigan, which had voted reliably for the Democratic nominee for the last several presidential election cycles (Robert P. Jones, "The Rage of White, Christian America," *New York Times*, November 10, 2016, http://www.nytimes.com/2016/11/11/opinion /campaign-stops/the-rage-of-white-christian-america.html?_r=0).

In fact, as Jones's colleague Daniel Cox points out, in spite of the popular narrative that Trump's victory was a function of a swell in support from white working-class voters, "the proportion of white Christians in each of the 50 states is more strongly correlated with support for Trump than is the proportion of white residents without a college degree in the state" (Daniel Cox, "Correlation between White Christians, Trump Win in Key States," PRRI.org, November 17, 2016, http://www.prri.org/spotlight/trump-triumphed-white-christian-states/).

Flawed candidates, deep convictions and fears, and a system that is indeed rigged and needs to be changed all contributed to the election results. But now we face a new political era. The question is, what should we do with the intense emotions that many feel? It's time to turn shock into strategy, anger into good work, fear into solidarity and protection, pain into resolve, loss into energy, faith into action, justice into healing, and despair into hope.

If I read my Scriptures right, people who are Christians, along with other people of faith and good conscience, should now turn toward solidarity with and support for people who feel afraid because they were targeted in the presidential campaign and, as noted above, are under attack in alarming and increasing ways since the election. That's what Christians are supposed to do: support the poor and vulnerable and defend those under attack. That's what the gospel says to do, no matter who you voted for. What does it mean to be "Matthew 25 Christians," pledging to focus on those whom Jesus called "the least of these" and treating *them* in the same way we would treat *him?* Protecting vulnerable people, especially those under the most immediate jeopardy, is unifying work that could help bring us back together again.

What are some ways to do that? We can *tell the truth*. We must replace fear with facts when it comes to public discussions about immigrants, refugees, Muslims, racial diversity, and national security. We must name racism and xenophobia as sins against our neighbors and against the God who made us all in God's image. Multiracial truth telling about race as America's *original sin* is urgently needed, and faith communities must always lift up the voices of diverse believers so that they can share their own stories. We need to clearly affirm diversity as a gift, blessing, and great opportunity for our churches and our nation—and reject the language of threats.

We can *love our neighbors* by protecting them from hate speech and attacks. We all must watch, report, and confront hate speech and behavior—against all ethnic and religious groups, women, LGBTQ people, immigrants, and all marginalized groups—and surround people being attacked with supportive community.

We must *welcome the stranger*, as our Scriptures instruct. We should block, interfere with, and obstruct the mass deportations of immigrants who are law-abiding and hard-working members of our communities. We all must accompany, advocate for, and invite immigrants and their families into our faith families and congregations, especially when they become vulnerable. If the federal deportation police forces being talked about were ultimately forced to arrest immigrants in our churches instead of in their homes, it might cause the political powers to reconsider.

We must *expose and oppose racial profiling in policing*. Local ecumenical and interfaith clergy councils should meet with sheriffs and police chiefs for open dialogue. But we must also make it clear that local faith communities will promise to watch and monitor the relationship of our police to our communities. If Washington doesn't hold police accountable for obeying the law with regard to people of color, then faith communities will have to—and should be doing that anyway.

We must *defend Muslims*. We all must embrace Muslims as fellow Americans, standing up against the fear of attack, joining with mosques in congregational solidarity, and protecting national security with our Muslim fellow citizens. We must also resist anti-Semitism as part of the white nationalism on the rise. If the registration of Muslims that has been talked about by the new administration is implemented, Christians and Jews should be the first ones in line.

It is time to listen. The nation is more divided and polarized than at any point most of us can remember. So we should all listen to one another if we desire healing. Our congregations should become safe and sacred spaces for hearing one another's stories, pains, fears, and hopes—as people who all want the same things for our families and children.

It is time for churches to emphatically renounce bigotry and become the multiethnic body of Christ that God wants us to be. It is time to nurture our children in a faith that unites and doesn't divide. And it is time to recommit ourselves to love, care for, and sustain one another as together we seek to be ambassadors for a new order that Jesus called the kingdom of God.

Simply increasing racial diversity isn't enough; we must change the narrative of racial division in America. That's why I wrote this book, which I hope will help you and your neighbors and fellow believers across racial boundaries to build the new relationships and reformations of public policy that will lead us to a country of fairness and flourishing—for us all.

It is imperative that faith communities come together to protect the vulnerable and afraid, speak the truth to power, act in prayer and discernment, and stand up in solidarity and support for those who are most in danger. We will also need to go deeper into our faith, as the actions we take become costlier and riskier. Our call and our ministry, for such a time as this, will be one of resistance to the bigotry that is still all too present in American life, but also one of healing that will bring new relationships, leading to new public commitments and policies that begin to build the bridge to a new America.

Visit www.bakerpublishinggroup.com/books/america-s -original-sin/343770 to access a downloadable discussion guide for this book.

Introduction

You Will Know the Truth, and the Truth
Will Set You Free

In John 8:32, Jesus says, "You will know the truth, and the truth will make you free,"[1] which is one of those moral statements that breaks through the confusion and chaos of our lives.

Untruths that we believe are able to control us, dominate us, and set us on the wrong path. Untruths are burdens to bear and can even be idols that hold us captive—not allowing us to be free people who understand ourselves and the world truthfully.

The question we need to ask is, will we seek, tell, and respond to the truth as we go deeper in our needed new national conversation and action on racism in America? For example, we have seen and heard painful revelations about how police—and, even more systematically, the criminal justice system—too often mistreat young men and women of color. These revelations are classic examples of how we handle truth questions. What is true, what is right, what holds us captive, and what can set all of us free?

What happened in these incidents? And are they *just* "incidents," or is there a pattern here? Is there really just one criminal justice system for all

1. The New International Version (NIV) uses the wording "the truth will *set* you free." I use the two wordings interchangeably for the purposes of this introduction.

of us—equally—or are there actually different systems for white Americans and for Americans of color? Can we look at that truthfully?

Are we hiding behind untruths that help make us feel more comfortable, or are we willing to seek the truth, even if that is uncomfortable? The Gospel text cited above is telling us that only by seeking the truth are we made *free,* and that hanging on to untruths can keep us *captive* to comfortable illusions.

And if the untruths are, more deeply, *idols*, they also separate us from God—which is, obviously, highly important for those of us who are people of faith.

The title of this book, *America's Original Sin*, is itself unsettling and, for many, provocative. We first used the phrase in a 1987 cover story for *Sojourners* magazine. The language of "America's original sin" helped me understand that the historical racism against America's Indigenous people and enslaved Africans was indeed a *sin,* and one upon which this country was founded. This helps to explain a lot, because if we are able to recognize that the sin still lingers, we can better understand issues before us today and deal with them more deeply, honestly, and even spiritually—which is essential if we are to make progress toward real solutions.

New York City police commissioner William Bratton acknowledged at a church breakfast in 2014 the negative role of police against African Americans throughout American history. "Many of the worst parts of black history would have been impossible without police," Bratton said.[2] You can imagine my surprise when he then used the language of original sin: "Slavery, our country's *original sin*, sat on a foundation codified by laws enforced by police, by slave-catchers."[3] Bratton is no theologian or liberal academic but rather an experienced, knowledgeable, and tough cop. In fact, Bratton has been a controversial figure in New York, coming under fire for his "broken windows" policing strategy that focuses on aggressively targeting low-level offenses in order to deter more serious crime—a strategy that many say disproportionately affects people of color.[4]

2. Ross Barkan, "Bratton: Police Made Worst Moments of Black History Possible," *Observer*, February 24, 2015, http://observer.com/2015/02/bratton-worst-parts-of-black -history-wouldnt-have-been-possible-without-cops/.

3. Ibid., emphasis added.

4. Christopher Mathias, "Bratton Says Police to Blame for 'Worst Parts' of Black History, but Reform Advocates Are Unimpressed," *Huffington Post*, February 24, 2015, http://www.huffington post.com/2015/02/24/william-bratton-nypd-slavery-history-broken-windows_n_6746906.html.

Bratton reminded fellow New Yorkers that the colonial founder of New York City, the Dutchman Peter Stuyvesant, was a supporter of the slavery system and created a police force to enforce and protect it. "Since then," said the commissioner, "the stories of police and black citizens have been intertwined again and again."[5] He called the role of the NYPD sometimes "corrosive" in race relations. Bratton was talking about how the "original sin" has lingered in our criminal justice system, which is a reality that many people of color experience.

I agree with Commissioner Bratton that telling the truth about America's original sin is the best way to deal with it and ultimately be free of it. That makes moral and practical sense. Yet the truth of systemic injustice in the past and present must also compel us to *action*. It remains to be seen whether Bratton's acknowledgment of the historical issues translates into a commitment to real and ongoing reforms in how his police do their jobs.

I wrote this book to talk honestly about America's original sin and how it still lingers in our criminal justice system and too many other areas of American life. To treat these issues as sin—which can be repented of and changed—is a deeper, more effective way to solve these problems than just seeing them as political issues in an illusory "post-racial" America.

On Wednesday, June 17, 2015, a young believer in white supremacy invaded the sanctuary of historic Emanuel African Methodist Episcopal (AME) Church in Charleston, South Carolina. There he murdered nine black Christians who were gathered for their Wednesday night prayer meeting. They were targeted and killed because they were black.

Charleston showed how painfully true it still is that there is no safe place for black people in America, even in the sacred space of their own churches. That must change absolutely, unequivocally, and fundamentally in every aspect of American life. Dealing with our lingering racial sins is the only way to truly honor those who died in that Charleston church. These victims exemplified the image and love of God among us and put the lie to white supremacy.

On the day that Dylann Roof appeared in court for the first time, family members of the people killed were there. Nadine Collier startled the

5. Barkan, "Police Made Worst Moments."

courtroom when she said, "I forgive you and have mercy on your soul."[6] Her mother, Ethel Lance, had been one of the shooter's victims. Alana Simmons, whose grandfather had been killed, then stood up and said, "We are here to combat hate-filled actions with love-filled actions. . . . And that is what we want to get out to the world."[7]

The anguish, grace, and forgiveness of one family member after another stunned the world. Those families are not just victims now. They set the tone for the new national conversation—and action—on race that is long overdue. They want and will require justice but are also offering forgiveness. They have told the country that love is stronger than hate, and that only love can defeat hate. We must fight the things that we know are wrong, but without being wrong ourselves.

The painful and combustible connection between poverty, crime, and hopelessness is another of our lingering national sins. Joblessness leads to hopelessness; if we don't do a better job of educating *all* our children, they will struggle to find decent jobs, and without education and jobs it's very hard to build the strong families that all humans so critically need.

I am often puzzled by the question that some middle-class white people ask when they see protests about economic inequality and unequal criminal justice. The question, asked directly or indirectly, usually seems to be, "What do they want?" And the "they" always implies people of color.

The best answer to that question I've heard lately came from a young black man I met in Ferguson, Missouri. He said, "What do I want? I want an education, a job, and a family." Well, that's what my two boys want, and that's what I want for them—it's what all parents want for their kids. And the undeniable fact is that those who are being *left out* without an education, a job, and a family are overwhelmingly people of color in America, black and Native Americans most of all—that's the strongest proof of the lingering power of America's original sin.

Recessions and recoveries come and go, while whole communities of people are left behind, never enjoying "recovery," in predominantly black and brown neighborhoods across the country. Law enforcement is then

---

6. Lizette Alvarez, "Charleston Families Hope Words Endure Past Shooting," *New York Times*, June 24, 2015, http://www.nytimes.com/2015/06/25/us/charleston-families-hope-words -endure-past-shooting.html?_r=0.

7. Ibid.

expected to control or at least contain the predictable outcomes of poverty's chaos, pain, anger, and hopelessness in those black and brown neighborhoods, while the rest of us evade our responsibility to end that poverty and hopelessness.

Our criminal justice system just can't control the results of such poverty, even when it militarizes to do so. Add to that mix the clear racial bias of too many police officers, departments, and *cultures*, and you get the explosive and even deadly results that we have witnessed across the nation. These are more than merely social issues; these are spiritual issues that speak to the lingering and, yes, *evil* power of America's original sin. Sin can be repented of and changed, but only when we acknowledge it for what it is.

One of the most central lingering sins that I focus on in this book is white privilege. I am a white man in America, and I write this book as a white male, a white dad, and a white Christian. For most of my adult life I lived in low-income neighborhoods that have been predominantly black. Confrontation with white racism in my childhood in Detroit and in white churches has been the primary converting experience in my own faith history. It set me on a path that has defined my understanding of faith ever since—a story this book lays out. Allies and companions in black churches and communities have been principal shapers of my direction and vocation.

But no matter where you go as a white person in American society, no matter where you live, no matter who your friends and allies are, and no matter what you do to help overcome racism, you can never escape white privilege in America if you are white. I benefit from white privilege (and male privilege as well) every single day, and I don't have any more say in that than black men and women who experience the opposite. What white responsibility means, in the face of these benefits, is a central theme of my book.

I wrote this book because I believe truth telling about America's original sin of racism must not be left to people of color alone. Crossing the bridge to a new America will be a multiracial task and vocation.

As I have talked with black friends about this book, especially with black parents, the line that has elicited the most response is this one: "If white Christians acted more Christian than white, black parents would have less to fear for their children." Some of their reactions have been,

"Are you really going to say that?" "Oh my, what are white Christians going to say about that?" "That's going to stir things up!" And, "You're going to need some of us to have your back on this one." Do I think white people and white Christians can hear this? I truly hope so. And if we can, I believe we might see a new day in our churches and help the nation move to a different kind of future.

Policing isn't our only issue, nor are the systemic reforms our criminal justice practices need. So this book is also a *primer* on the underlying racism that still exists in America and that lies beneath the deep tensions related to the police killings that have recently refocused the nation's attention. We will try to look truthfully at underlying racial injustices, misunderstandings, and conflicts that continue to hold us back from being the country we can and should be. We will look at these crucial questions both structurally and spiritually. The book also describes how a new generation, of all races, is ready to deal with America's original sin in new and hopeful ways.

In the following pages we will take a positive, hopeful, and forward-looking approach. We will talk about what it means to "repent" of our original sin—and repentance means more than just saying you're sorry. It means turning in a new and better direction, which I believe we can do. We look backward in order to look forward. And this book makes a spiritual statement: our racial diversity and social pluralism are a great strength and a gift for our future, because our *primary* identity is as the children of God—all of us are created in God's image. Thinking about ourselves in that deeper way helps us to sort out a lot of things.

So what can the truth do for us?

You will know the truth, and the truth will make you *defensive*? I think we can do better than that.

You will know the truth, and the truth will make you *dishonest*? I don't think we want to keep doing that.

You will know the truth, and the truth will make you *deceptive*? We've seen way too much of that from public officials, and many people are now calling for accountability.

You will know the truth, and the truth will make you *bitter*? That just makes us miserable, and miserable to live with.

You will know the truth, and the truth will make you *angry*? Anger can be a positive thing, but only if it is channeled toward constructive change and gives us energy instead of hatred. We can eventually move beyond that too.

You will know the truth, and the truth will make you *free*. I truly believe that would be the best thing for all of us.

To become more *free* because of the truth.

To become more *honest* because of the truth.

To become more *responsible* because of the truth.

To become *better neighbors* because of the truth.

To become more *productive and contributing citizens* because of the truth.

To become *better Christians, Jews, Muslims, Buddhists, people of other faiths, or people of conscience with no religion*—all better because of the truth.

To become a *better and freer country for all of us* because of the truth.

And a big issue for me, as the father of two teenage boys, is how we can all become *better parents who are more supportive of other parents* because of the truth.

Finally, to *become better and freer human beings* because of the truth. I think that's what Jesus was getting at in the Gospel passage.

We can no longer be afraid of the truth about race in this country—past, present, and future—because our fears will keep us captive to all kinds of untruths.

This book is about how to find the truth together in these difficult, challenging, and complicated matters of race in America.

We will try to answer the question Dr. Martin Luther King Jr. named in the title of his last book, released just months before we lost him: *Where Do We Go from Here: Chaos or Community?* A new generation will answer that question for a new time.

I crossed the famous Edmund Pettus Bridge in Selma, Alabama, on the fiftieth anniversary of the historic march that helped bring voting rights to all our fellow citizens. It was then I realized that the answers to these questions will be found in crossing another bridge—the bridge to a new America that will soon be a majority of minorities. This book seeks to describe that new bridge and how we and our children can cross it together.

We need to better understand the past so we can cross the bridge to a new, freer American future where our growing diversity is experienced as a great benefit and not as a great threat. I hope you will take this book as an invitation—to explore the truth of America's racial past, present, and hopeful future so that, yes, together, we might all become more free, our congregations more faithful, and the state of our union "more perfect."

You will know the truth, and the truth will set you free.

1 | Race Is a Story

Race is about the American story, and about each of our own stories. Overcoming racism is more than an issue or a cause—it is also a story, which can be part of each of our stories, too. The story about race that was embedded into America at the founding of our nation was a lie; it is time to change that story and discover a new one.

Understanding our own stories about race, and talking about them to one another, is absolutely essential if we are to become part of the larger pilgrimage to defeat racism in America. It is also a biblical story, and now a global story in which we play a central role. We all start with our own stories about race, so I will begin with mine.

My Story

Fifty years ago I was a teenager in Detroit. I took a job as a janitor at the Detroit Edison Company to earn money for college. There I met a young man named Butch who was also on the janitorial staff. But his money was going to support his family, because his father had died. We became friends. I was a young white man, and Butch was a young black man, and the more we talked, the more we wanted to keep talking.

When the company's elevator operators were off, Butch and I would often be the fill-ins. When you operated elevators, the law required you to take breaks in the morning and in the afternoon. On my breaks, I'd go into Butch's elevator to ride up and down and talk with him. On his breaks, Butch came to ride and talk with me. Those conversations changed the way I saw Detroit, my country, and my life. Butch and I had both grown up in Detroit, but I began to realize that we had lived in two different countries—in the same city.

When Butch invited me to come to his home one night for dinner and meet his family, I said yes without even thinking about it. In the 1960s, whites from the suburbs, like me, didn't travel at night into the city, where the African Americans lived. I had to get directions from Butch. When I arrived, his younger siblings quickly jumped into my lap with big smiles on their faces, but the older ones hung back and looked at me more suspiciously. Later, I understood that the longer blacks lived in Detroit, the more negative experiences they had with white people.

Butch was very political, and even becoming militant—he always carried a book he was reading, such as Frantz Fanon's *The Wretched of the Earth*, stuffed into the back pocket of his khaki janitor's uniform—but his mom certainly wasn't. She was much like my own mother, focused on her kids and worried that her son's ideas would get him into trouble.

As we talked through the evening about life in Detroit, Butch's mom told me about the experiences all the men in her family—her father, her brothers, her husband, and her sons—had with the Detroit police. Then she said something I will never forget as long as I live. "So I tell all of my children," she said, "if you are ever lost and can't find your way back home, and you see a policeman, quickly duck behind a building or down a stairwell. When the policeman is gone, come out and find your own way back home." As Butch's mother said that to me, my own mother's words rang in my head. My mom told all of her five kids, "If you are ever lost and can't find your way home, look for a policeman. The policeman is your friend. He will take care of you and bring you safely home." Butch and I were becoming friends. And I remember his mother's advice to her children as vividly today as I heard those words fifty years ago.

Five decades ago, revelations about race in my hometown turned my life upside down—and turned me in a different direction. Encounters with black Detroit set me on a new path, on which I am still walking. My own white church ignored and denied the problem of race. People there didn't want to talk about the questions that were coming up in my head and heart—questions that suggested something very big was wrong about my city and my country.

As a teenager, I was listening to my city, reading the newspapers, having conversations with people. I wondered why life in black Detroit seemed so different from life in the white Detroit suburbs. I didn't know any hungry people or dads without jobs, and I didn't have any family members who had ever been in jail. Why were all these things happening in the city? Weren't there black churches in the city too? Why had we never visited them or had them come to visit us? Who was this minister in the south named King, and what was he up to? Nobody in my white world wanted to talk about it—any of it.

All of this drew me into the city to find answers to questions that nobody wanted to talk about at home. When I got my driver's license at age sixteen, I would drive into the city and just walk around, looking and learning. I took jobs in downtown Detroit, working side by side with black men, and I tried to listen to them. That's how I met Butch and many young men like him who had grown up in an entirely different city from me—just a few miles away.

In Detroit, I found the answers I was looking for, and I made new friends. I also met the black churches, which warmly took in a young white boy with so many questions and patiently explained the answers. When I came back to my white church with new ideas, new friends, and more questions, the response was painfully clear. An elder in my white church said to me one night, "Son, you've got to understand: Christianity has nothing to do with racism; that's political, and our faith is personal."

That conversation had a dramatic effect on me; it was a real conversion experience, but one that took me out of the church. That was the night that I left the church I had been raised in and the faith that had raised me—left it in my head and my heart. And my church was glad to see me go.

During my student years I joined the civil rights and antiwar movements of my generation and left faith behind. But that conversation with the church elder was indeed "converting," because it led me to the people who would later bring me back to my Christian faith—"the least of these" whom Jesus talks about in Matthew 25, which would ultimately become my conversion text.

How we treat the poorest and most vulnerable, Jesus instructs us in that Gospel passage, is how we treat *him*: "Just as you did it to one of the

least of these . . . you did it to me" (v. 40). My white church had missed
that fundamental gospel message and, in doing so, had missed where to
find the Jesus it talked so much about. My church, like so many white
churches, talked about Jesus all the time, but its isolated social and racial
geography kept it from really knowing him.

At the same time, black churches were leading our nation to a new
place. Their more holistic vision of the gospel was transforming my understanding of faith, and my relationship to the churches was forever changed.

I had to leave my white home church to finally discover Christ himself
and come back to my faith. In doing so, I discovered something that has
shaped the rest of my life: I have always learned the most about the world
by going to places I was never supposed to be and being with people I was
never supposed to meet. What I discovered by driving from the white suburbs
to the city of Detroit every day, and going into neighborhoods and homes
like Butch's, were some truths about America that the majority culture
didn't want to talk about—truths that are always more clearly seen from the
bottom of a society than from the top. This different perspective continues
to change me, and Matthew 25 continues to be my conversion passage.

As a teenager, I didn't have the words to explain what happened to me
that night with my church elder, but I found them later: God is always
personal, but never private. Trying to understand the public meaning of
faith has been my vocation ever since. How that personal and public gospel
can overcome the remaining agendas of racism in America is the subject
of this book.

Much Has Changed, but Much Still Hasn't

A half century later, much has changed. Reverend Martin Luther King Jr.
and the black churches of America led a civil rights movement that changed
the country and impacted the world. The historic Civil Rights Act passed
in 1964 and the Voting Rights Act in 1965. Black elected officials moved
into office around the country for the first time since Reconstruction. And
Barack Obama was elected the first black president of the United States
and reelected four years later. African Americans have achieved much
in every area of American society, from law and medicine to business
and labor, from education and civil service to entertainment, sports, and,

always, religion and human rights. A new generation, of all races, is more ready for a diverse American society than any generation has ever been.

But much still hasn't changed. Too many African Americans have been left behind without good education, jobs, homes, and families—and these factors are all connected. Perhaps most visibly and dramatically, the treatment of black men by police and a still-racialized criminal justice system in America became a painful and controversial national issue over the last few years, making visible what has been true for decades. The cases of Trayvon Martin in Sanford, Florida; Michael Brown in Ferguson, Missouri; Eric Garner in New York; Tamir Rice in Cleveland; and Freddie Gray in Baltimore, along with countless other black men whose names didn't receive national attention, have provoked a raw and angry racial debate in our nation. As I finish the final edits on this book, yet another story has drawn national attention, this time involving a young black woman named Sandra Bland, who was on her way to take a new job at Prairie View A&M University, her alma mater in Texas, until she was arrested in a routine traffic stop and died three days later in police custody.[1]

The facts in specific cases are often in great dispute. But the reality that young black men and women are treated *differently* than are young white men and women by our law enforcement system is beyond dispute. A half century after my relationship with my friend Butch's family, there is still not equal treatment under the law for black and white Americans. And that is the great moral and religious failure we must now address.

I feel a deep sadness at recent revelations that show how deep our racial divides still go. The stories of young black men, in particular, are still so different from the stories of my young white sons. As a dad who is also a person of faith, I believe that is an unacceptable wrong it is time to right. That's also why I wrote this book.

The Talk

All the black parents I have ever spoken to have had "the talk" with their sons and daughters. "The talk" is a conversation about how to behave and

1. Mitch Smith, "At Sandra Bland Funeral, Mourning a Life Cut Short in Texas," *New York Times*, July 25, 2015, http://www.nytimes.com/2015/07/26/us/sandra-bland-funeral-texas .html?_r=0.

not to behave with police—"Keep your hands open and out in front of you, don't make any sudden movements, shut your mouth, be respectful, say 'sir,'" as my friend and regular cab driver, Chester Spencer, said he told his son. "The talk" is about what to do and say (and what *not* to do and say) when you find yourself in the presence of a police officer with a gun.

White parents don't have to have this talk with their kids. That's a radical difference between the experiences of black and white parents in America. Why do we continue to accept that?

As a Little League baseball coach, I know that all the parents of the black kids I have coached have had the talk, while none of the white parents have had such conversations with their children. And most white parents don't have a clue about those talks between their children's black teammates and their parents.

It's important now that we white people begin to understand "the talk." Even white couples who have adopted black sons and daughters have that same conversation with their kids. As a white dad, that is a talk I don't need to have with my two white sons, Luke and Jack, who are now ages sixteen and twelve. The fact that most white parents don't know that this talk is even occurring is a big problem.

Not being able to trust the law enforcement in your community—especially in relationship to your own children—is a terrible burden to bear. The stark difference in the way young black men and women are treated by police and our criminal justice system compared to white children is a deeply personal and undeniable structural issue for every black family in American society. For many white Americans, the tragic deaths of young black men at the hands of white police officers are "unfortunate incidents" that can be explained away. But for most black families, they are indicative of systems they have lived with their entire lives. Therein lies the fundamental difference: a radical contrast in experience and, therefore, perspective.

If the mistreatment of young black men by law enforcement officials is true, if black lives are worth less in our criminal justice system than white lives are, then this is a fundamental and unacceptable wrong that it is time to correct. I know it is true. The overwhelming evidence on the operations of our criminal justice system proves it is true, even beyond the individual facts of particular cases.

Believing that black experience is different from white experience is the beginning of changing white attitudes and perspectives. How can we get to real justice if white people don't hear, understand, and, finally, believe the real-life experience of black people? Families have to listen to other families. If white children were treated in the ways that black children are, it would not be acceptable to white parents; so the mistreatment of black children must also become unacceptable to those of us who are white dads and moms.

The old talk is still necessary—and it's time to start talking together. If we do, I believe we can change the underlying patterns of personal and social prejudice that hold up the larger structural injustices in our society.

Building Racial Bridges

The best way to change that *old talk* that black parents have with their children is to start a *new talk* between white and black parents. These conversations will make people uncomfortable, and they should. White parents should ask their black friends who are parents whether they have had "the talk" with their children. What did they say? What did their children say? How did it feel for them to have that conversation with their children? What's it like not to be able to trust law enforcement in your own community?

Pay attention, read, listen. If you are white and have African American colleagues at work or friends at your church, ask them to talk with you about this, to tell you their stories—then listen. If you don't have any black people or other people of color in your church, it's time to ask why. Reach out, and ask your pastor to reach out, to black and Latino churches in your community. We must find safe and authentic ways to hear one another's stories across the racial boundaries that insulate and separate us from others. Reach out sensitively to black parents at your children's schools. Ask to hear their stories. Talk to the black parents of your children's teammates if they play a sport. Or maybe it's time to realize that not having children of color at your children's school or on their teams is a big part of the problem. Parents talking to parents and hearing one another's stories may be one of the most important ways of moving forward in the church and in the nation. But white Americans must also take responsibility for their self-education and preparation before these talks so as to not put the whole burden of their learning on their colleagues and friends of color.

White people need to stop talking so much—stop defending the systems that protect and serve us and stop saying, "I'm not a racist." If white people turn a blind eye to systems that are racially biased, we can't be absolved from the sin of racism. Listen to the people the criminal justice system fails to serve and protect; try to see the world as they do. Loving our neighbors means identifying with their suffering, meeting them in it, and working together to change it. And, for those of us who are parents, loving our neighbors means loving other people's kids as much as we love our own.

Racism as a Faith Issue

To put this in a religious context: overcoming the divisions of race has been central to the church since its beginning, and the dynamic diversity of the body of Christ is one of the most powerful forces in the global church. Our Christian faith stands fundamentally opposed to racism in all its forms, which contradict the good news of the gospel. The ultimate answer to the question of race is our identity as children of God, which we so easily forget applies to all of us. And the political and economic problems of race are ultimately rooted in a theological problem. The churches have too often "baptized" us into our racial divisions, instead of understanding how our authentic baptism unites us above and beyond our racial identities.

Do we believe what we say about the unity of "the body of Christ" or not? The New Testament speaks of the church as one body with many members.

> For just as the body is one and has many members, and all the members of the body, though many, are one body, so it is with Christ. . . . For the body does not consist of one member but of many. . . . As it is, there are many parts, yet one body . . . that there may be no discord in the body, but that the members may have the same care for one another. If one member suffers, all suffer together; if one member is honored, all rejoice together. (1 Cor. 12:12, 14, 20, 25–26 RSV)

Another version of 1 Corinthians 12:26 reads, "If one part of the body suffers, all the other parts share its suffering" (GW). What would it mean to share in the suffering of our brothers and sisters of color who are subjected to a racialized criminal justice system? So let's be honest. As I said in the introduction to this book, if white Christians in America were ready to act more Christian than white when it comes to race, black parents would be less fearful for their children.

Racial healing is a commitment at the heart of the gospel. If we say we belong to Christ, that mission of reconciliation is ours too. What does racial healing and reconciliation mean in the face of America's racial divide over policing and the criminal justice system? Churches, in particular, can offer leadership in navigating us through these difficult issues.

The American Pilgrimage

The United States has the most racial diversity of any country in the world. This diversity is essential to our greatness, but it has also given us a history of tension and conflict. It has always been the resolving and, ultimately, the reconciling of those tensions that makes us "a more perfect union." However, that cannot happen when we ignore, deny, or suppress our racial history and journey; it can occur only when we talk about it, engage it, embrace it, and be ready to be transformed by it.

Ironically and tragically, American diversity began with acts of violent racial oppression that I am calling "America's original sin"—the theft of land from Indigenous people who were either killed or removed and the enslavement of millions of Africans who became America's greatest economic resource—in building a new nation. The theft of land and the violent exploitation of labor were embedded in America's origins. Later immigration of other racial minorities was also driven—at least in part—by the need for more cheap labor. Therefore, our original racial diversity was a product of appalling human oppression based on greed. Many people have come to America, involuntarily in chains or voluntarily in the hope of a better life. And our great diversity is the key to our brightest and most transforming future. Indeed, it has already been one of America's greatest contributions to the world.

I believe that most police are good cops, but it would take more than a few "bad apples" to produce all the stories that *almost every black person in America* has about their experience with the police. Those stories are about a system, a culture, old structures and habits, and continuing racial prejudice, and how the universal but complex relationship between poverty and crime is made worse by racism. All of that can and must change with reforms that begin with better training and transparency and more independent prosecution in incidents of lethal police violence—and end with making police more relational and accountable to the diverse communities they serve.

But underneath the flaws and injustices of the criminal justice system is our unfinished business of challenging and ending racism, an agenda that is not finished and never will be. We are not now, nor will we ever be, a "postracial" society. We are instead a society on a journey toward embracing our ever-greater and richer diversity, which is the American story. The path forward is the constant renewal of our nation's ideal of the equality of all our citizens under the law—which makes the American promise so compelling, even though it is still so far from being fulfilled.

Our highest and most inspirational points as a nation have been when we have overcome our racial prejudices; our lowest and ugliest points have been when we have succumbed to them. In 2013, *Time* magazine did a cover story on the fiftieth anniversary of the "I Have a Dream" speech. In it, *Time* rightly said that Martin Luther King Jr. is now understood to be a "father" of our nation because he helped shape its course as much as the founding fathers did.[2] King and the movement he led opened a new door of opportunity for the future of America. But as we are becoming, for the first time, a country with no single racial majority—having been from our beginnings a white-majority nation—we stand at another door, which many white Americans are still very fearful of passing through. In this book I call that the *bridge* to a new America, and we will explore how to cross it together.

Race is woven throughout the American story and each of our own stories. All of our stories can help to change the racial story of America. I hope you will join me in this hard but critical—and ultimately transforming—conversation. Only by telling the truth about our history and genuinely repenting of its sins, which still linger, can we find the true road to justice and reconciliation. That is the premise and promise of this book.

---

2. Jon Meacham, "Founding Father: Martin Luther King Jr., Architect of the 21st Century," *Time*, August 26, 2013, http://content.time.com/time/magazine/article/0,9171,2149610,00.html.

2 | The Parables of Ferguson and Baltimore

When Trayvon Martin was shot and killed in Sanford, Florida, in 2012, I felt it was past time for white people—especially white parents—to listen and learn from the terribly painful loss of this young man. The loss of this young man and the way it happened filled me with lament.

The Lament of a White Father

Everyone knows that if my white sixteen-year-old son, Luke, had walked out that same night, in that same neighborhood, just to get a snack, he would have come back to his dad and mom unharmed—and would still be with Joy and me today. But when black seventeen-year-old Trayvon Martin went out that night, just to get a snack, he ended up dead—and is no longer with his dad and mom. We must try to imagine how that feels to them. It was a political, legal, and moral mistake not to put race at the center of that historic trial because it was at the center from the beginning of this terrible case. Afterward, many said, "The trial results must be accepted." How well the case against the shooter, George Zimmerman, was prosecuted, how fair the tactics of the defense were, the size and selection of the jury, how narrowly their instructions were given—all will be the subject of legal discussions and history for a long time.

But the Trayvon Martin case was not just about verdicts; it was also about values. The impact of race on that case and the response to it around the country must all be centrally and morally addressed.

The tragedy began with the racial profiling of Trayvon Martin. In Zimmerman's comments, rationales, and actions, the identity of Martin as a young black man was absolutely central. Both sides in the courtroom admitted that. It really said it all when the defense put up as a witness a white woman who had been robbed by a black man as an "explanation" for why Zimmerman picked out Martin to follow and stalk. Was she robbed by Trayvon Martin? No. So why should he be considered suspect because of another black robber? That is racial profiling—period.

As Martin Luther King Jr. said in his "I Have a Dream" speech, whose fiftieth anniversary has now passed, "I have a dream that my four little children will one day live in a nation where they will not be judged by the color of their skin, but by the content of their character."[1] King's dream failed that night in Florida when Zimmerman decided to follow Martin because of the color of his skin.

What exactly happened between Zimmerman and Martin will never be known. We will likely never hear the truth of how a black boy responded to a strange man who was following him, and what the stranger did with that. But regardless of the verdict that rests on narrow definitions of self-defense and reasonable doubt, it is absolutely clear that racial profiling was present in this incident.

Racial profiling is a sin in the eyes of God, as we will later explore theologically. It should also be a crime in the eyes of our society and reflected in the laws we enact to protect one another and our common good.

White parents should ask black parents what they were talking about with their children the weekend after Martin's death. As we discussed in the last chapter, black parents have long had conversations with their children about how to behave carefully in the presence of police officers with guns. Now they must add any stranger who might have a gun and could claim he or she was fearful of a black person and had to shoot. The

1. Martin Luther King Jr., "I Have a Dream," August 28, 1963, http://www.americanrhetoric .com/speeches/mlkihaveadream.htm.

spread of legalized open-carry and concealed weapons and the generous self-defense laws that accompany the guns will certainly lead to more tragic deaths, and to the deaths of more black men in particular.

Death is horrible enough. But systematic injustice—one that allows white boys to assume success, yet leads black boys to cower from the very institutions ostensibly created to protect *everyone's* well-being—is a travesty. In the weeks after Martin's death, I heard stories of twelve-year-old black boys who asked to sleep in bed with their parents because they were afraid. If black youths in America can't rely on the police, the law, or their own neighborhood for protection, where can they go?

This was one of those painful moments that reveal an utterly segregated society, in reality and perception alike. Most white people, conservatives and liberals, had almost no idea what was happening in virtually every black family and black church in America over the weekend following the Trayvon Martin tragedy.

There is a religious message here for Christians. If there ever was a time that demonstrated why racially and culturally diverse congregations are needed, this was that time. The body of Christ is meant, instructed, and commanded to be racially inclusive (Gal. 3:28). If white Christians stay in our mostly white churches and talk mostly to one another, we will never understand how our black brothers and sisters feel after a terrible incident like this one.

White Christians must not leave the sole responsibility of telling the truth about America's criminal justice system solely to their African American brothers and sisters in Christ. It's time for white Christians to listen to their black and brown brothers and sisters, to learn their stories, and to speak out for racial justice and healing. The country needs multiracial communities of faith to show us how to live together.

Why Ferguson Is a Parable

Jesus often told parables. A parable is just a story, but often one with a simple but important point. What is the story of Ferguson, beyond the details of the situation? What is the point of the story? What does the parable reveal? What are we learning from it?

The stories of young black men killed by police have sparked a national conversation. However, public responses to these painful stories reveal an alarming racial divide. From an unarmed teenager killed in Ferguson, Missouri, to a twelve-year-old boy shot dead in Cleveland and a white police officer on video choking a black man to death in New York City—as well as a startling number of similar stories across the country and over many decades—our reactions show great differences in white and black perspectives. As I described in the last chapter, the heart of the difference is that many white Americans tend to see unfortunate *incidents* based on *individual* circumstances, while most black Americans see *systems* in which their black lives matter less than white lives.

White Americans talk about how hard and dangerous police work is—that most cops are good and are to be trusted. Black Americans agree that police work is dangerous and difficult, and want good policing in their neighborhoods, especially in lower-income neighborhoods where poverty often leads to more crime. But the vast majority of African Americans, unlike most white Americans, have also experienced systemic police abuse of their families.

Are there police uses of force that are understandable and justifiable? Of course there are. If our society wasn't steeped in a gun culture, even many of these "justifiable" shootings could be avoided. But has excessive, unnecessary, lethal force been used over and over again, all across the country, with police killing unarmed black civilians? One heartbreaking story after another strongly suggests that the answer is yes.

It's indefensible that no accurate national data currently exist describing how many people are killed by the police each year. The FBI estimates that about four hundred people are killed by law enforcement officers each year, but this is *at best* a low estimate;[2] a recent study commissioned by the Bureau of Justice Statistics suggests that number is at least nine hundred.[3] Yet even these limited data show that black people are disproportionately killed by police: African Americans represent 31 percent of deaths by law enforcement officers reported to the FBI in 2012 while making up only 13 percent of the US population.[4] FBI director James Comey has acknowledged the problem of the lack of good data: "It's ridiculous that I can't

2. Dara Lind, "The FBI Is Trying to Get Better Data on Police Killings. Here's What We Know Now," Vox.com, April 10, 2015, http://www.vox.com/2014/8/21/6051043/how-many -people-killed-police-statistics-homicide-official-black.

3. Duren Banks, Lance Couzens, Caroline Blanton, and Devon Cribb, "Arrest-Related Deaths Program Assessment," *RTI International*, March 2015, http://www.bjs.gov/content/pub/pdf /ardpatr.pdf.

4. Lind, "FBI Is Trying to Get Better Data."

tell you how many people were shot by the police in this country."[5] But will those of us who are white agree that this is "ridiculous" and demand better reporting from local police departments and better data collection from the federal government?

A Tale of Two Reports

The shooting in Ferguson of Michael Brown, an unarmed, eighteen-year-old black man, by white police officer Darren Wilson happened on August 9, 2014. Almost immediately, the city of Ferguson exploded in protest of what many residents believed was a completely unjustified use of force against an unarmed black teenager. Outrage was particularly intense because several witnesses told the media that Brown had been trying to surrender when he was killed, raising his hands and begging the officer to stop shooting.[6] The protests quickly gained momentum and soon attracted national and international media attention, particularly when the police responded to the protests in a militarized manner more suitable for a war zone than the streets of an American city.

Seven months later, the US Department of Justice released two reports about Ferguson. The first reported the results of the DOJ's investigation to determine whether Darren Wilson could be charged with a crime under federal civil rights law.[7] The second report was a broader investigation into the policies and practices of the Ferguson Police Department and Municipal Court.[8] Taken together, the two reports show why Ferguson is such a parable for people on various sides of the debates that emerged after Michael Brown's death.

5. Sari Horwitz, "FBI Director Acknowledges 'Hard Truths' about Racial Bias in Policing," *Washington Post*, February 12, 2015, http://www.washingtonpost.com/world/national-security /fbi-director-acknowledges-hard-truths-about-racial-bias-in-policing/2015/02/12/023c6c6e -b2c6-11e4-854b-a38d13486ba1_story.html.

6. Jonathan Capeheart, "'Hands Up, Don't Shoot' Was Built on a Lie," *Washington Post*, March 16, 2015, http://www.washingtonpost.com/blogs/post-partisan/wp/2015/03/16/lesson -learned-from-the-shooting-of-michael-brown/.

7. "Department of Justice Report regarding the Criminal Investigation into the Shooting Death of Michael Brown by Ferguson, Missouri Police Officer Darren Wilson," US Department of Justice, March 4, 2015, http://www.justice.gov/sites/default/files/opa/press-releases/attachments /2015/03/04/doj_report_on_shooting_of_michael_brown_1.pdf.

8. "Investigation of the Ferguson Police Department," US Department of Justice Civil Rights Division, March 4, 2015, http://www.justice.gov/sites/default/files/opa/press-releases/attachments /2015/03/04/ferguson_police_department_report.pdf.

The first report challenged the early narrative that Brown was shot with his hands up while trying to surrender—a narrative that provided the origin for the protest slogan "Hands Up, Don't Shoot." It was not particularly surprising that the Justice Department did not find cause to bring civil rights charges against Darren Wilson—as the report makes clear, the bar of evidence that the department would have to meet to pursue charges in a case like this is extremely high.[9] The report, which contained an exhaustive review of physical and forensic evidence, autopsy reports, and witness testimony, did not corroborate the "hands up" account of the initial story. Instead it described a confrontation between Brown and Wilson—that Wilson felt threatened by Brown—and concluded that the totality of the evidence and the witness testimony showed that Officer Wilson did not use "objectively unreasonable force"[10] in his confrontation with Brown. Evidence suggested, the report said, that Brown fought with Wilson for control of his gun, then later, after fleeing the site of the initial altercation, turned around and was advancing toward Wilson when he was killed.[11] The report could not conclusively prove that Wilson did not feel himself to be in danger.

I visited the scene weeks later, and it was a somber experience, especially listening to the many members of the community who felt outraged by the killing of Brown and the response of the Ferguson police. After visiting the site of the tragedy, hearing the evidence, and reading the report, it is my view that nobody should have died that day; there were other procedures and alternatives that could and should have been followed. But there was insufficient evidence to prosecute the police officer because of what officers are allowed to do in such situations of conflict.

The second report told the rest of the story; it explained why the protests exploded into a movement after the shooting. The investigation into the Ferguson Police Department and Municipal Court was detailed and thorough. It relied in large part on documents obtained directly from the police department and court.[12] This devastating report revealed a police force and court system in Ferguson that verified almost everything that the protesters and other local residents had been saying about their city

9. "Shooting Death of Michael Brown," 9–12.
10. Ibid., 5.
11. Ibid., 5–7.
12. "Investigation of the Ferguson Police Department," 1.

in the wake of the shooting. This report should be read by anyone who believes in racial justice and healing, because it shows us what we are still up against in 2016.

Instead of focusing on protecting the public, the Ferguson Police Department's mission was revenue generation—extracting money from the black residents of the town, using methods that were often legally questionable, sometimes outright unlawful,[13] and certainly morally reprehensible. The report painstakingly reveals unconstitutional and consistently abusive policing aimed at balancing the city budget on the backs of its poorest citizens. The Ferguson police went beyond even racial profiling to direct racist targeting and exploitation for a profit, with city and police leadership apparently more concerned about "fill[ing] the revenue pipeline"[14] than protecting public safety. The use of traffic stops, citations, court appearances, fines, and even arrests that overwhelmingly affected black residents revealed a profound contempt for black people, with repeated racial slurs and verbal abuse also reported by residents. Disgusting racist "jokes," even aimed at the president and the first lady, circulated in the emails of police supervisors and court officials.[15] One joked about a black mother getting a crime prevention award for having an abortion.[16]

Blacks make up 67 percent of the population of Ferguson yet constituted 85 percent of vehicle stops, 90 percent of citations, 93 percent of arrests, 88 percent of cases with the use of force, 92 percent of cases in which arrest warrants were issued, and 96 percent of the people held at the Ferguson jail for more than two days. Stopping people for no apparent reason was common in Ferguson, using Tasers and other force if they objected. Dubious municipal ordinances were used as excuses to generate citations, said the report—again, almost entirely against black residents—for "Manner of Walking" (95 percent), "Failure to Comply" (94 percent), and "Peace Disturbance" (92 percent). One hundred percent of police-dog bite victims were black.[17]

13. Ibid., 5.
14. Ibid., 13.
15. Mark Berman, "The Seven Racist E-Mails the Justice Department Highlighted in Its Report on Ferguson Police," *Washington Post*, March 4, http://www.washingtonpost.com /news/post-nation/wp/2015/03/04/the-seven-racist-e-mails-the-justice-department-highlighted -in-its-report-on-ferguson-police/.
16. "Investigation of the Ferguson Police Department," 72.
17. Ibid., 4–5, 56, 62.

It was heartbreaking to learn from the report about specific people's experiences, such as the formerly homeless woman who ended up owing more than $1,000 and spending six days in jail because her car was parked in the wrong place.[18] It seemed as if every black person in Ferguson had a similar story. The Justice Department found that the stark racial disparities could not be explained, even when controlling for other variables such as age, gender, or the reason the person was initially stopped, concluding, "Ferguson law enforcement practices are directly shaped and perpetuated by racial bias."[19]

Then-attorney general Eric Holder summed up better than anyone what the two reports mean when taken together:

> Seen in this context—amid a highly toxic environment, defined by mistrust and resentment, stoked by years of bad feelings, and spurred by illegal and misguided practices—it is not difficult to imagine how a single tragic incident set off the city of Ferguson like a powder keg.[20]

In other words, when you get beyond the specific circumstances of the Brown shooting and look at the larger context of law enforcement in Ferguson, it's impossible to disagree with Holder's statement that "some of those protestors were right."[21]

One of the things I value most about the Justice Department's careful work on both of these reports is that it has allowed for some breaking down of the battle lines that were drawn in the months following Brown's death. Some conservatives dismissed the report on the broader Ferguson Police Department, calling it a "witch hunt" or a "farce."[22] And given the lack of a video record of the incident, the subjectivity of Darren Wilson's decision to use deadly force, and the often-justified racial mistrust engendered by biased law enforcement against the black community, there will be many

---

18. Ibid., 4.

19. Ibid., 70.

20. Mark Berman, "Holder: Report Shows Why Michael Brown's Death Set Off Ferguson like 'a Powder Keg,'" *Washington Post*, March 4, 2015, http://www.washingtonpost.com/news/post-nation/wp/2015/03/04/holder-report-shows-why-michael-browns-death-set-off-ferguson-like-a-powder-keg/.

21. Ibid.

22. Conor Friedersdorf, "Where's the Conservative Outcry on Ferguson Police Abuses?" *Atlantic Monthly*, March 10, 2015, http://www.theatlantic.com/politics/archive/2015/03/the-conservative-ambivalence-about-abuses-in-ferguson-department-of-justice-michael-brown/387196/.

who will always feel that Wilson was not justified in killing Brown, and that he should have been charged with a crime. However, people from all sides have accepted the credibility of both reports and the more complex parable that they represent.

For example, *The Washington Post*'s Jonathan Capeheart was an early critic of the Ferguson police and sympathetic with the early "hands up" narrative. But the Justice Department reports convinced him that the narrative was much more complicated. He accepted the facts presented by the report of Michael Brown's behavior before the shooting. But he went on to say:

> Yet this does not diminish the importance of the real issues unearthed in Ferguson by Brown's death. Nor does it discredit what has become the larger "Black Lives Matter." In fact, the false Ferguson narrative stuck because of concern over a *distressing pattern* of other police killings of unarmed African American men and boys around the time of Brown's death. . . .
>
> It is imperative that we continue marching for and giving voice to those killed in racially charged incidents at the hands of police and others. But we must never allow ourselves to march under the banner of a false narrative on behalf of someone who would otherwise offend our sense of right and wrong. And when we discover that we have, we must acknowledge it, admit our error and keep on marching. That's what I've done here.[23]

That kind of honesty in the face of such difficult truths is extremely difficult but imperative for the overall progress of the movement to bring justice to our broken criminal justice system.

On the Right, RedState.com ran an excellent piece by Leon H. Wolf explaining why conservatives who care about personal liberty should be outraged by what the Department of Justice report on the Ferguson Police Department revealed. He also made these important points about the dangers of our ideology getting in the way of the facts:

> It's unfortunate, the way news is consumed and interpreted in the age of twitter [*sic*]. Everyone feels tremendous pressure to form an opinion *quickly* and state it loudly and with certainty. Once this has been done, people are highly resistant to changing their minds and they become impervious to new evidence, often dismissing out of hand outright facts just because they are reported by a given source (e.g., "the media is untrustworthy" or "you can't trust the Holder

23. Capeheart, "'Hands Up, Don't Shoot' Was Built on a Lie."

Department of Justice"). Perhaps nowhere has this phenomenon been more obvious (or regrettable) than in Ferguson, Missouri, in the wake of the shooting death of Michael Brown. Interpreting the news out of Ferguson has become a part of ideological tribalism in which, if you are a conservative you stand for the Ferguson PD and if you are a liberal you stand against them. Thus, liberals have become highly resistant to assimilating information that strongly suggests that "hands up, don't shoot" never happened. Conservatives, on the other hand, have become highly resistant to assimilating information that strongly suggests that the Ferguson PD—as with many other municipal police departments in the country—truly is out of control, in that it recklessly violates the constitutional rights of the citizens of Ferguson and does so in a manner that has a clearly disproportionate impact on minorities.[24]

Conservatives and liberals need to take facts—and the lives impacted by those facts—seriously, by committing themselves to correcting and changing the racialized behaviors of our policing and criminal justice systems— and doing that together.

Complicated Parables and Deeper Truths

In some ways, Ferguson makes a good parable not *in spite of* how complicated the narrative is regarding what happened that day but precisely *because* the situation was so complicated. Life is complicated. Faith is complicated. The issue of race is certainly complicated. So why should we expect easy lessons about any of these topics? Yet the lessons are there, even if they aren't easy to understand or accept.

The Ferguson parable also teaches us that racially biased criminal justice systems and practices don't need "perfect victims" to be wrong. Even if criminal suspects are guilty of crimes or are running away from the scene of a crime, this doesn't excuse police officers for using lethal force when other methods might be used to deescalate conflict and still protect public safety. Even when force must be used, it does not always need to be deadly force, and seldom should be.

In early 2015, the nation witnessed another white police officer shooting and killing another unarmed black man, this time in North Charleston,

24. Leon H. Wolf, "Many Conservatives Are Blowing It on the Ferguson DOJ Report," RedState.com, March 15, 2015, http://www.redstate.com/2015/03/15/many-conservatives -blowing-it-ferguson-doj-report/.

South Carolina. Officer Michael T. Slager stopped Walter L. Scott for a malfunctioning brake light. After their initial conversation, when Slager went back to his car, Scott got out of his and began to run away from the scene, allegedly because he was behind in child-support payments and feared he might get into trouble. After a brief tussle, Slager drew his .45 caliber pistol and fired on Scott as he tried to flee, shooting him in the back multiple times and killing him.[25]

What made this incident stand out was that a local barber, who was walking by on his way to work, saw the incident evolving and turned on his cell phone camera.[26] His video caught the officer shooting Scott in the back as he ran away and then appearing to try to cover up the evidence. The officer was charged with murder, an unusual decision that was praised by the community. But as a lawyer for the Scott family put it, "What happened today doesn't happen all the time. What if there was no video?"

The tragedy of Ferguson revealed deep truths about race and the criminal justice system. Of course, many already knew these truths, particularly the people of color for whom they are a daily reality. But for those who were unaware of these truths or in denial about them, Ferguson offered a much-needed wake-up call. The story of Ferguson allowed other stories to get attention in ways they never would have otherwise—stories of other young black men and women who paid the ultimate price at the hands of law enforcement. For most of these, there is much less reason to believe the police had reasonable justification for what they did. If it weren't for the killing of Michael Brown and the community's reaction to the Ferguson police, many of the other incidents since Ferguson would never have come to national attention. Ferguson put a national spotlight on the violence of police against black men and women.

As someone who became deeply engaged as soon as I heard about Ferguson, I want to share some of the stories I heard and experienced in the days and months after Michael Brown was killed. I believe they show how the Ferguson parable went from a *moment* to a *movement* and why it is so important for the future of America that this movement continues until it prevails.

25. David von Drehle, "Line of Fire," *Time*, April 20, 2015, 24–28.
26. "Feidin Santana, Who Recorded Police Shooting of Walter Scott, Speaks Out," NBCnews.com, April 8, 2015, http://www.nbcnews.com/news/latino/feidin-santana-who-recorded-man-shot-police-officer-speaks-out-n338171.

A Moment to a Movement

Despite intense disagreements over the St. Louis County grand jury decision not to indict Darren Wilson, for many African Americans the verdict on America's criminal justice system was already in: guilty, for treating young black men differently than young white men.

For many, the decision by the grand jury was predictable in a nation where police officers are almost never indicted for the use of deadly force[27]— especially when it is white police officers killing black people. The special relationship that prosecutors have with police departments has become a real issue, and the need for special and independent prosecutors in cases of lethal police force has been raised as a possible reform.[28]

The night the grand jury decided not to indict Wilson was a sad night for America because of the way the peaceful protests were hijacked by a small number of people intent on violence. St. Louis-area pastor Rev. Traci Blackmon's words reflected that pain the next morning: "I hurt for all the people in my community, and I hurt for the many young people who did everything they could . . . to make sure that last night was not violent and make sure their voices were heard. And unfortunately, the pain and the rage of a few have made a different narrative this morning."[29]

Even though most of the protests in Ferguson and later around the country were peaceful, it was painful to watch President Obama speaking to the nation on a split screen with scenes of violent reactions in Ferguson. In his speech, the president said, "We need to recognize that this is not just an issue for Ferguson; this is an issue for America."[30] He also reminded the nation of the words of Michael Brown Sr., the dead boy's dad, before the grand jury decision, words that deeply touched many people—especially those of us who are parents.

27. Kimberly Kindy and Kimbriell Kelly, "Thousands Dead, Few Prosecuted," *Washington Post*, April 11, 2015, http://www.washingtonpost.com/sf/investigative/2015/04/11/thousands -dead-few-prosecuted/.

28. "Lujan Grisham Co-Sponsors Bill Requiring Special Prosecutor for Police Shootings," Office of Rep. Lujan Grisham, February 4, 2015, https://lujangrisham.house.gov/media-center /press-releases/lujan-grisham-co-sponsors-bill-requiring-special-prosecutor-police.

29. Dallas Franklin, "Streets of Ferguson Smolder after Grand Jury Declines to Indict Officer," KFOR-TV online, November 24, 2014, http://kfor.com/2014/11/24/ferguson-protests -turn-ugly-following-grand-jury-decision/.

30. Lindsay Holst, "President Obama Delivers a Statement on the Ferguson Grand Jury's Decision," *The White House Blog*, November 24, 2014, http://www.whitehouse.gov/blog/2014/11/24 /president-obama-delivers-statement-ferguson-grand-jurys-decision.

Brown Sr. offered these powerful words: "Hurting others or destroying property is not the answer. No matter what the grand jury decides, I do not want my son's death to be in vain. I want it to lead to incredible change, positive change, change that makes the St. Louis region better for everyone."[31]

Watching buildings burn the night of the announcement of the grand jury's decision, I remembered that Martin Luther King Jr., the nation's apostle of nonviolence, once said, "A riot is the language of the unheard."[32] But King also showed us that, ultimately, only disciplined, sacrificial, and nonviolent social movements can change things.

It is indeed time to right the unacceptable wrong of black lives being worth less than white lives in our criminal justice system. Of course, all lives matter, but "Black Lives Matter" is the message that most needs to be heard right now. The broken relationships between law enforcement officials and their communities are deeply felt and very real. How law enforcement interacts with communities of color raises fundamental, legitimate issues that must be addressed by the nation if we are to move forward. The changes we need in both policies and practices must be taken up in detail, which we will do in chapter 7. Our neglect has led to anger and hopelessness for many in the new generation, but the activism from that same generation will also help lead us to new places.

I interviewed Brittany Packnett, a dynamic young leader who emerged from the Ferguson protests. She shared her thoughts with me on how the movement came to be and described the energy and commitment of her peers to continuing this fight for justice:

> These were not preformed marches; these were not rallies that [had] been planned for the last six months and we got all of the right people and all of the news cameras. People just literally got out of their homes and wouldn't go back inside, and they kept coming back night after night even though they were putting their lives in danger. . . . They felt like they had no other choice, because they wouldn't be heard unless they put their bodies on the line. . . . [It's] different from movements in the past . . . not only is that okay, but it's necessary given where we are now.[33]

31. "Michael Brown, Sr., Discusses Moving St. Louis Forward," YouTube video, 0:54, November 20, 2014, https://www.youtube.com/watch?v=x4LkX7PZCoo.

32. "MLK: A Riot Is the Language of the Unheard," *60 Minutes Overtime*, August 25, 2013, http://www.cbsnews.com/news/mlk-a-riot-is-the-language-of-the-unheard/.

33. Brittany Packnett, interview with the author, March 27, 2015.

The young people who took to the streets around St. Louis vowed to turn Ferguson from a moment to a movement. On one hand, they obviously wanted to call to account the deeply unjust and corrupt governance and policing of Ferguson. More important, these young leaders vowed to spur a broader movement toward racial justice in the criminal justice system. But they knew that also depended on how the rest of the country would respond.

Retreats and Responsibility

I was in Ferguson when, in a morally stunning decision, a Staten Island grand jury announced it would not bring criminal charges against a white police officer who choked a black man to death in July 2014. Stopping Eric Garner for allegedly selling some loose and therefore untaxed cigarettes, Officer Daniel Pantaleo put a "chokehold" on Garner, despite the fact that such a move is against NYPD rules. Video of the incident shows the struggling Garner uttering his last words, "I can't breathe," which subsequently spread to protests around the country and to the shirts of professional athletes. New York's medical examiner officially called the case a homicide, but the grand jury said no charges would be filed.

The Garner decision came just ten days after the Ferguson grand jury decision not to indict Darren Wilson.

That afternoon, Sojourners was convening a retreat in Ferguson for national faith leaders and local pastors. We were looking deeply at the historical and theological foundations of the Ferguson events and reflecting on the church's response. Emotional calls came from colleagues in New York City with the horrible news about the Staten Island decision. People around me began to weep; one young man wailed, "This time it was all on video, and it still didn't matter! How can I as a black man bring a black son into this world?" Lament and prayers followed, with a resolve from an extraordinary two days on the ground in Ferguson for faith leaders to act.

Experts in St. Louis County had helped us understand the deliberate segregation and damage done to their local communities for decades, which led to the response that erupted after the killing of Michael Brown. We also went to a local church to meet with seven young leaders of the Ferguson protest movement. In just 116 days, these young people had become extraordinary leaders, and we listened to a compelling analysis of their urgent situation and how they were trying to apply the history of social movements to change their oppressive circumstances. Their chilling stories of police harassment and brutality, especially toward the new leaders, were reinforced by a compelling narrative of the educational and economic brutality that black young people like them experience daily.

These were transforming words for those of us who listened. As I heard these young leaders, I realized America would be converted by these young people's honest and earnest conversation—they would clearly win a national debate about our criminal justice system's response to young people of color—if the nation could really see and hear them. That is why they have been deliberately marginalized and painted with the brush of false narratives that polarize our responses to them, a polarization so painfully and starkly along racial lines.

Some of these young people had just returned from Washington, DC, where they met in the Oval Office with President Obama. Later I joined them for a meeting at the White House, where the president convened faith leaders, law enforcement officials, legal scholars, the vice president, and some of his cabinet secretaries to discuss a new task force and national commission to deal with what he called "a real problem" in our law enforcement system between too many police departments and their communities of color.

These young leaders were powerfully articulate at our retreat, calling Ferguson a historic moment and asking us all how we were going to respond to it. We could see the serious and costly commitments that they had made. They asked us what commitments we were willing to make and what risks we were willing to take as faith leaders.

The faith leaders' retreat in Ferguson resulted in new and determined commitments to change, beginning with the churches themselves and extending to the criminal justice system. That commitment will go beyond our racial and political differences and could hopefully provide a most needed multiracial, nonpartisan political force for fundamental change.

Conservative white Southern Baptist leader Russell Moore said this in the wake of Ferguson:

> In the public arena, we ought to recognize that it is empirically true that African-American men are more likely, by virtually every measure, to be arrested,

sentenced, executed, or murdered than their white peers. We cannot shrug that off with apathy. Working toward justice in this arena will mean consciences that are sensitive to the problem. But how can we get there when white people do not face the same experiences as do black people?[34]

After the Eric Garner decision, Moore made another powerful statement:

A government that can choke a man to death on video for selling cigarettes is not a government living up to a biblical definition of justice or any recognizable definition of justice. . . . It's time for us in Christian churches to not just talk about the gospel but live out the gospel by tearing down these dividing walls not only by learning and listening to one another but also by standing up and speaking out for one another.[35]

When the decision about Eric Garner was announced, the young people we had met the night before called and asked us to join them in the protest they had just organized at a US courthouse in downtown St. Louis, and we did. Faith leaders and pastors stood alongside black and white young people who chanted "I can't breathe" in front of a line of police.

We do have a problem, and it is past time to fix it. Our communities and our churches must stand alongside a new generation of young leaders and help the nation find the way forward.

"Leader-full," Not Leaderless

Brittany Packnett talked about leadership and the role she and her peers have played in bringing national attention to the fundamental injustices of the criminal justice system. It's my judgment that had the new genera-tion of leaders in St. Louis County and elsewhere not been in the streets protesting every day, doing all the heavy lifting for all of us who believe in this cause, these issues would not have gained the attention they so urgently need. President Obama might not have convened his task force

34. Elizabeth Bristow, "ERLC President Russell Moore Responds to Grand Jury Decision in Ferguson," The Ethics and Religious Liberty Commission of the Southern Baptist Convention, November 24, 2014, http://erlc.com/article/erlc-president-russell-moore-responds-to-grand -jury-decision-in-ferguson.

35. Elizabeth Bristow, "ERLC's Russell Moore Responds to Eric Garner Case," The Ethics and Religious Liberty Commission of the Southern Baptist Convention, December 3, 2014, http://erlc.com/article/erlcs-russell-moore-responds-to-eric-garner-case.

on twenty-first-century policing. There might not have been any Department of Justice reports about Ferguson or Michael Brown. Ferguson, and specifically these young leaders, changed the national conversation on race.

Packnett described the diversity of gifts these young people have brought to the table and how they have built on the legacy of the civil rights movement:

> When we talk about leadership . . . we like to talk about the idea that our movement is not leaderless, as it's so often been described, but rather "leader-full." . . . Because the work of the midcentury civil rights movement has allowed for black people to be successful and to emerge in so many different spaces, we now have the opportunity to have people contributing in many different ways. Now we've got people of color and black people specifically in new and mainstream media, in all levels of politics, all the way up to the White House, and in various spaces at the local level. We've got people working in education and in social justice, we've got people working in engineering and the sciences and business. . . . That structural diversity allowed us to pull on people's expertise and networks. . . . It really is this more leader-full impact model that says everyone needs to make a contribution, but everybody's contribution doesn't have to be the same. . . . This is a new age, a new era, and the way that we communicate with people and the way that we agitate and the way that we organize can be different, it can be of our generation.[36]

Packnett also talked about some of the local clergy, and how some had been much more helpful than others. She called attention to clergy like Rev. Traci Blackmon, whom I also had the honor to work with in Ferguson and who helped convene our faith leaders retreat there:

> I remember [Traci Blackmon] leading a march and . . . she said in front of everyone, "I need to apologize to the young people, because we treated you like you should have come to the church, and we should have brought the church to you." And what she meant by that was not just having the march, but having the march actually get out there behind young people instead of in front of them, instead of speaking over what they had built, instead of saying, "Well, here's how you need to do things," actually listening and determining to follow the creative leadership of young people.[37]

These words rang true for me. In all my decades of organizing and protesting for social justice across the country, I have always found that we've

36. Brittany Packnett, interview with the author, March 27, 2015.
37. Ibid.

had much more success when we *listen* to local leaders, ask them questions instead of giving them our "answers," and, most important, follow their lead.

As Packnett's comments above about Blackmon suggest, she and other young leaders in the movement are also sensitive to the role of women, as well as broader issues of gender and male privilege. Here is how Packnett explained it to me:

> There is in particular an epidemic that is affecting young black men, but young women are losing their lives too. . . . [What] people have seen in terms of the leadership of the movement is the continuation of a cultural history that has centered around the strengths of the black woman. We have often been the ones holding families together, holding congregations together. Even in times of extreme patriarchy we have often been the backbone. . . . What I actually think has formed is the extent to which black women in this movement are absolutely and fundamentally not going to deal with the patriarchy. And so we have been uncompromising in how we have not allowed people to silence us, to diminish our contribution, to tell our stories for us—all of those kinds of very typical attributes of male privilege. We will call them out every single time we see them. Right within the movement! . . . Women are dying too in this situation, and if I'm not dying I'm worried about my son, I'm worried about my uncle, I'm worried about my brother, so I'm going to be out here too.[38]

These young women and men are the civil rights leaders of their generation. They are multiracial, and their cry for justice is one that we must hear. If we do, it will help us cross the bridge to the new America, which will look more like all of them than it will look like me.

The Parable of Baltimore

In the spring of 2015, the city of Baltimore, just fifty miles north of where I live, exploded. Baltimore is also a parable, a story that can teach us important lessons, and one in which we should see that we are, for the most part, still missing the most important lessons.

The Baltimore story began with yet another incident between a young black man and the police. A twenty-five-year-old African American named Freddie Gray was picked up by the Baltimore police (for reasons still not

38. Ibid.

clear as I write this) and died of injuries he received in police custody after being put into a police van and not receiving the medical help he needed. In response, protests rose up that were disciplined, articulate, and nonviolent. They lasted for many days and focused attention on Gray and what happened to him.

Around the time of Gray's funeral, lawbreakers took control of the streets and began looting, burning businesses and cars, and attacking police. The national media swooped in to cover the "riots," the National Guard was called in, Orioles baseball games were postponed or closed to the public, and Baltimore made national headlines. But soon citizens from all over Baltimore, led by faith, community, and African American political leaders, moved in to condemn the violence, take back the streets, begin to clean up their city, and call for both healing and justice. It was one of the best examples I have seen of the church stepping up to be the church.

Persistent, deeply rooted bad behavior on the part of Baltimore's police force in relation to the black community was brought to light, as it has been in many similar cases; but the parable of Baltimore needs to go deeper. In Baltimore, unlike Ferguson, the mayor and the police chief at the time were African Americans, as is a significant portion of the police force.[39] Unfortunately, other cities with black leaders and diverse police officers also have problems with the use of excessive force against young black men and women, and the lessons learned here must go deeper than just the diversity of local police forces and political leaders.

Just two weeks before, I had taken my son Luke on a college-visit tour. As we visited Johns Hopkins University in Baltimore, Luke and I both noticed how poor the area around the academically prestigious university was. Sadly, many young African American men in neighborhoods such as East and West Baltimore were not taking college tours that spring.

In neighborhoods across the country, we are not providing a decent education to black and brown young people—and society is accepting that. Baltimore, like many cities, used to have manufacturing jobs that paid enough to support a family. Such employment has been replaced with low-paying jobs or no jobs at all, a situation that often leads to the disintegration of family life.

39. Ralph Blumenthal, "Integrating Baltimore's Police Force," *Baltimore Sun*, April 30, 2015, http://www.baltimoresun.com/news/opinion/oped/bs-ed-police-race-freddie-gray-201 50430-story.html.

Joblessness leads to hopelessness, lack of education leads to more joblessness, and the lack of education and jobs leads to family breakdown,
which leads to so many other problems. Add substance abuse to hopelessness, replace real industry with a drug industry, and everything gets worse
and more violent.[40] Then law enforcement comes in, with the expectation
of containing crime in the midst of those hopeless circumstances. Then
add racial bias, both explicit and implicit,[41] in police forces around the
country, and you have recurring incidents, lethal consequences, protests,
and "riots," one after another. That's the pattern, and that's the lesson: a
very combustible combination of social factors that we—again—accept
in particular neighborhoods across the country. And we are all responsible
for that passive acceptance.

Young people in those neighborhoods feel left out—and some will participate in self-destructive and community-destructive behavior that is
clearly wrong and counterproductive, even distracting from the real issues
of racial policing that usually are the catalytic factors that produce the
unrest. If we just focus on the "riots," or even just on policing behavior,
we will not be addressing the root causes of these problems. I've heard
pastors in Baltimore ask why many in the media were more concerned with
people's reactions to their conditions than with the conditions themselves.

Two of my favorite columnists, E. J. Dionne of *The Washington Post*
and Nicholas Kristof of *The New York Times*, were among the few media
voices who got it right in the wake of the Baltimore events. In his column
titled "Baltimore's Downfall," Dionne wrote:

> The obvious flashpoints involve race and policing. But since at least the 1970s,
> the economy's invisible hand has also been diligently stripping tens of thousands
> of blue-collar jobs from what was once a bustling workshop where steel, cars,
> and planes were made. Baltimore has tried to do its best in a post-industrial
> economy, but when work disappears, the results are catastrophic.[42]

Nick Kristof has been one of the few white columnists writing regularly and honestly about race and policing. In his piece "When Baltimore

40. We will discuss these topics in detail in chap. 3.
41. Implicit bias (also known as unconscious bias) will be discussed in detail in chap. 5.
42. E. J. Dionne Jr., "The Labor Roots of Baltimore's Anguish," *Washington Post*, April
29, 2015, http://www.washingtonpost.com/opinions/the-economic-roots-of-baltimores
-anguish/2015/04/29/91a4415c-eea2-11e4-a55f-38924fca94f9_story.html.

Burned," he spoke of the failure of the media in response to events like this, and what we should *all* be protesting:

> We focus television cameras on the drama of a burning CVS store but ignore the systemic catastrophe of broken schools, joblessness, heroin, oppressive policing—and maybe the worst kind of poverty of all, hopelessness. . . . If wealthy white parents found their children damaged by lead poisoning, consigned to dismal schools, denied any opportunity to get ahead, more likely to end up in prison than college, harassed and occasionally killed by police—why, then we'd hear roars of grievance. And they'd be right to roar: Parents of any color should protest, peacefully but loudly, about such injustices.[43]

This is the parable of Baltimore, and accepting responsibility for the things we have "accepted" and that clearly involve race is the first honest step.

President Obama's words about Baltimore were some of the most honest of his presidency. He too addressed Baltimore's systemic poverty and lack of opportunity:

> In those environments, if we think that we're just going to send the police to do the dirty work of containing the problems that arise there, without as a nation and as a society saying what can we do to change those communities, to help lift up those communities and give those kids opportunity, then we're not going to solve this problem. . . . And we'll go through the same cycles of periodic conflicts between the police and communities and the occasional riots in the streets. And everybody will feign concern until it goes away and then we go about our business as usual. . . .
>
> If we are serious about solving this problem, then we're going to not only have to help the police, we're going to think about what can we do, the rest of us, to make sure that we're providing early education to these kids, to make sure that we're reforming our criminal justice system so it's not just a pipeline from schools to prisons, so that we're not rendering men in these communities unemployable because of a felony record for a non-violent drug offense, that we're making investments so that they can get the training they need to find jobs.
>
> But if we really want to solve the problem, if our society really wanted to solve the problem, we could. It's just it would require everybody saying this is important, this is significant, and that we don't just pay attention to these communities when a CVS burns and we don't just pay attention when a young man gets shot or has his spine snapped. We're paying attention all the time

---

43. Nicholas Kristof, "When Baltimore Burned," *New York Times*, April 29, 2015, http://www.nytimes.com/2015/04/30/opinion/nicholas-kristof-when-baltimore-burned.html.

because we consider those kids our kids and we think they're important and they shouldn't be living in poverty and violence.[44]

As Nicholas Kristof wrote, "The greatest problem is not with flat-out white racists, but rather with the far larger number of Americans who believe intellectually in racial equality but are quietly oblivious to injustice around them. Too many whites unquestioningly accept a system that disproportionately punishes blacks. . . . We are not racists, but we accept a system that acts in racist ways."[45]

Let me add a personal conclusion to my white brothers and sisters: you can't continue to say you are not racist when you continue to accept and support systems that are. It's time for white people to take responsibility for our acceptance of racist systems.

The time for zero tolerance of racialized policing has come. It's time for white citizens and parents to join with black citizens and parents to right an unacceptable wrong, to say that black lives matter. These kids are not just God's kids; they are *our* kids. Will Ferguson and Baltimore become teaching parables that serve as wake-up calls to white parents too—or just as another warning to black parents?

Jesus proclaimed, "Blessed are the peacemakers, for they will be called children of God" (Matt. 5:9). Martin Luther King Jr. reminded us, "True peace is not merely the absence of tension: it is the presence of justice."[46] These are not just nice sentiments to be dismissed when tensions and conflicts arise. Rather, they are wise words of truth that should guide our thinking in moments of distress. We need to make Jesus's instruction real and consider King's words a practical exhortation for ensuring peace and public safety in so many places, from Ferguson to Baltimore.

44. Barack Obama, "Remarks by President Obama and Prime Minister Abe of Japan in Joint Press Conference," White House Office of the Press Secretary, April 28, 2015, https://www .whitehouse.gov/the-press-office/2015/04/28/remarks-president-obama-and-prime-minister -abe-japan-joint-press-confere.

45. Nicholas Kristof, "When Whites Just Don't Get It, Part 3," *New York Times*, October 11, 2014, http://www.nytimes.com/2014/10/12/opinion/sunday/nicholas-kristof-when-whites -just-dont-get-it-part-3.html?_r=0.

46. Martin Luther King Jr., *Stride toward Freedom: The Montgomery Story* (Boston: Beacon, 2010), Google Play edition.

3 | The Original Sin and Its Legacy

The most controversial sentence I ever wrote was not about abortion, gay marriage, the wars in Vietnam or Iraq, elections, or anything to do with national or church politics. It was a statement about the founding of the United States. Here's the sentence: "The United States of America was established as a white society, founded upon the near genocide of another race and then the enslavement of yet another."

The comments were overwhelming, with many calling the statement outrageous and some calling it courageous. But it was neither. The sentence was simply a historical statement of the facts. It was the first sentence of a *Sojourners* magazine cover article, published in November 1987, titled "America's Original Sin: The Legacy of White Racism."

America's Original Sin

I believe this book's title is very important. Racism is rooted in sin—or evil, as nonreligious people might prefer—which goes deeper than politics, pointing fingers, partisan maneuvers, blaming, or name calling. We can get to a better place only if we go to that morally deeper place. There will be no superficial or merely political overcoming of our racial sins—that will take a *spiritual* and moral transformation as well. Sin must be named, exposed, and understood before it can be repented of.

This chapter is about honestly naming the sin and its many implications in our nation's life. The criminal justice system's failure at the point of race is best understood as an example of the lingering of America's original sin. Only if we go deeper than politics will we be able to get beyond politics to practical and nonpartisan solutions that will work for us all.

Let's start our discussion of America's original sin by looking at some of the typical white responses to this title, *America's Original Sin*, and to the controversial sentence I wrote many years ago to describe what it means.

Over and over, I hear defensive white reactions such as: "*I* never owned slaves," or "*My* family never owned slaves," or "*My* ancestors never owned slaves," or "*My* immigrant forefathers and mothers came long after slavery was abolished. Why am I to blame for racism?" Perhaps the most common response is "I am not a racist." I am not a bad person; don't blame me for this bad thing. That's partly because most white people don't feel themselves to be racists. They are indeed genuinely opposed to the overt expressions of racism we sometimes still see and hear. Another common question white people have and sometimes express is, what do "they" (black and brown people) want?

As a white person, my response to these questions from my white brothers and sisters is twofold.

First, we must look more deeply into our inner selves, which is a practice people of faith and moral conscience are rightly expected to do. And we must go deeper than the individually overt forms of racism to the more covert forms, especially in our institutions and culture. We have new and compelling social research that is teaching us about the "implicit bias" that most people have with regard to race, as we will discuss in chapter 5. Awareness of our biases, personal introspection, empathy, and retraining our ways of thinking are all difficult, but they are necessary to take the first steps toward the real and needed changes in our personal and public lives. This kind of intervention can make racial progress in our communities, congregations, and country.

Second, and perhaps even more unconscious to white people, is the *white privilege* that has come from our nation's history. Whether we or our families or our ancestors had anything to do with the racial sins of

America's establishment, *all white people* have benefited from them. No matter who you are, where you live, how you have acted—and even if you have fought hard against racism—*you can never escape white privilege in America if you are white*.

To benefit from oppression is to be responsible for changing it. The conversations and the "new talks" I propose will not be easy. But they are necessary. Why? Not to make white people feel guilty and defensive about the past but to free all of us to take responsibility for a new and better future—especially for our children. So I am asking my fellow white Americans to stay in this important discussion about America's future, and my fellow white Christians to engage the true meaning of sin and repentance.

What I hear from black friends and allies is also twofold.

First, when issues such as racialized policing or the injustice of America's criminal justice system come up, *it matches their experience*—experiences white people don't have. And when white people are defensive and disbelieve the experience of blacks, it turns them away from white people. It makes black and brown people frustrated and angry that their experience is not being taken seriously by so many white people, even by their white friends. Respect and dignity are important. When both are denied to people of color, and especially to their children, black and brown people are going to push back—as well they should—as would white parents if their children were so treated.

Second, the concern of many people of color is not just about history and the need to teach it accurately, as important as that is. Their concern is for *the current situation*—what they want and fear for their children.

A recent *New York Times* video includes a striking series of comments by young black boys about their feelings—how they feel about their lives in America, their fear of the police, and the painful things they hear from other people around them. As a dad, it moved me to tears, as I believe it would other parents, black and white. You can watch this video op-ed, "A Conversation about Growing Up Black," by visiting: http://www.ny times.com/2015/05/07/opinion/a-conversation-about-growing-up-black .html.

Here are some samples of what these young boys say:

"I've been in situations where, you know, I had to cross the street, because I didn't want to scare the white lady that was walking."

"My mom has to be afraid, when I walk outside, [of] the people who are meant to protect me. . . . I don't like when my mother feels like that, you know, I love my mother, I want her to always be happy."

"How can I not be afraid when I feel like I'm being hunted?"

"I want people to know that I'm perfectly fine, and I'm not going to hurt anybody or do anything bad."

"I should be judged about who I am and what kind of person I am."

"[Mom and Dad], I want you to know that I will act in an appropriate manner, and do everything that you told me to do, because I do love you, and I know that everything you say is for a reason, and not just to talk the talk. And I love you."[1]

In my experience the motivation of black friends and colleagues isn't to make white people feel guilty, to beat us up over our racial history, or to just complain about it. What I hear is deep concern for their children and for their future, and the reasonable expectation that white people not defend themselves from the past but rather join efforts to build a better multiracial future.

Here is where the language of "sin" can be helpful, not just as an old religious category but as a way to become more honest and go to a deeper place. In traditional Christian theology, we know that we are all sinners. The apostle Paul says in Romans 3:23, "All have sinned and fall short of the glory of God." And earlier in the same chapter he writes, "There is no one who is righteous, not even one" (Rom. 3:10). This makes a lot of sense to me in regard to our racial sins. We are often not fully aware of our sins or the collective sins that advantage some and disadvantage others. And all have sinned, so no one is completely righteous here—not one. Whites have benefited from racism, but that doesn't make people of color sinless even in the midst of our nation's sins against them.

Our scriptures and our democratic principles call all of us—across all of our racial diversity—to both personal and social responsibility in fixing the sins our nation was founded upon. There is no moral equivalence in the national white sins committed against people of color and human, angry, and sometimes sinful reactions to them, but there is the opportunity for multiracial integrity and responsibility in repairing and healing those sins. All that starts by being honest.

1. Joe Brewster and Perri Peltz, "A Conversation about Growing Up Black," *New York Times*, May 7, 2015, http://www.nytimes.com/2015/05/07/opinion/a-conversation-about-growing-up -black.html.

What We Tolerate

An extraordinary film called *12 Years a Slave* came out in 2013, and Sojourners hosted a premiere for the faith community in Washington, DC. Reverend Otis Moss III was on the panel afterward that reflected on the film. Dr. Moss is not only a dynamic pastor and preacher at Trinity United Church of Christ in Chicago, but he is also a longtime student and admirer of film. He put this compelling story about Solomon Northup—a free man from New York who was kidnapped and sold into slavery—into the context of all the American films ever done on slavery. Moss told us that, in his view, *12 Years* is the most accurate and best-produced drama of slavery ever done.[2]

In her *New York Times* review titled "The Blood and Tears, Not the Magnolias," Manohla Dargis wrote that *12 Years a Slave* "isn't the first movie about slavery in the United States—but it may be the one that finally makes it impossible for American cinema to continue to sell the ugly lies it's been hawking for more than a century."[3] Instead of the Hollywood portrayal of beautiful plantations, benevolent masters, and simple, happy slaves, it shows the utterly brutal violence of a systematic attempt to dehumanize an entire race of people for economic gain. It reveals how morally outrageous the slave system was, and it is very hard to watch.

That's why we need to see it—especially white people. Many white people, even white people who care about social justice, told me they didn't want to see the film. "Too violent," I heard them say. "Sounds too intense for me." The enslavement of millions of people of African descent by white Americans was always too violent and intense for most white people to accept the truth, even now.

So here is the truth: most white people—the vast majority in both the South and the North, including our "founding fathers"—accepted slavery. Most white people, white Christians, and white churches tolerated slavery in North America for 246 years, from 1619 to 1865.[4] This historically

2. Jim Wallis, "The Most Controversial Sentence I Ever Wrote," *God's Politics* (blog), *Sojourners*, October 24, 2013, http://sojo.net/blogs/2013/10/24/most-controversial-sentence-i-ever-wrote.

3. Manohla Dargis, "The Blood and Tears, Not the Magnolias," *New York Times*, October 17, 2013, http://www.nytimes.com/2013/10/18/movies/12-years-a-slave-holds-nothing-back-in-show-of-suffering.html?_r=0.

4. "Slavery in America," History Channel Online, http://www.history.com/topics/black-history/slavery.

horrendous evil existed because we tolerated it. That's why evil always continues to exist: because we tolerate it.

What do we still tolerate today? The film *12 Years a Slave* is so breathtaking, I worry that it might be seen as a museum movie, a film about a horrible past that is, thankfully, all over now. But we did tolerate this evil institution, and we still tolerate the devaluing of black lives today. Would we tolerate completely dysfunctional urban schools if they were full of young white children? Would we tolerate racialized policing if it were being done to white children? And would we tolerate deliberate political efforts to diminish the votes of minority communities if it were happening to whites?

A Changing America

When people of color speak the truth about the realities of race in our culture and politics, they are often accused of "playing the race card." White racists accuse other white people of doing the same. As a white man and an evangelical Christian, I want to join with my African American brothers and sisters in telling the truth about race in American politics today. That truth telling must become more and more multiracial.

In about thirty years, the majority of Americans will be descended from Africans, Asians, and Latin Americans. Many white Americans are clearly not ready for that profound demographic change in their country. The white fear of who "we" Americans will be is at the heart of much of the resistance to immigration reform, in my view, as well as underlying the criminal justice controversies and other political issues such as voter suppression.

Many older, conservative white voters are acutely aware of being in a country that is becoming less white with each passing year. Congressional districts have been gerrymandered along racial lines to protect dominant racial majorities. Shutting down a government that they believe to be too generous to minorities becomes a cause. "Obamacare" becomes a great threat of government providing medical insurance disproportionately to poor people of color. Giving food stamps to poor families becomes another racial flashpoint for conservative white voters (even though whites constitute the largest racial group of recipients of the Supplemental Nutrition

Assistance Program).[5] For some, a black president has become a symbol of the demographic changes they fear.

Historically Systemic Racism

Remember my controversial sentence, "The United States of America was established as a white society, founded upon the near genocide of another race and then the enslavement of yet another."

To make such a statement today is to be immediately accused of being rhetorical or, worse yet, of being stuck in the 1960s. The reaction is instructive and revealing. The history of how white Europeans conquered North America by almost destroying the native population and by building the new nation's economy on the backs of kidnapped Africans can hardly be denied. Yet to speak honestly of such historical facts is to be charged with being polemical, divisive, or out of date.

Native Americans suffered near extinction as a result of the European "discovery" of their lands. Before European contact in 1492, an estimated 5 million people lived in what is now the continental United States.[6] By 1900, 95 percent of the precontact population had been wiped out by European-borne diseases, war, forced relocation, forced labor, dietary changes, and other causes related to European colonialism.[7] The Europeans who colonized North America and their descendants also waged cultural genocide against the Native Americans over the next five centuries, attempting to force Native peoples to adopt a "civilized" lifestyle, which included Western Christianity.

Richard Twiss, an evangelical Native American leader who championed a vision of Christianity that integrated and honored Native traditions and culture, observed that traditional Native American rituals and music were long thought to be incompatible with Christianity due to the legacy of colonialism and cultural genocide:

5. Arthur Delaney and Alissa Scheller, "Who Gets Food Stamps? White People, Mostly," *Huffington Post*, February 28, 2015, http://www.huffingtonpost.com/2015/02/28/food-stamp -demographics_n_6771938.html.

6. Russell Thornton, "Native American Demographic and Tribal Survival into the Twenty-First Century," *American Studies* 46, nos. 3/4 (Fall–Winter 2005): 24, https://journals.ku.edu /index.php/amerstud/article/viewFile/2951/2910.

7. Russell Thornton, *American Indian Holocaust and Survival: A Population History since 1492* (Norman: University of Oklahoma Press, 1987), 43–44.

Participation in traditional powwows, with their key features of drumming/
singing and dancing, for many Native Christians has been discouraged or forbid-
den. Long considered a seditious threat to government control and an obstacle
to the evangelization of tribal people, there was a long-concerted effort on the
part of the U.S. government and missionary organizations and workers to put
an end to these practices.[8]

The legacy of five centuries of colonialism and genocide continues to
linger in the appalling conditions on many Native American reservations
and the treatment of Indigenous people in the larger society. In 2012, the
median income of Native American households was $35,310, compared
to $51,371 for the nation.[9] Also in 2012, 29.1 percent of Native Americans
lived in poverty—the highest rate of any racial group—compared to 15.9
percent for the nation as a whole.[10]

This legacy of oppression also reveals itself in how Native people are
portrayed in popular culture today. For example, it is past time to change
my current hometown's NFL team name. The word "Redskins" is dis-
paraging and offensive—it says as much in the dictionary.[11] But the team
name represents something much deeper, as young Native American leader
Peggy Flanagan, who recently became a mother, writes:

> As a Native American woman and mother, I am concerned about how my
> infant daughter will see herself represented and portrayed in popular culture
> and the media as she grows up. Multiple studies have shown that American
> Indian sports mascots and other negative stereotypes are detrimental to the
> self-esteem and development of Native American youth and exacerbate racial
> inequities. The continued use of the Washington Redsk*ns mascot sends my
> daughter, and other Native and non-Native youth, the message that somehow
> it's okay for her to be called a racial slur. In her formative years, she will con-
> tinually see herself portrayed as less than human. . . . When you deny people
> their humanity, it is easier to disrespect them and their culture. I am not a
> mascot. My daughter is not a mascot. My people are not mascots. We are
> human beings. We are still here.[12]

8. Richard Twiss, "A Sacred Beat," *Sojourners*, June 2015, 39.
9. "Statistics on Native Students," National Indian Education Association, http://www
.niea.org/Research/Statistics.aspx.
10. Ibid.
11. "Redskin," Dictionary.com, http://dictionary.reference.com/browse/redskin.
12. Peggy Flanagan, "Sacking the 'Redsk*ns,'" *Sojourners*, February 2014, http://sojo.net
/magazine/2014/02/sacking-redskns.

We must acknowledge that not only are Native Americans "still here," they are our neighbors, made in the image of God. We should not tolerate the fact that five hundred years after the arrival of Europeans, the institutions of our society—economic, political, and cultural—continue to disadvantage, marginalize, and trivialize the lives and images of Native people.

Like Native Americans, Asian Americans also suffer today from having their images and cultures mocked, misunderstood, misappropriated, and trivialized. Although Asians arrived in the United States later than European colonizers and African slaves, the legacy of European domination and exploitation of nonwhites has also affected Asian people. The exploitation of Asians as a cheap source of labor, decades of immigration laws that prohibited Asians from settling in the United States, other laws that prohibited Asians who were already here from becoming naturalized citizens, and the internment of Japanese Americans during World War II are just a few examples of the historical mistreatment and exclusion of people with Asian ancestry.

In recent decades, Asian Americans have as a group succeeded economically but still often feel marginalized. American popular culture, which is still mostly dominated at the upper levels by whites, routinely and casually propagates offensive, insensitive, and inaccurate stereotypes of Asian people. Perhaps most distressing to me are the instances where this has happened within the Christian community.

For example, in 2009 a book about character and integrity in Christian leadership began to gain popularity in some circles of primarily white evangelical men. The book, released by Zondervan, a Christian publishing house, was called *Deadly Viper Character Assassins: A Kung Fu Survival Guide for Life and Leadership*. Although the message of the book about the importance of moral character was admirable, it was packaged, marketed, and themed around Asian culture and martial arts in ways that reflected a poor and caricatured understanding of Asian culture and traditions. At times, the marketing materials veered into blatantly offensive stereotypes of Asian people. As Soong-Chan Rah, a theologian and professor at North Park Seminary who is Asian American, put it in an open letter to the authors and publisher:

> You [the authors] are two white males who are inappropriately co-opting another culture and using it to further the marketing of your book. . . . In other words,

you are using what are important and significant cultural symbols to make a
sale or to make your point. . . . You are taking a caricature of Asian culture
(the martial arts warrior, the ninja, etc.) and furthering the caricature rather
than engaging Asian culture in a way that honors it. . . . You are representing a
culture that you do not know very well to thousands of people. You are using
another culture to make your message more fun. That is offensive to those of
us who are of that culture and seek to honor our culture.[13]

Rah also pointed out that the offensive marketing campaign for the book
was only possible because the entire editorial and publishing staff at
Zondervan at the time was white.[14]

This particular story does have a positive ending. After Rah and a
coalition of other Asian American Christian leaders expressed their concerns through honest dialogue with both the authors and the publishers,
Zondervan agreed to permanently remove the book from stores and work
with the authors to repackage their material on character and integrity
in a culturally appropriate way. Zondervan also appointed a new editor
in chief, whom the CEO charged with making changes at the company
that would prevent this sort of mistake in the future.[15] This was a genuine
act of repentance on Zondervan's part and a great example of how truly
listening to people with different cultural and racial backgrounds can lead
to changes in perspectives and actions.

When it comes to the experience of African Americans in our country,
until the recent controversies surrounding black men being shot by white police officers, racism wasn't a hot topic. In fact, many claimed that the United
States had become a "postracial" society. After the so-called "racial crisis" of
the '60s, white America, including some of those involved in the civil rights
movement, had moved on to other concerns. The legal victories of black
Americans in that period, as far as most white Americans were concerned,
had settled the issue and left many asking, "What more do blacks want?"

Racial attitudes toward African Americans have changed among whites,
a fact attested to by opinion polls and accelerated by generational progress.

13. Soong-Chan Rah, "How Deadly Viper Character Assassins Undermines Its Message with
Co-opted Culture," *God's Politics* (blog), *Sojourners,* November 11, 2009, http://sojo.net/blogs
/2009/11/04/how-deadly-viper-character-assassins-undermines-its-message-co-opted-culture.
    14. Ibid.
    15. Soong-Chan Rah, "Tremendous Act of Repentance by Zondervan," *God's Politics* (blog),
Sojourners, November 20, 2009, http://sojo.net/blogs/2009/11/20/tremendous-act-repentance
-zondervan.

One reason for the change in popular attitudes is the increased number of black faces appearing in the very visible worlds of the mass media, politics, entertainment, and sports.

In the decades since the passage of the momentous civil rights legislation of the 1960s, *some things have changed and some things haven't*. What has changed are the personal racial attitudes of many white Americans and the opportunities for some black Americans to enter the middle class. The word "middle" is key here, insofar as fewer blacks have yet been allowed into the upper echelons and decision-making positions of business, the professions, the media, or even sports and entertainment, where black "progress" has so often been celebrated.

Legal segregation has been lifted off the backs of black people, which has also contributed to changes in white attitudes. But de facto economic and housing segregation still exists for the majority of African Americans, and the geography of race still separates most black Americans from most white Americans. Public Religion Research Institute's 2013 American Values Survey found that the social networks of white Americans are an astonishing 91 percent white, with fully 75 percent of whites having *entirely* white social networks.[16]

What has not changed is the *systematic* and pervasive character of racism and the conditions of life for what many call the "black underclass." Profound racial inequality continues to exist. In 2011, the median household income for a white family was $67,175, compared to $40,007 for a Latino household and $39,760 for a black household.[17] The wealth gap is even more staggering: the median net worth of white households in 2013 was $141,900, compared to $13,700 for Latino households and $11,000 for black households.[18] In other words, the median white household is thirteen times wealthier than the median black household and ten times wealthier than the median Latino household.

16. Robert P. Jones, "Self-Segregation: Why It's So Hard for Whites to Understand Ferguson," *Atlantic Monthly*, August 21, 2014, http://www.theatlantic.com/national/archive/2014/08/self-segregation-why-its-hard-for-whites-to-understand-ferguson/378928/.

17. Drew Desilver, "5 Facts about Economic Inequality," Pew Research Center, January 7, 2014, http://www.pewresearch.org/fact-tank/2014/01/07/5-facts-about-economic-inequality/.

18. Rakesh Kochhar and Richard Fry, "Wealth Inequality Has Widened along Racial, Ethnic Lines since End of Great Recession," Pew Research Center, December 12, 2014, http://www.pewresearch.org/fact-tank/2014/12/12/racial-wealth-gaps-great-recession/.

Of course, economic inequality is both caused by and can be measured by factors beyond mere dollars and cents. For example, in 2013 the homeownership rate for white households was 73.9 percent, compared to 47.4 percent for minority households.[19] The unemployment rate for African Americans has never been less than 66 percent higher than the unemployment rate for whites.[20] In fact, more than half of the time since 1972, the black unemployment rate has been at least double the white unemployment rate.[21] Even when black families manage to reach the middle class, children of these families are less likely to stay there than white children of middle-class families, according to a study done by the Federal Reserve Bank and reported in *The Atlantic*. The report noted that "about 60 percent of black children whose parents had income that fell into the top 50 percent of the distribution saw their own income fall into the bottom half during adulthood. This type of downward slide was common for only 36 percent of white children."[22]

Our education system is another part of American society with vast racial inequalities. According to Richard Reeves at the Brookings Institute, "the school system remains highly segregated by race and economic status: Black students make up 16 percent of the public school population, but the average black student attends a school that's 50 percent black." The average black student, Reeves said, "attends a school at the 37th percentile for test score results whereas the average white student attends a school in the 60th percentile."[23] And only 17 percent of African American kids graduate from college, compared to 31 percent of white kids.[24]

The area of society where we see perhaps the greatest racial inequalities is our criminal justice system, which we will take up in detail in chapter 7.

19. Ibid.

20. Phillip Bump, "Black Unemployment Is Always Much Worse Than White Unemployment. But the Gap Depends on Where You Live," *Washington Post*, September 6, 2014, http://www.washingtonpost.com/blogs/the-fix/wp/2014/09/06/black-unemployment-is-always-much-worse-than-white-unemployment-but-the-gap-depends-on-where-you-live/.

21. Ibid.

22. Gillian B. White, "How Black Middle-Class Kids Become Poor Adults," *Atlantic Monthly*, January 19, 2015, http://www.theatlantic.com/business/archive/2015/01/how-black-middle-class-kids-become-black-lower-class-adults/384613/.

23. Richard V. Reeves and Edward Rodrigue, "Five Bleak Facts on Black Opportunity," Brookings Institute, January 15, 2015, http://www.brookings.edu/blogs/social-mobility-memos/posts/2015/01/15-mlk-black-opportunity-reeves.

24. Richard V. Reeves and Quentin Karpilow, "The College Bottleneck in the American Opportunity Structure," Brookings Institute, May 8, 2014, http://www.brookings.edu/blogs/social-mobility-memos/posts/2014/05/08-college-bottleneck-american-opportunity-structure-reeves.

Historically, racism originated in domination and provided the social rationale and philosophical justification for debasing, degrading, and doing violence to people on the basis of skin color. Many have pointed out how racism is sustained by *both personal attitudes and structural forces*. Racism can therefore be brutally overt or invisibly institutional, or both.

Individual statements and acts of racism obviously still exist. The most horrible example in decades was the murder of nine black Christians in their Charleston church by a young white supremacist on June 17, 2015. But many other cases of overtly expressed racism still abound.

For instance, in a well-publicized case in 2014, LA Clippers basketball team owner Donald Sterling was caught on tape telling his girlfriend not to post pictures on Instagram of herself with black players or bring black people with her to Clippers games (as a result, he was banned for life from the NBA).[25] Statements such as Sterling's are considered embarrassing today. But the institutional character of racism still remains, even in sports—despite one owner getting banned and losing his team. The scope of racism extends to every area of human society, economy, psychology, and culture.

Prejudice may indeed be a universal human sin that all races can exhibit, but racism is more than an inevitable consequence of human nature or social accident. Rather, racism is a system of oppression for social and economic purposes. As many analysts have suggested, *racism is prejudice plus power*.[26]

In the United States, the original purpose of racism was to justify slavery and its enormous economic benefit. This particular form of racism, inherited from the English to justify their own slave trade, was especially venal, for it defined the slave not merely as an unfortunate victim of bad circumstances, war, or social dislocation but rather as less than human, as a thing, an animal, a piece of "chattel" property to be bought, sold, used, and abused. In contrast, Greek slaves often had roles as tutors to the wealthiest Roman families and were hardly denied their humanity.

American slaves did not have to be treated with any human consideration whatsoever. Even in the founding document of our nation, the

25. Braden Goyette, "LA Clippers Owner Donald Sterling's Racist Rant Caught on Tape: Report (Updates)," *Huffington Post*, April 26, 2014, http://www.huffingtonpost.com/2014/04/26/donald-sterling-racist_n_5218572.html.

26. See, for example, Don Operario and Susan T. Fiske, "Racism Equals Power Plus Prejudice," in *Confronting Racism: The Problem and the Response*, ed. Jennifer Lynn Eberhardt and Susan T. Fiske (Thousand Oaks, CA: Sage, 1998), 33–53.

famous constitutional compromise defined the slave as only three-fifths
of a person. The professed high ideals of Anglo-Western society could
be allowed to exist side by side with the profitable institution of slavery
only if the humanity of the slave was denied and disregarded. Recently,
I've heard black young people in Ferguson and other places describe their
status in the criminal justice system with the same fraction: "We are still
three-fifths of a person."

The heart of racism was and is economic, though its roots and results
are also deeply cultural, psychological, sexual, religious, and, of course,
political. Due to 246 years of brutal slavery and an additional 100 years
of legal segregation and discrimination, no area of the relationship between black and white people in the United States is free from the legacy
of racism.

All of this has especially affected black youth, whose rate of unemployment is alarmingly high. In the year before March 2015, between 25
and 35 percent of black teenagers from sixteen to nineteen years old who
looked for work couldn't find jobs.[27] The human meaning of such grim
statistics can be seen in the faces of the kids in the inner-city neighborhoods where I have lived and spent time. They know they have no job, no
place, no future—and can therefore feel no real stake in this country. In
the introduction to this book I quoted the young man who said he just
wanted a "good education, a good job, and a good family." He went on to
say, "I want to be able to 'green light' something. Right now I can't green
light anything." For many young people of color, society has ceased to
be a society for them, with very little ownership or sense of belonging.

The economy itself enforces the oppression of racism. It happens invisibly and impersonally in the changing economic order. When I was
growing up in Detroit, many black families had manufacturing jobs that
were later lost to automation or to cheaper labor markets in the Third
World. Family farm labor, which also had supported many black families,
has become almost extinct, lost to big agriculture. Both were historically
important to black workers and families.

In the new "high-tech" world and "service economy," many blacks have
been relegated to the lowest-income jobs at places such as McDonald's.

27. "The Employment Situation—March 2015," US Department of Labor Bureau of Labor
Statistics, April 3, 2015, http://www.bls.gov/news.release/pdf/empsit.pdf.

Many young blacks today feel they have been educationally and economically marginalized, but they still have a real desire for better jobs and lives in the new economy.

Increasingly, we see a two-tiered economy: one tier being a highly lucrative level of professionals, managers, investors, technicians, and high-end consumers who operate and run the system, and the other tier an impoverished sector of unemployed, underemployed, and unskilled labor from which the work of servicing the system can be done. That black and brown people are disproportionately consigned to the lowest economic tier is a continuing proof of racism. The existence of a vast black and brown underclass, inhabiting the inner cities of our nation, is a testimony to the tenacity of white racism, decades after legal segregation was officially outlawed.

The cold economic savagery of racism has led to declines in the quality of life in low-income black communities. The rate of infant mortality for black babies is more than twice that of white babies.[28] More than 70 percent of black children are now born outside of marriage.[29] The leading cause of death for black men and women ages fifteen to thirty-four is homicide.[30] For young black men ages fifteen to twenty-four, almost 50 percent of all deaths are due to homicide (just 8 percent of young white men of the same age group who die do so from homicide).[31] African Americans make up 40 percent of the incarcerated population, despite making up only 13 percent of the population.[32]

Despite landmark court decisions and civil rights legislation, nearly 30 percent of black Americans still live in poverty,[33] suffering from education

28. "QuickStats: Infant Mortality Rates, by Race and Hispanic Ethnicity of Mother—United States, 2000, 2005, and 2010," Centers for Disease Control and Prevention, January 10, 2014, http://www.cdc.gov/mmwr/preview/mmwrhtml/mm6301a9.htm.

29. Joyce A. Martin et al., "Births: Final Data for 2013," Centers for Disease Control and Prevention, *National Vital Statistics Reports* 64, no. 1 (January 15, 2015), http://www.cdc.gov/nchs/data/nvsr/nvsr64/nvsr64_01.pdf.

30. "Deaths, Percent of Total Deaths, and Death Rates for the 15 Leading Causes of Death in 5-Year Age Groups, by Race and Sex: United States, 2013," Centers for Disease Control and Prevention, December 31, 2014, http://www.cdc.gov/nchs/data/dvs/LCWK1_2013.pdf.

31. Ibid.

32. Leah Sakala, "Breaking Down Mass Incarceration in the 2010 Census: State-by-State Incarceration Rates by Race/Ethnicity," Prison Policy Initiative, May 28, 2014, http://www.prisonpolicy.org/reports/rates.html.

33. Carmen DeNavas-Walt and Bernadette D. Proctor, "Income and Poverty in the United States: 2013," US Census Bureau, September 2014, http://www.census.gov/content/dam/Census/library/publications/2014/demo/p60-249.pdf.

and housing that is both segregated and inferior. Such conditions, along with diminishing social services due to state and local budget deficits and the lack of jobs that pay a living family wage, inevitably and easily lead to despair and criminality. Historically, many other countries and cultures show that poverty, and especially growing inequality, leads to family breakdown and crime. The fact that this reality is still surprising or incomprehensible to many white Americans raises the question of how much racial attitudes have really changed.

Reading these appalling statistics can feel devastating. And it is even more impactful when you realize that all these numbers have very human faces. To move forward, we need to get personal about all of this, to regard the children in these statistics as *our* children. Statistics should not disempower or disengage us. On the contrary, these realities can wake up our hearts and minds and set us on the path to change them, and that's what I see a new generation of young people doing around the country.

The connection of racism to American militarism should by now also be painfully clear. First, massive military spending causes cuts in social services to low-income people who need some support and assistance in escaping poverty, and the most vulnerable are disproportionately people of color.

Second, the primarily military definition of national security puts a prior claim on vast material, scientific, and human resources that could otherwise be directed toward achieving economic opportunity with the expansion of jobs and critically needed improvements in our society's infrastructures that would create many more jobs.

The building of a new clean and renewable energy grid would conserve energy and protect us from increasing climate change. And the jobs created by retrofitting all our existing commercial and residential buildings and renovating our energy economy would produce generations of constructive new work and good jobs. As Van Jones wrote in *The Green Collar Economy*: "We should use the transition to a better energy strategy as an opportunity to create a better economy and a better country all around."[34]

But all that is proclaimed as not being a practical financial option because of budget deficits, corporate subsidies (even to extremely profitable

34. Van Jones, *The Green Collar Economy: How One Solution Can Fix Our Two Biggest Problems* (New York: HarperCollins, 2009), e-book edition, 19.

oil and gas companies), and the continuing human and material cost of American military spending, which is about $640 billion per year, greater than the military spending of the next seven highest-spending countries combined.[35] What's most needed is a whole new debate about what really creates national security.

The failure of the mostly white, middle-class peace movement in the United States to make such connections and enter into a vital political partnership with racial minorities is a primary reason for the ineffectiveness of that movement. Even in the peace movement, racism becomes a debilitating force that robs us of opportunities to work toward a more just and peaceful nation and foreign policy.

Benefit and Responsibility

The strategies for how black and brown people will challenge and finally overcome the ever-changing face of white racism must always originate within communities of color themselves. White allies can play a significant role in the struggle against racism in partnership with people of color. But an even more important task for white Americans is to examine ourselves, our relationships, our institutions, and our society for the ugly persistence of racism.

Whites in America must admit the realities of racism and begin to operate on the assumption that ours is still a racist society. Positive individual attitudes are simply not enough, for, as we have seen, racism is much more than just personal.

White people in the United States have benefited from the structures of racism, whether or not they have ever committed a racist act, uttered a racist word, or had a racist thought (as unlikely as that is). Just as surely as blacks suffer in a white society *because* they are black, whites benefit *because* they are white. And if whites have profited from a racist system, we must try to change it. To go along with racist institutions and structures such as the racialized criminal justice system, to obliviously accept the economic order as it is, and to just quietly go about our personal business within institutional racism is to participate in white racism.

35. "The U.S. Spends More on Defense Than the Next Seven Countries Combined," Peter G. Peterson Foundation, April 13, 2015, http://pgpf.org/Chart-Archive/0053_defense-comparison.

Racism has to do with the power to dominate and enforce oppression, and that power in America is mostly still in white hands. Therefore, although there are instances of black racial prejudice against whites in the United States today, that is really not "black racism." Remember, racism is "prejudice plus power." By and large, black people in America do not have the power to enforce that prejudice.

Racism in white institutions must be challenged and eradicated by white people and not just by black people. In fact, white racism is primarily a white responsibility.

We must not give in to the popular temptation to believe that racism existed mostly in the Old South or before the 1960s. Neither can any of our other struggles against poverty, hunger, homelessness, or sexism be separated from the reality of racism. There are always connections.

The church must, of course, get its own house in order. It is still riddled with racism and segregation. The exemplary role of the black church in the struggle against racism offers a sharp indictment of white churches, which still, sadly, mostly reflect the racial attitudes, geography, and structures around them. Multiracial congregations offer hope that such factors are beginning to change.

The church has the capacity to be a much-needed prophetic interrogator of a system that has always depended upon racial oppression. The gospel is clear. The church can be a spiritual and social community where the ugly barriers of race are finally torn down to reveal the possibilities of a different American future.

The First Black President

"What racism?" many pundits and people cry. "Didn't we just elect a black president?" The implication being: "Doesn't that prove that racism is over in America?"

A few responses. First, on November 4, 2008, the United States did what very few countries have ever done—democratically elect a chief executive from a minority race in a country with a different majority race. That a still predominantly white United States would elect a black man as head of state was stunning. It made me think that the country was better than I thought it was. That historic accomplishment is a sign of great progress and a hope of better things to come for racial equality and justice in the United States.

Second, the majority of Americans, even of white Americans—whether they voted for Obama or not—seemed to feel positive and even proud that the nation had finally reached this amazing milestone. Inaugurating Barack Obama on that cold and historic day made most Americans feel good about themselves and about their country. The new president's approval rating climbed up to 70 percent in the week after his inauguration, which obviously meant that even some of those who voted against him were impressed by the fact of the first black president.

Third, there are many people, most of whom voted against Obama, who have basic disagreements with the president on substantive political issues. Clearly, to disagree with a black president on policy questions does not mean that you are racist. All the people who initially approved of the president's job performance but now disapprove did not suddenly turn into racists. Many of my conservative friends, who admire Obama personally but disagree with him politically, can hardly be called racists.

But fourth, and equally important, there was and still is a hard core of racially motivated white people in this nation who voted against Obama because he is black and who virulently oppose him as president because he is black. That racist core of angry white Americans resides on the extreme political right of American politics.

The far-right wing in America has never supported racial equality. Its political representatives voted against both the Civil Rights Act of 1964 and the Voting Rights Act of 1965, and most have never repented of it. The loudest voices of right-wing talk radio and cable television appeal directly to that core with subtle and not-so-subtle racial messages, as has the right wing of the Republican Party, and now the Tea Party, for many years.

We see many racial subtexts in the intensity of the attacks on Obama—not in the disagreements per se but in the viciousness of the rhetoric. Racism shows itself in disrespect, and many African American citizens feel that the first black president has been widely disrespected. They see it in the disrespect shown a black president by white members of Congress, many from the South. Many see it in the "birthers" movement, who try to stir up doubts about Obama's citizenship. Questioning Barack Obama's birthplace and parentage, calling him a Muslim (of course, there's nothing wrong with being a Muslim, but Obama has been more outspoken about his Christian faith than many other presidents), and naming him as a "foreigner" and not a "real American" are all ways to define this president as "the other" and not one of "us." The hatred goes far beyond Obama's policies and extends to his very person as the wrong kind of American. Obama shows them that they are losing national elections, and they fear that means losing "their" country.

We all know that racism still exists in America today. We also know that there is a hard core of our white fellow citizens who simply will not accept their black or brown brothers and sisters—especially one in the White House. So while we should not call every disagreement an issue of racism, it is time to call out the racism that really does still exist, that wounds our soul as a nation, and that obstructs the promise of the United States.

"Listen Up" and "We Forgive You"

Much of American racism as it is experienced today is rooted in the broader structures of society such as education, employment, housing, and the criminal justice system. In this way, racism is more subtle than open, interpersonal bigotry and at least as destructive. Unfortunately, many whites, even those in highly visible leadership positions in the church, seem to be in deep denial about these structural inequalities. As a result, they sometimes say things that, even if they are meant well, are in fact deeply hurtful because they reveal an ignorance born of a failure to truly listen and interact with people from different races and backgrounds. How we listen and who we listen to is critically important for the future of our country. There is a right way and a wrong way. Here is an example of the wrong way by an old evangelical leader and the right way by a multiracial new generation of evangelicals who responded to him.

On March 12, 2015, evangelist Franklin Graham posted a remarkable message on Facebook. In response to the controversial police shootings of young black men, Graham had this to say:

> Listen up—Blacks, Whites, Latinos, and everybody else. Most police shootings can be avoided. It comes down to respect for authority and obedience. If a police officer tells you to stop, you stop. If a police officer tells you to put your hands in the air, you put your hands in the air. If a police officer tells you to lay down face first with your hands behind your back, you lay down face first

with your hands behind your back. It's as simple as that. Even if you think the police officer is wrong—YOU OBEY. Parents, teach your children to respect and obey those in authority. Mr. President, *this* is a message our nation needs to hear, and they need to hear it from you. Some of the unnecessary shootings we have seen recently might have been avoided. The Bible says to submit to your leaders and those in authority "because they keep watch over you as those who must give an account."[36]

When I read Graham's comments, I felt personally compelled to respond about what it means to "listen up." His father, Rev. Billy Graham, was known for racial sensitivity in insisting that his evangelistic crusades be racially integrated, even in the South in the 1950s; he had personally met with and supported Martin Luther King Jr. during the civil rights movement. But that racial sensitivity was not present in his son's extremely insensitive remarks. So on Facebook, I posted this response:

Dear Franklin,
    The real issue here goes much deeper than obedience to the police or lack thereof. We all need and should obey good police officers whose important mission is to serve and protect—but that must be done equally and without racial bias. Most African American men, in particular, could tell you their own personal stories of mistreatment by white police officers; which had nothing to do with them not obeying them. Many black women and other people of color could tell you stories too. You should be listening to them. . . .
    It's time to listen to and learn from Americans of color, including our black brothers and sisters in Christ. Listen to why all black parents have to have "the talk" about white police with their sons and daughters. Your Facebook post makes you seem, at best, oblivious to the racial inequity in this country's policing and criminal justice system, which is also still deeply embedded in our American society. At worst, your post reflects your own racial biases—unconscious or conscious. It makes me sad to read such things coming from a leader in your position. So until you are equally willing to "listen up," please stop making such embarrassing and divisive statements.[37]

On March 19, an open letter was sent to Graham, written by young, black evangelical leaders—and signed by many other black, Latino, Asian American, and white evangelicals—which explained the sin the older white

---

36. Franklin Graham, "Listen Up," Facebook post, March 12, 2015, https://www.facebook.com/FranklinGraham/posts/883361438386705.
    37. Jim Wallis, "Last Thursday," Facebook post, March 16, 2015, https://www.facebook.com/permalink.php?story_fbid=10152653035032441&id=207206302440.

evangelical leader had committed, and then went on to say, "We forgive you." It's a powerful letter, and I invite you to read an excerpt from it below:[38]

Dear Rev. Graham,

We write to you in the spirit of Matthew 18: we aim to reconcile with you. You have sinned against us, fellow members of the body of Christ. . . . Your words hurt and influenced thousands. Therefore, we must respond publicly so that those you hurt might know you have received a reply and the hundreds of thousands you influenced might know that following your lead on this issue will break the body of Christ further.

Frankly, Rev. Graham, your insistence that "Blacks, Whites, Latinos, and everybody else" "Listen up," was crude, insensitive, and paternalistic. . . . Your instructions oversimplified a complex and critical problem facing the nation and minimized the testimonies and wisdom of people of color and experts of every hue, including six police commissioners that served on the president's task force on policing reform. . . .

The fact that you identify a widely acknowledged social injustice as "simple" reveals your lack of empathy and understanding of the depth of sin that some in the body have suffered under the weight of our broken justice system. It also reveals a cavalier disregard for the enduring impacts and outcomes of the legal regimes that enslaved and oppressed people of color, made in the image of God—from Native American genocide and containment, to colonial and antebellum slavery, through Jim Crow and peonage, to our current system of mass incarceration and criminalization. . . .

Rev. Graham, as our brother in Christ and as a leader in the church, we forgive you and we pray that one day you will recognize and understand the enduring legacy of the institution of race in our nation. . . .

Ultimately, we invite you to join us in the ongoing work of the ministry of reconciliation.[39]

In spiritual and biblical terms, racism must be named as a perverse sin that cuts to the core of the gospel message. Put simply, racism negates the reason for which Christ died—the reconciling work of the cross, first to God and then to one another. It denies the purpose of the church: to bring together, in Christ, those who have been divided from one another— particularly, in the early church's case, Jew and Gentile—a division based on racial ethnicity, culture, and religion.

38. You can read the whole letter at http://sojo.net/blogs/2015/03/19/open-letter-franklin -graham.
39. Lisa Sharon Harper et al., "An Open Letter to Franklin Graham," *God's Politics* (blog), *Sojourners*, March 19, 2015, http://sojo.net/blogs/2015/03/19/open-letter-franklin-graham.

There is only one remedy for such a sin, and that is repentance. If genuine, it will always bear fruit in concrete forms of conversion and changed behavior, with both rejections and reversals of racism. Although the United States may have changed in regard to some of its racial attitudes and allowed some of its black citizens into the middle class, white America has yet to recognize the extent of its racism, especially institutionally—that we always have been a racist society, still are, and have yet to fully repent of our racial sins.

Because of that lack of repentance and, indeed, because of the economic, social, and political purposes still served by the oppression of black and brown people, systematic racism continues to shadow American life. Although often denied by white social commentators and the media, evidence of the persistent and endemic character of racism still painfully abounds.

It is to the true meaning of repentance, in response to the sin of white racism, that we now turn.

4 | Repentance Means More Than Just Saying You're Sorry

When it comes to a sin with the magnitude of America's original sin of white racism, the only adequate response prompts the deepest meaning of *repentance*—and only in the fullest magnitude of that transforming word. Yet few religious words have been more misunderstood, misinterpreted, and minimized—especially in the churches.

If the near genocide and historic oppression of America's Native American peoples and the enslavement and debasing of African peoples for profit were both sins—America's original sin—how can we possibly respond today? And if the consequences of those sins still linger in the many ways we have been discussing, what do we do now?

Spiritually and theologically, the necessary response to sins, large and small, is always repentance. But what does that mean, especially for a sin as big as racism?

Repentance, clearly, is more than just saying you're sorry, or even just feeling guilty—which are popular misconceptions of the word. The biblical meaning of repentance is far more challenging than that, and the true meaning of the word is often not well understood. Repentance is not just expressing sorrow or admitting guilt; it is about turning completely around and going in a whole new direction.

In Scripture, repentance means literally to stop, make a radical turnaround, and take an entirely new path. It means a change of mind and heart and is demonstrated by nothing less than transformed behavior. Repentance means we now have to think, act, and live differently than we did before, when we were still under sin.

The Biblical Meaning of Repentance

In the Hebrew Scriptures, the Old Testament, the word for repentance is *sub*. *Baker's Evangelical Dictionary of Biblical Theology* says, "Two requisites of repentance included in *sub* are to turn from evil, and to turn to the good."[1] Here is the central idea of turning away from evil, turning around, and turning (returning) to God. The article points to the prophet Ezekiel's call from God to the children of Israel and to the demands and invitations of many other biblical prophets:

> "Repent! Turn from your idols and renounce all your detestable practices!" ([Ezek.] 14:6); "Repent! Turn away from all your offenses" ([Ezek.] 18:30); "Turn! Turn from your evil ways" ([Ezek.] 33:11). Such a call was characteristic of the prophets (see, e.g., Isa. 45:22; 55:7; Joel 2:12–13). The Septuagint underlines this idea by usually translating *sub* by *epi* (*apo-*)*strepho* (to turn about, or to turn away from). To be abandoned are both evil intentions and evil deeds, and both motive and conduct are to be radically changed. A striking example is found in Isaiah 1:16–17: "Take your evil deeds out of my sight! Stop doing wrong, learn to do right! Seek justice, encourage the oppressed. Defend the cause of the fatherless, plead the case of the widow."[2]

Words, like intentions, deeds, and practices, are critical here. "Conduct" is to be "radically changed." And the biblical language isn't as nuanced as ours normally is about sin, especially big sins such as racism. Evil is named, as is doing "wrong," and repentance is about learning to do "right." And justice for the oppressed is named as a fruit of repentance.

1. Walter M. Dunnett, "Repentance," in *Baker's Evangelical Dictionary of Biblical Theology*, ed. Walter A. Elwell, http://www.biblestudytools.com/dictionaries/bakers-evangelical-dictionary /repentance.html.
2. Ibid.

We need to apply these clear prophetic commands to America's original sin of racism: from 246 years of slavery to 100 years of racial discrimination in the Jim Crow system; and from the incredibly violent white resistance to the civil rights movement in the 1950s and '60s—and to every black attempt to change systematic racism—to today's structural racial injustice in criminal justice, economics, education, housing, and politics, including the racial gerrymandering of voting districts and the attempted suppression of black voting rights as recently as the last election.

These "evil intentions and evil deeds" have been upheld not just by culture and politics but also by the legal systems of the United States—including the brutal enforcement of slavery, the violent application of segregation laws, the long history of racialized policing, and the racially disproportionate exercise of mass incarceration and the death penalty. Clearly, Isaiah's call to "stop doing wrong" by seeking justice and encouraging the oppressed remains as relevant today as ever.

In the New Testament, the primary word for repentance in the Greek is *metanoia*. It's such a wonderful and rich word, whose roots are also in our word "metamorphosis," meaning a *transformation*. Repentance is what leads to conversion. Repentance "turns us from sin, selfishness, idols, habits, bondages, and demons, both private and public."[3] The repentance of stopping our present path in the wrong direction and turning completely around is what opens the door to conversion.

"Repentance leads to conversion," and "deeds consistent with repentance" are to follow.[4] Repentance, remember, was the first proclamation of the sermons of John the Baptist, the forerunner of Jesus. Jesus began his own ministry with the call to repent in Matthew 4:17: "From that time Jesus began to preach, saying, 'Repent, for the kingdom of heaven is at hand'" (ESV).

A whole new order called the kingdom of God is about to break into the world, Jesus is saying here, and if you want to be part of it, to join it and him, you must go through a transformation so fundamental that Jesus would later refer to it as a "new birth" (John 3:3–8). Old things will pass away, new things will come, and a whole new community will be created.

3. Jim Wallis, *The Call to Conversion: Why Faith Is Always Personal but Never Private*, 2nd ed. (San Francisco: HarperSanFrancisco, 2005), 5.
4. "Repentance."

From the beginning of his ministry, Jesus led his disciples to people outside their traditional boundaries. He lifted up a "good Samaritan" from a different ethnic group as his best example of what it means to be a good neighbor and fulfill the laws of God. And, of course, one of the fundamental tasks of the early church was the establishment of a new community with both Jews and Gentiles at the center—opening up and inviting every race of God's children to join the new community called the body of Christ. So from the beginning of the call to repentance and the beginning of the church, responding to God also meant responding in a new way to different racial groups. That is very important.

The English expression closest to the word *metanoia* is "a change of mind." Nineteenth-century commentator Treadwell Walden wrote that *metanoia* is a change

> not of essence, of course, but of consciousness. We understand by a change of place the occupation of another place; a change of condition, another condition; a change of form, another form. We can imagine the otherwise unchangeable man undergoing, in like manner, a "Change of Mind." . . . The Mind, when placed in a new situation, thinks new thoughts, receives new impressions, forms new tastes, inclinations, purposes, develops new aptitudes.[5]

James Glentworth Butler, in his 1897 *Topical Analysis of the Bible*, wrote that the word *metanoia* occurs more than fifty times in the New Testament and "is one of the most significant and vital words of Inspiration; one of immense breadth in its meaning and in its relations."[6] According to Butler, in the originally intended meaning of *metanoia*,

> there is absolutely no trace of sorrow or regret, no single element contained in the word Repentance. Hence its translation by that word has been, from the first until now, an utter *mis*translation. For the perpetuation of this grave error the sole excuse of the Revisers is that no other single word can fully or rightly interpret *Metanoia*. Literally, the word signifies *Change of Mind*, a change in the trend and action of the whole inner nature, intellectual, affectional and moral, of the man, a reversal of his controlling estimates and judgments, desires and

5. Treadwell Walden, *The Great Meaning of Metanoia: An Underdeveloped Chapter in the Life and Teaching of Christ* (New York: Thomas Whittaker, 1896), 4–5.

6. James Glentworth Butler, *Topical Analysis of the Bible: A Re-Statement of Its Moral and Spiritual Truths, Drawn Directly from the Inspired Text* (New York: Butler Bible Work Company, 1897), 443.

affections, choices and pursuits, involving a radical revolution in his supreme life aims, purposes and objects.[7]

This "change of mind," which is central in all the commentaries, always leads to a "change of direction." The more one studies about and reflects on the word *metanoia*, the deeper it becomes in terms of transformation: turning from the old to the new. It's like finding a new path with a new moral compass. Christ becomes the new starting point, and his new order, called the kingdom of God, will now set a different trajectory for one's life in the world. And it is indeed a "revolution" of thought, life, values, and behavior.

What does it mean to apply that deeper understanding of *metanoia* to our cultural, economic, and political acceptance of racism, in all its historical and present-day manifestations? The need for repentance for these sins is especially acute for white churches, which have accepted them for a very long time. Repentance is the beginning of conversion for white churches on the matter of white racism.

What Repentance Means and Doesn't Mean

New Testament scholar N. T. Wright writes about repentance and how it ultimately relates to our very humanity before God. "When we see ourselves in the light of Jesus' type of kingdom," Wright says, "and realize the extent to which we have been living by a different code altogether, we realize, perhaps for the first time, how far we have fallen short of what we were made to be."[8]

Wright is known for bringing churches back to Jesus's preaching and teaching of the "kingdom of God," and not just more recent and narrowly privatized notions of individual salvation. Wright directly relates Jesus's proclamation of the kingdom to the real meaning of repentance: "This realization is what we call 'repentance,' a serious turning away from patterns of life which deface and distort our genuine humanness. It isn't just a matter of feeling sorry for particular failings, though that will often be true as well. It is the recognition that the living God has

7. Ibid., emphasis original.
8. N. T. Wright, "Believing and Belonging," http://ntwrightpage.com/Wright_Believing _Belonging.htm.

made us humans to reflect his image into his world, and that we haven't done so."[9]

This gets to the definition of "sin," which has been personalized and privatized by so many contemporary churches. Wright says,

> The technical term for [failing to reflect God's image in the world] is "sin," whose primary meaning is not "breaking the rules" but "missing the mark," failing to hit the target of complete, genuine, glorious humanness. Once again, the gospel itself, the very message which announces that Jesus is Lord and calls us to obedience, contains the remedy: forgiveness, unearned and freely given, because of his cross. All we can say is, "Thank you."[10]

Too often, in many of our churches, especially evangelical churches like the one I grew up in, repentance was more related to an acceptance of doctrine than to a change of behavior. Often only internal sins—mostly private and sexual sins—were involved. What was missed is how the biblical texts on repentance focus on both a personal and a public change in attitudes, actions, directions, and purpose. I gained little knowledge from my home church in Detroit about how my Christian faith leads me to behave in the world (other than to abstain from sex). Repentance would never have been applied to the racism and racial conflicts going on in Detroit that the whole world would learn about in the Detroit "riots" of 1967. To that momentous social uprising, my church was clueless about our response as Christians, so it just reacted in the ways that most white Detroiters did—with fear, condemnation, and a complete lack of empathy.

Wright comments on the tendency to focus on personal sins—so starkly exhibited by my church as I was growing up—and explains the broader perspective that Christians need to have:

> Jesus invited his hearers to "repent and believe the gospel." In our world, telling people to repent and believe is likely to be heard as a summons to give up personal sins and accept a body of dogma or a scheme of religious salvation. This is a classic occasion where we have to unlearn our normal readings (including our faith readings) of first-century texts. As we see in Josephus [a first-century Jewish historian], the phrase means, basically, "Give up your agendas and trust me for mine." This is not to say that Jesus did not give this challenge what we would call a religious or spiritual dimension. It is to insist that we cannot use

9. Ibid.
10. Ibid.

that to screen out *the practical and political challenge* that the words would convey . . . to give up [our] agendas and trust him for his way . . . of bringing the kingdom, his kingdom agenda.[11]

Cheap Grace on Racism

Dietrich Bonhoeffer, the brilliant German theologian whose influence is on the rise again in our time, speaks directly to this issue of *naming the sins* from which we must repent. For publically addressing and naming the sins of National Socialism and of Nazism, and for leading other pastors to form the "Confessing Church" in the midst of the Third Reich, Bonhoeffer was executed by Adolf Hitler.

In his classic book *The Cost of Discipleship*, Bonhoeffer speaks of the problem of "cheap grace" and the realities of repentance, faith, and sin. That kind of "cheap" grace—rather than the "costly" grace that Jesus invites us into—is exactly what I encountered from the evangelical church in which I was raised, especially when they ignored and denied America's sins of racism.

Bonhoeffer writes,

> Cheap grace is the preaching of forgiveness without requiring repentance, baptism without church discipline, Communion without confession, absolution without personal confession. Cheap grace is grace without discipleship, grace without the cross, grace without Jesus Christ, living and incarnate. Costly grace is . . . the call of Jesus Christ at which the disciple leaves his nets and follows him. Costly grace is the gospel which must be sought again and again, the gift which must be asked for, the door at which a man must knock.[12]

The martyred German faith leader explains that "costly grace" means a genuine repentance from sin that is historically and specifically named. Bonhoeffer insists that "the preaching of forgiveness must always go hand-in-hand with the preaching of repentance."[13]

> If the Church refuses to face the stern reality of sin, it will gain no credence when it talks of forgiveness. . . . It is an unholy Church, squandering the precious

11. N. T. Wright and Marcus Borg, *The Meaning of Jesus: Two Visions* (San Francisco: HarperSanFrancisco, 2000), 38 (emphasis added).

12. Dietrich Bonhoeffer, *The Cost of Discipleship* (New York: Simon & Schuster, 2012), Google eBook edition, 44–45.

13. Ibid., 287.

treasure of the Lord's forgiveness. Nor is it enough simply to deplore in general terms that the sinfulness of man infects even his good works. It is necessary to point out concrete sins, and to punish and condemn them.[14]

Unless the sins we repent of are not just "general" but "concrete," writes Bonhoeffer, genuine forgiveness is "squandered." When the church "refuses to face the *stern reality of sin*," it will have no credibility when it talks about its faith, forgiveness, and salvation. Indeed, the white churches in America lost their credence when they failed to face the "stern" realities of racism in the United States.

One wonders if that lack of credibility of America's white churches was on Bonhoeffer's mind as one example of what he was trying to say. His involvement with Harlem's Abyssinian Baptist Church while he was studying at Union Theological Seminary in New York City gave him a perspective on American Christianity different from that of most visiting international students in those days. I have tried to imagine what was going through the mind of likely one of the few white people listening to the sermons each Sunday at Abyssinian.

I had the privilege of writing the foreword to *A Year with Dietrich Bonhoeffer: Daily Meditations from His Letters, Writings, and Sermons*, in which I said this:

> It was Bonhoeffer's radical allegiance to Jesus Christ that engendered his criticism of the narrow and false religion of his day. For him, the religious demands of German nationalism gave way to the lordship of Christ. During a stint at Union Seminary in New York City, Bonhoeffer's response to theological liberalism was tepid, but he became inspired by his involvement with the Abyssinian Baptist Church in Harlem. Meeting the black church in America showed the young Bonhoeffer again that the real Christ was critical of the majority culture.[15]

For Bonhoeffer, faith had to be lived out in the everyday world, what he called "living in the full this-worldliness of life."[16] Repentance must be practically applied to the life of the world, and not just the spiritual inner life. He writes:

14. Ibid., 287–88.
15. Jim Wallis, foreword to *A Year with Dietrich Bonhoeffer: Daily Meditations from His Letters, Writings, and Sermons*, ed. Carla Barnhill (San Francisco: HarperSanFrancisco, 2005), ix.
16. Dietrich Bonhoeffer, *Letters and Papers from Prison* (Minneapolis: Fortress, 2010), Google eBook edition, 486.

One throws oneself completely into the arms of God, and this is what I call this-worldliness: living fully in the midst of life's tasks, questions, successes and failures, experiences, and perplexities—then one takes seriously no longer one's own sufferings but rather the suffering of God in the world. Then one stays awake with Christ in Gethsemane. And I think this is faith; this is *metanoia*. And this is how one becomes a human being, a Christian.[17]

Repentance from Oppression

In the years since then, some of our best black liberation theology has come from Union Theological Seminary. The great theologian James Cone writes this about repentance in his classic *God of the Oppressed*:

> There can be no forgiveness of sins without repentance, and no repentance without the gift of faith to struggle with and for the freedom of the oppressed. When whites undergo the true experience of conversion wherein they die to whiteness and are reborn anew in order to struggle against white oppression and for the liberation of the oppressed, there is a place for them in the black struggle of freedom. Here reconciliation becomes God's gift of blackness through the oppressed of the land.[18]

For Cone, we cannot "separate love from justice and reconciliation from liberation."[19] The powerful thing Cone is saying here is that participation in the struggle to overcome racism is less about skin color and more about repentance. In order for white people to join the struggle, they need to "die to whiteness" and be "reborn." That again is the biblical language of repentance and conversion. This also means that the foundation of genuine racial reconciliation becomes the acts of true white repentance from racism.

In his 2011 book *The Cross and the Lynching Tree*, Cone compares the cross of Christ to the lynching tree for black Americans and describes how the former could transform the latter into "triumphant beauty." But that depends on the repentance of white Christians and churches from the "great sin" of white racism. Repentance and reparation provide the hope to redeem this tragedy. Writes Cone: "Yet, God took the evil of the cross and the lynching tree and transformed them both into the triumphant

17. Ibid.
18. James Cone, *God of the Oppressed* (Maryknoll, NY: Orbis, 1997), 222.
19. Ibid.

beauty of the divine. If America has the courage to confront the great sin and ongoing legacy of white supremacy with repentance and reparation there is hope 'beyond tragedy.'"[20]

One of the greatest modern experiments with repentance, forgiveness, and reconciliation was the Truth and Reconciliation Commission (TRC) process in South Africa, which followed the beginning of democracy in that country with the election of Nelson Mandela in 1994. The TRC "created a unique space for perpetrators of violence and their victims to meet, share their stories, and confess wrongdoing. In many cases victims forgave their perpetrators, so that healing was the outcome for both perpetrator and victim."[21] The church also played an important role in that process, as Julie Clawson has argued: "It was only through the church working directly with the state . . . that healing was able to begin. The church as a prophetic voice had to call the state (and its own members) to justice and at the same time grant healing through the transformative power of Jesus Christ."[22]

Under the apartheid regime, there were so many horrendous acts by whites against blacks that it would have been impossible to identify and prosecute all those past crimes. But something substantial and creative had to be found to begin to heal the nation's wounds and lay the groundwork for a more unified society. The grand, ambitious project of the TRC had both successes and flaws and is still morally, politically, and economically uncompleted. But it opened up a new and dynamic global conversation on truth and forgiveness, repentance and reconciliation. With the direct and crucial support of President Mandela, who believed in reconciliation over retribution, the TRC was in effect led by the only moral leader in the country with the credibility to do so: Archbishop Desmond Tutu.

Here is what Tutu said about the theology involved:

> Theology reminded me that, however diabolical the act, it did not turn the perpetrator into a demon. We had to distinguish between the deed and the perpetrator, between the sinner and the sin, to hate and condemn the sin while being filled with compassion for the sinner. The point is that if perpetrators

20. James Cone, *The Cross and the Lynching Tree* (Maryknoll, NY: Orbis, 2011), 166.

21. Nontando Hadebe, "Truth and Reconciliation," *God's Politics* (blog), *Sojourners*, September 9, 2009, http://sojo.net/blogs/2009/09/09/truth-and-reconciliation-zimbabwe.

22. Julie Clawson, "The Church Must Retain a Prophetic Voice," *God's Politics* (blog), *Sojourners*, October 1, 2010, http://sojo.net/blogs/2010/10/01/church-must-retain-prophetic-voice.

were to be despaired of as monsters and demons, then we were thereby letting accountability go out the window because we were then declaring that they were not moral agents to be held responsible for the deeds they had committed. Much more importantly, it meant that we abandoned all hope of their being able to change for the better. *Theology said they still, despite the awfulness of their deeds, remained children of God with the capacity to repent, to be able to change.*[23]

Tutu said that the TRC was "operating on the premise that people could change, could recognize and acknowledge the error of their ways and so experience contrition or, at the very least, remorse, and would at some point be constrained to confess their dastardly conduct and ask for forgiveness."[24] This is a crucial concept for our own dealing with America's past. It is impossible to identify and prosecute all the previous acts of brutality over the course of America's history of white racism, but we need clear admission of those sins and an asking for forgiveness on the part of white Americans, followed by deeds and behaviors that signify real change.

If racism is a sin, the reactions to it can also be sins, and those reactions can come from all sides, even from the victims. Perpetrators or beneficiaries of such sin can be redeemed from it only by way of genuine truth, honesty, and repentance. And the potentially sinful and violent reactions to the sin of racism, by its many victims, can also be redeemed in the process of truth and reconciliation. That is what Tutu and the other South African leaders believed.

But one critical mistake that can be made in the conversation about repentance concerns the time frame of change and the fraudulent assumption that changing our responses to sin is somehow inevitable. Martin Luther King Jr. struggled with these issues of sin, guilt, repentance, and change—perhaps as much as any American leader has—and offers us some important warnings:

> Let nobody give you the impression that the problem of racial injustice will work itself out. Let nobody give you the impression that only time will solve the problem. That is a myth, and it is a myth because time is neutral. It can be used either constructively or destructively. And I'm absolutely convinced that the people of ill will in our nation—the extreme rightists—the forces committed to

23. Desmond Tutu, *No Future without Forgiveness* (New York: Crown, 2009), Google eBook edition, 95 (emphasis added).
24. Ibid.

negative ends—have used time much more effectively than the people of good will. It may well be that we will have to repent in this generation, not merely for the vitriolic works and violent actions of the bad people who bomb a church in Birmingham, Alabama, or shoot down a civil rights worker in Selma, but for the appalling silence and indifference of the good people who sit around and say, "Wait on time." *Somewhere we must come to see that human progress never rolls in on wheels of inevitability. It comes through the tireless efforts and the persistent work of dedicated individuals.* Without this hard work, time becomes an ally of the primitive forces of social stagnation. So we must help time and realize that the time is always right to do right.[25]

The Hard Work of Repentance

Repentance requires action, and it is hard work. That hard work often requires a leap of faith. In his book *The Early Preaching of Karl Barth*, William Willimon, a professor of theology at Duke Divinity School, explains that Barth believed that only those who truly are willing to turn themselves over to God will ever understand the true meaning of repentance. Barth, a leading German theologian who opposed Hitler, wrote:

> Those who can truly say, "The Lord is my shepherd," have made that leap [of repentance]. They have not resisted God, who judges the world, but thrown themselves into God's arms and become God's captives. They have not swum with the current of opinion in the world, but against it. In them something has turned from the idols to God; they have submitted to judgment; they have let the truth rule in their hearts. . . . They have begun at least to think differently, to look in a different direction. . . . But for us it is not simply and immediately true, for it is not simply and immediately certain that we are and want to be participants in this process of transformation.[26]

Barth summarized the challenge of repentance: "Repentance is turning around to that which is nearest and which we always overlook; to the center of life which we always miss; to the simplest which is still too high and hard for us."[27]

25. Martin Luther King Jr., "Remaining Awake through a Great Revolution" (commencement address to Oberlin College, June 1965), http://www.oberlin.edu/external/EOG/BlackHistory Month/MLK/CommAddress.html (emphasis added).

26. Karl Barth, *The Early Preaching of Karl Barth: Fourteen Sermons with Commentary by William H. Willimon* (Louisville: Westminster John Knox, 2009), Google eBook edition, 91–92.

27. Karl Barth, *Come Holy Spirit: Sermons* (New York: Round Table, 1933), 67.

Sometimes the church's opposition to genuine repentance is at the heart of the problem, as it has been with white churches' lack of response, frequent denial, general conformity, and even direct support of white racism. Barth contrasts such disobedience to the call of Christ. "The call of Jesus resounds despite the church. But the church is a great, perhaps the greatest, hindrance to repentance. If we wish to hear the call of Jesus, then we must hear it despite the church."[28] "Despite the church" has too often painfully been my experience of working for racial and economic justice in America. But imagine how powerful it would be if white and multicultural churches could now join in helping to lead the way to repentance at a new moment in American racial history, remembering how black churches led the nation during the civil rights movement.

Reinhold Niebuhr, who was teaching at Union when Bonhoeffer was there, made clear the central meaning of repentance. "In classical Christianity," Niebuhr wrote, "it is suggested again and again that repentance is the beginning of redemption, even that it is synonymous with redemption."[29]

All this suggests that repentance isn't possible until we name the sin to be repented of. Admitting, naming, and confessing sin is the first step in repentance. The sin of white racism must be named, directly and publically, especially by white people, for the process of genuine repentance to begin. Just saying we are sorry won't be enough.

The new generation of young leaders from all racial backgrounds that is calling on society to reverse the sins of a racialized criminal justice system could embody the true repentance that we so critically need.

A Weekend of Resistance and Repentance

In November 2014, thousands of young people from around the country came to Ferguson, Missouri, for a "weekend of resistance." For many of us faith leaders, it was also a weekend of *repentance*.

I went to Ferguson as a faith leader—but in particular as a white faith leader, because challenging the fundamental injustices in our criminal justice system must not be left only to black and brown faith leaders. It

---

28. Ibid., 71.
29. Reinhold Niebuhr, *The Essential Reinhold Niebuhr: Selected Essays and Addresses*, ed. Robert McAfee Brown (New Haven: Yale University Press, 1987), 70.

is indeed time for us white Christians to repent—to turn around and go in a new direction. The tragic events in Ferguson offered an opportunity to express that repentance.

In the case of Ferguson, repentance had to mean more than merely acknowledging the tragic death of Michael Brown. It also means more than lamenting the loss of another young black man or being sympathetic to his grieving mother. True repentance means *changing* the direction of the *practices* and *policies* that led to his death and to so many others. But we had seen little evidence that public officials in Ferguson and St. Louis County had the courage to alter their behavior and the systemic treatment of young men and women of color in their communities.

Several faith leaders came to participate in the process of repentance. We began with ourselves. Many black and brown young people have been left alone, subject to educational failures and economic forces that have marginalized them, a judicial system that disproportionately punishes them, and police departments that regularly brutalize them. They have either left the churches or were never there in the first place, and few of our churches had reached out to them. Some of the clergy in Ferguson were repenting of that now and promised to change that reality. Mike Kinman, dean of Christ Church Cathedral in St. Louis, went even further, saying that the faith leaders not only need to go out and meet the young people but that those young people have a message to teach the faith leaders. He said:

> John the Baptist is alive in the young women and men who are protesting on the streets of Ferguson every night. The call is the same. The question is—will we go out and see them. Will we heed the call to change our life, the life we all live together? Will we as the church lead our people out to this new Jordan River? Will we lead our people into bearing fruit worthy of a common life changed?[30]

After much confessing, praying, and singing in a Ferguson church, we marched to the Ferguson police station that had been the headquarters for much of the brutality against the black people in their community. Two hundred of us walked to police headquarters, where we were met by the Ferguson police.

---

30. "Local Religious Leaders Respond to Ferguson," *Religion & Politics*, December 1, 2014, http://religionandpolitics.org/2014/12/01/local-religious-leaders-respond-to-ferguson/.

A young black man lay down on the ground in front of the police station, and chalk was drawn around him. When he got up, a dramatic picture remained—a memorial to Mike Brown and to others who have been shot and killed. Many of their names were read in a painful but powerful liturgy, which brought many tears to those present who had lost family members, loved ones, and young friends to police violence. Together we repented those losses in the presence of Ferguson police officers, whom many wanted to hold accountable for moving in new directions.

Then, one by one, clergy approached the police officers who were blocking our path to the police station, and we began to speak quietly and personally to them face-to-face, asking them to become part of this repentance too. In my previous arrests in acts of nonviolent civil disobedience, I had never asked a police officer to join in repentance. The officer facing me was a thirty-six-year veteran of the police force. He admitted he was a Christian, too, and said the last two months had been the hardest in his almost four decades of service. "I didn't want it to end like this," he told me. "What would you like to see happen now?" I asked him. The officer said he hoped all this could "end peacefully." I suggested that would take a lot of big changes. He nodded his head.

We then asked to see the Ferguson chief of police and began to move forward to do so. That's when we were arrested. We had decided to accept the consequences of prayerful, nonviolent civil disobedience. Twenty national and local faith leaders spent the next five hours in police custody being processed in Ferguson, and then we were taken to the county courthouse in St. Louis. We had the opportunity to speak to many police officers. Several, especially some of the African American officers in St. Louis, admitted there were some real racial problems in local police departments and said they would be praying for change. Some of them even thanked us as we left.

As faith leaders we were, of course, treated very well—in sharp contrast to the ways young black men are often treated in those same facilities. We were eventually released without bond or bail, while young black men and women sometimes have to pay hundreds of dollars to get out of jail. But the action, as intended, did bring more national attention to the issues of Ferguson.

As we have discussed in this chapter, racism must be clearly named as a sin—against young black men and women, and against fairness and justice in our law enforcement system. From a religious perspective, racism is also a sin against God, who requires fairness and justice for all God's children, and even against oneself, as it is contrary to the image of God in which we are created and hinders us from becoming fully human, conformed to the fullness of Christ (Eph. 4:13). Quite simply, this American sin must be repented of and turned from; and the American faith community cannot rest until that repentance is done.

We marched together with young leaders in Ferguson, whose calling, as many of them put it to me, is making sure the world knows that black lives matter and ensuring that all lives are treated equally in our criminal justice system. We were arrested together—for an act of repentance.

5 | Dying to Whiteness

Having seen what repentance means biblically and theologically, let's go deeper now into what repentance means in relationship to "whiteness." In the deepest and most honest sense, the real issue at stake in US racial history is the persistence of white privilege, which is profoundly rooted in the ideology of white supremacy. The existence and persistence of white identity itself, with the accompanying assumption of white privilege, is still a major obstacle to real change in the racial climate. Borrowing a phrase from James Cone, what would it mean for us to "die to whiteness"?

Europeans Becoming "White People"

During sessions of antiracism training I did years ago, we began by asking the white people what ethnic groups they were from. "White" Americans are often startled by that question, and it quickly becomes clear that many haven't really thought much about their European ethnic roots, especially if their families have been in the United States for a long time.

But eventually people would begin to respond when you ask for a show of hands for who was "English," "French," "German," "Polish," "Dutch," "Swedish," and so on. People would start to smile and begin lifting up their hands—even with a little pride, "Yeah Italian!" or "Go Irish!" But the ethnic pride of white people from Europe had obviously diminished, especially if their families had been "American" for many generations.

In our antiracism training sessions, I would then say something like this: "You know, I can never tell you Swedes and Italians apart. You act just like each other. Or you Germans and Irish, same personality for both of your cultures!" Many people would begin to laugh at the idea that diverse European ethnicities were exactly the same—as if there were no difference between German control and Irish expressiveness, for example, or quiet Swedes and verbal Italians, if we go by the stereotypes. "So tell me," I would finally ask, "how did you all become 'white people' when you came to America?"

English, Italians, Swedes, Irish, Dutch, Germans, and the rest were never a common ethnic group in Europe. There is really no such thing as a white race in Europe, which is very much a mixture of cultures and shades of skin colors. But all became *white* when they arrived in America, taking on not only a new national identity but also a new white cultural identity. Indeed, being "white" meant being part of the "white race," which in reality was merely a social and political construction, *created* to supply the ideology and justification for slavery and racial oppression. Because if you were "white" in America, that meant that you were *not* "black" or "brown" or "yellow." You were not African, Latino, or Asian. You and all the other European cultures were "white" and therefore *different* and *better* than all the people of "color" who would also be found in America.

Today, still, the people of different ethnicities in Europe have little common understanding of being "white," but that is beginning to change as immigrants from North Africa, Asia, and other places are entering European countries. Preserving native and white ethnic identity is part of the message and appeal of the New Right groups in many European countries.

Supremacy and Privilege

Historically, slavery was often not based on race at all. For example, Greek "slaves" were tutors and mentors for the children of elite families in ancient Rome. Never did anyone think Greeks were inferior to the Romans; on the contrary, they were looked to with respect—they had just lost wars, which was often the reason for slavery. Losing cultural battles was often the reason that the losers became slaves and the winners became masters.

But given the English (and later American) ideals and rhetoric about human rights, equality, freedom, and democracy, slavery had to be justified by making the slaves less "human." The ideology of white supremacy, of course, was economically motivated—slavery was enormously profitable—but it had to be philosophically and religiously tied to false ideas of white superiority and black inferiority. To put it most bluntly, racial ideologies had to be created to cover up greed. It was always a myth and an exceptionally cruel and brutal one to deny a group of people their human identity, their worth, their family integrity, and ultimately their standing before God.

It's important to understand where this history comes from, especially the idea of white supremacy. Allan G. Johnson is a sociologist and author. In an essay called "Where White Privilege Came From," which is excerpted from his book *The Forest and the Trees: Sociology as Life, Practice, and Promise*, Johnson says this:

> We begin with the long history of the British struggle to conquer Ireland and subjugate its people. This structural relation of dominance along with British frustration in the face of stubborn resistance, gave rise to a cultural belief that the Irish were an inferior and savage people, not merely in the organization of their societies, but in their very nature as human beings. The British came to view the Irish as something like a separate species altogether, possessing inferior traits that were biologically passed from one generation to the next. In this, the British were inventing a concept of race that made it a path of least resistance to see other peoples as subhuman if not nonhuman, making it easier to objectify them and more difficult to feel empathy for them as members of their own kind, both integral to the exertion of control over others.[1]

The very categories of "white" and "color" that have shaped and structured American society since the beginning (our "original sin") stem directly from this history. Johnson goes on:

> It's important to emphasize that prior to the British experience with the Irish and the enslavement of Africans in North America, the concept of race, including

---

1. Allan G. Johnson, "Where White Privilege Came From," http://www.agjohnson.us/essays/whiteprivilege/.

categories such as "white" and "color" as social markers of inferiority and superiority, did not exist. Notice, then, how cultural ideas can come into being as a way to justify structural arrangements, and how those same ideas can go on to play a role in shaping other systems in various ways, such as the subordination of Africans and Native Americans when English migrants came to North America to make new lives for themselves. This kind of interaction among the various characteristics of social systems is basic to understanding how social life happens—everything is connected to and has the potential to affect everything else.[2]

Johnson helps us to see not only how the cultural idea of white supremacy came into being but also how such a concept can spread roots and tentacles, infiltrate every area of social interaction, and be extremely difficult to get rid of.

After Slavery

Of course, white identity and supremacy lasted long after slavery. During the Reconstruction period following the Civil War, freed black slaves made enormous progress in setting up their own economic and family lives and even electing many blacks to public office in the South. According to Richard Wormser, who cowrote and produced the PBS series *The Rise and Fall of Jim Crow*,

> This uneasy coalition of black and white Republicans passed significant civil rights legislation in many states. Courts were reorganized, judicial procedures improved, and public school systems established. Segregation existed but it was flexible. But as blacks slowly progressed, white Southerners resented their achievements and their empowerment, even though they were in a political minority in every state but South Carolina.[3]

By 1877, Reconstruction had been defeated. White Southerners intent on returning to white supremacy and removing newly established rights for blacks had retaken control of state legislatures across the former Confederacy, "backed up by mob and paramilitary violence, with the Ku Klux Klan, the White League, and the Red Shirts assassinating pro-Reconstruction

2. Ibid.
3. Richard Wormser, "Reconstruction," *The Rise and Fall of Jim Crow*, PBS.org, http://www.pbs.org/wnet/jimcrow/stories_events_reconstruct.html.

politicians and terrorizing Southern blacks."[4] In Washington, a severe economic downturn and allegations of corruption by black politicians led to anti-Reconstruction Democrats taking control of Congress in 1874.[5] The heavily disputed presidential election of 1876 was the final blow, as "the Republicans agree[d] to abandon Reconstruction policies in exchange for the presidency,"[6] in a backroom political deal officially put into place in March 1877.

White supremacy was systematically reestablished throughout the South through "Jim Crow" segregation policies. The Constitutional Rights Foundation lists many appalling examples of what this practically meant in the daily lives of black people:

> In South Carolina, black and white textile workers could not work in the same room, enter through the same door, or gaze out of the same window. Many industries wouldn't hire blacks: Many unions passed rules to exclude them.
>
> In Richmond, one could not live on a street unless most of the residents were people one could marry. (One could not marry someone of a different race.) By 1914, Texas had six entire towns in which blacks could not live. Mobile passed a Jim Crow curfew: Blacks could not leave their homes after 10 p.m. Signs marked "Whites Only" or "Colored" hung over doors, ticket windows, and drinking fountains. Georgia had black and white parks. Oklahoma had black and white phone booths.
>
> Prisons, hospitals, and orphanages were segregated as were schools and colleges. In North Carolina, black and white students had to use separate sets of textbooks. In Florida, the books couldn't even be stored together. Atlanta courts kept two Bibles: one for black witnesses and one for whites. Virginia told fraternal social groups that black and white members could not address each other as "Brother."[7]

These laws, along with the wide array of unwritten social codes that accompanied them, were violently enforced. Whites beat blacks with impunity, relying on all-white police, prosecutors, judges, and juries to protect them.

4. "Reconstruction vs. Redemption," National Endowment for the Humanities, February 11, 2014, http://www.neh.gov/news/reconstruction-vs-redemption.

5. "Reconstruction Timeline: 1867–1877," *Reconstruction: The Second Civil War*, PBS.org, http://www.pbs.org/wgbh/amex/reconstruction/states/sf_timeline2.html.

6. Ibid.

7. "A Brief History of Jim Crow," Constitutional Rights Foundation, http://www.crf-usa .org/black-history-month/a-brief-history-of-jim-crow.

And *at least* 3,440 black men, women, and children were lynched—publicly murdered by white mobs.[8]

Amid systematic disenfranchisement and discrimination, between 1910 and 1970 an estimated 6 million African Americans migrated to northern cities, where prospects were also brighter for better jobs.[9] Tragically, although life in the North was better in many instances, the ideology of white superiority was alive and well there, too. Blacks encountered plenty of long-standing racial discrimination in the North. In housing and other areas, de facto segregation replaced the legal segregation of the South.

The fundamental battle of the civil rights movement—legally, philosophically, and even religiously, given the strong role that black churches played in the movement—was that black people should be treated equally, because black people are as human as white people are, and their humanity must be defended morally and not just politically.

We are all equal and valued before God, and should also be equal and valued in an American democracy, the civil rights movement and its preachers said. Black people, like all people, are made in "the image of God" and should be treated that way. Not a partial image, nor a secondary image, nor a "three-fifths" image—black men, women, and children are created in the full image of God. And that powerful assertion was converting to the white people, in the North and the South, who joined the civil rights movement.

The movement's gains were never just about rights but were more deeply a challenge to the ideology of white supremacy, with a strong assertion of the moral equality of all Americans, no matter the color of their skin. It was about the humanity of black people, but white people's own human souls and human rights were also at stake, and not just legal civil rights.

White privilege is a more nuanced term than white supremacy, but it amounts to the same thing. *It continues* to be an unspoken and sometimes stated assumption in American life—that whites do or even should enjoy, benefit from, and even depend upon privileges that blacks and other people of color don't have or deserve. As the legal basis of those white privileges has historically diminished, the majority white culture has still tried to preserve its privileges culturally, economically, politically, and societally.

---

8. David Pilgrim, "What Was Jim Crow?," Jim Crow Museum, Ferris State University, September 2000, http://www.ferris.edu/jimcrow/what.htm.

9. Richard Wormser, "The Great Migration," *The Rise and Fall of Jim Crow*, PBS.org, http://www.pbs.org/wnet/jimcrow/stories_events_migration.html.

All of this can be very subtle, but it is no less real and no less brutally oppressive—and it can easily explode into violence.

Unconscious and "Normal"

White privilege is often unconscious. In fact, when many white people hear about the problems of *race*, they tend to think those problems are about "other people." Even if whites feel affinity with the plight of people of color, they still often feel that the issues concerning race are mostly not about themselves. We want to offer rights generously to others, but we don't see the problems rooted in our own racial identity. It becomes more about how we help people who are black and brown than how we confront our own white racial privilege.

We still assume "whiteness" in American society, in ways that are both implicit and explicit. White privilege is *normal* in American society. And it is the most normal thing in the experience of white Americans to expect privilege—even when we would not think to call it that. I would name white privilege as the actual practice of modern-day white supremacy.

The unspoken but everyday assumption is that America is still a white society and that it has minorities who have problems in regard to race. Some well-known pundits regularly say or write things that suggest they truly believe whites are superior to other races. For example, Rush Limbaugh has a long history of racist comments, remarking in 2009 that "the days of them [minorities] not having any power are over, and they are angry. And they want to use their power as a means of retribution."[10] In December 2014, a professor at Florida State University resigned after a Facebook exchange was publicized in which she wrote, "Obama has single-handedly turned our once great society into a Ghetto Culture, rivaling that of Europe. France is almost at war because of his filthy rodent Muslims who are attacking Native Frenchmen and women."[11] Overseas, there are ostensibly intelligent academics, such as Andrew Fraser in Australia, who

10. Joan Walsh, "You Heard Me: Rush Limbaugh Is 'a Racist Troll,'" Salon.com, September 10, 2013, http://www.salon.com/2013/09/10/you_heard_me_rush_limbaugh_is_%E2%80%9Ca _racist_troll%E2%80%9D/.

11. Bill Cotterell, "FSU Professor Resigns after Racist Facebook Comments," *Huffington Post*, December 9, 2014, http://www.huffingtonpost.com/2014/12/10/fsu-professor-facebook -comments_n_6298288.html.

with a straight face say things like, "I think Australia would have been better off to follow Japan's lead and retain its ethnic homogeneity."[12]

In this view, racial problems are never mostly about us, as white people; rather, they are about the problems that other people are having—people who aren't white, white being "normal." Even though some of us are sympathetic to the problems those *other* people are having, it doesn't directly affect us—unless we choose, admirably, to be involved.

But we *are involved*—all of us who are "white" people. In fact, the ideology of white supremacy and the more subtle assumptions of white privilege and normality are at the heart of "the racial problem" in America today. Racism in America is still rooted in the identity of "whiteness"; it is about us as white people.

The approach that "we are all racists and all need to repent" is neither good theology nor honest history. We have already said that racism is prejudice plus power—the power that, by and large, white people have and people of color don't—and racism is rooted in the identity of whiteness. White supremacy is the ideology, and white privilege is the assumption and practice, that must be dismantled if racial progress is to be made in America.

For American democracy to be real for all its citizens, we must die to "whiteness." Only by morally dying to our false identity as white people—an identity created for violent, oppressive profit—can we come alive to our true identity as human beings. That false identity is well articulated by Ta-Nehisi Coates as "those Americans who believe that they are white."[13] And for white Christians, dying to whiteness is essential to our spiritual integrity and to our salvation from the sin of racism. It will mean nothing less than giving up what has become an idol and casting it away in returning to God.

Idolatry

Whiteness is not just an ideology; it is also an idol. For people of faith, this is not just a political issue but a religious one as well. Idols separate us from God, and *the idolatry of "whiteness" has separated white people from God.*

12. "Racist Professor Tells Africans Their Intellectual Ability Not Good Enough for White Australia," *Atlanta Black Star*, July 11, 2014, http://atlantablackstar.com/2014/07/11/racist -white-professor-tells-black-africans-their-intellectual-ability-is-not-good-enough-for-white -australia/.

13. Ta-Nehisi Coates, *Between the World and Me* (New York: Spiegel and Grau, 2015), 6.

It gives us an identity that is false, one filled with wrongful pride, one that perpetuates both injustice and oppression. Whiteness is an idol of lies, arrogance, and violence. This idol blinds us to our true identity as the children of God, because, of course, God's children are of every color that God has made them to be. To believe otherwise is to separate ourselves from God and the majority of God's children on this planet who are people of color.

> So God created humankind in his image, in the image of God he created them; male and female he created them. God blessed them, and God said to them, "Be fruitful and multiply, and fill the earth and subdue it; and have dominion over the fish of the sea and over the birds of the air and over every living thing that moves upon the earth." (Gen. 1:27–28)

The original creation account in Genesis makes our sin of racism painfully and theologically clear. *All* human beings were created in God's image, not just some of them, and not just the ones whose skin color is the lightest. To suggest otherwise is nothing short of a heresy. And *all* human beings are to have "dominion" over the earth and all its other creatures.

But they are not to have dominion over one another—that is against the very meaning of creation. Note also that the word "dominion" here in the text means not to dominate the earth but rather to serve and be good stewards of the earth and all its created life. Any notion of white supremacy and domination of other people is nothing less than a denial of God's creation and its stated purpose.

In a *Washington Post* article published soon after the police killing of Walter Scott in North Charleston, South Carolina, Lisa Sharon Harper spoke about the truth of Genesis 1 and the spiritual lie that plagues our nation: "Black people and other people of color are *simply* less human than white people, and, as a result, they have less character, capacity, and calling to steward and lead. On the flip side of the same theological coin, is the other lie that white people are more like God than others—uniquely equipped and called to exercise dominion on American soil."[14]

The false idol of white supremacy and its practice of white privilege require conversion of us all, and especially of white people. I would say

14. Lisa Sharon Harper, "How Religion Became a Destructive—and a Redemptive—Force for 'Black Lives Matter,'" *Washington Post*, April 9, 2015, http://www.washingtonpost.com /news/acts-of-faith/wp/2015/04/09/how-religion-became-a-destructive-and-redemptive-force -for-black-lives-matter/.

we need an "exorcism," for the sake of our spiritual and theological integrity. Overcoming racism is not only necessary for the sake of black souls in America. Rejecting the idols of white supremacy and privilege, and casting away the false identity of "whiteness," is a prerequisite for white Americans *to get our own souls back*. Only by rejecting the concept and category of "whiteness" can Americans of European ancestry once again find our true identity—as the children of God and as Americans among other Americans. Will white Christians demonstrate the faith to overcome racism by first rejecting the idols that have captured our identities away from God? That, ultimately, will be the test of racial healing.

I'm Not a Racist, Am I?

This is a question that we hear from many white people: "I am not a racist, am I?"

That's really the wrong question. This is not just an individual matter, as I have been demonstrating. These issues are historical and structural and have to do with how our racial groupings as human beings have been deliberately manipulated for social and economic purposes. Therefore, most of us have been socialized, instructed, and formed along the patterns of our racial groups, which is especially true of those of us who have been raised to think of ourselves as "white." Understanding how we have been categorized, and why, is the first step toward breaking free of oppressive categories.

When I was a little boy, I loved to listen to musicals. *South Pacific*, based on a book by James Michener, was my favorite. The musical contained a clear message on racism. In the plot, a young American nurse falls in love with a middle-aged French plantation owner with mixed-race children, and an American lieutenant courts a young Tonkinese Asian woman. Both Americans, and the people around them, struggle with the racial issues in their romances and fear the consequences of marrying the ones they love. Racial prejudice is honestly explored in the musical and the film, which comes out most pointedly in the song "You've Got to Be Carefully Taught."

The song explains that racial prejudice—manifested as hatred and fear of people from different ethnic backgrounds—is not an innate quality that people are born with. Instead, the song explains that "you've got to be taught to be afraid / of people whose eyes are oddly made, / and people whose skin is a different shade, / you've got to be carefully taught."[15] The songwriters also point out that racial prejudice is something young children learn from their elders and role models: "You've got to be taught before it's too late, / before you are six or seven or eight, / to hate all the people your relatives hate, / you've got to be carefully taught!"[16]

The Broadway musical had enormous success at the box office and won ten Tony Awards, including best musical and best score. It was the second-longest-running musical in its time on Broadway, behind only Rodgers and Hammerstein's *Oklahoma*. Its great success led to the film a decade later, and it has had popular revivals ever since. In the 1950s, the attention to race was quite controversial, especially in the South, but the authors were reportedly never apologetic about the script and score.[17]

I still remember the clear message that racism had to be taught—and it was. Racism taught becomes racism learned—and racism lived as both overt behavior and, even more subtly, as unconscious bias. White people have been taught racism, more explicitly in the past but still implicitly today. And what we have been taught we need to unlearn.

Implicit Bias

We are learning more and more about "implicit" racial bias. Underneath the explicit racial attitudes and behaviors that we can see lie the implicit or unconscious attitudes that we have. The more overt expressions of racism are now mostly condemned in our society, and when such incidents happen people often name them as "appalling" or "unacceptable." But more covert, subtle, and implicit racial bias continues and is seldom really addressed or exposed. And recent research shows that those implicit biases exist in most all people—white, but also black and other people of color.

Some remarkable research has been done about implicit racial bias, and some of the results are now available in the form of a short test. It's called the Implicit Association Test, developed by Harvard and several

15. Richard Rogers and Oscar Hammerstein II, "You've Got to Be Carefully Taught," Metrolyrics.com, http://www.metrolyrics.com/youve-got-to-be-carefully-taught-lyrics-south-pacific.html.

16. Ibid.

17. Michele Norris, "Six Words: 'You've Got to Be Taught' Intolerance," NPR.org, May 19, 2014, http://www.npr.org/2014/05/19/308296815/six-words-youve-got-to-be-taught-intolerance.

other schools, including a group called the Kirwan Institute for the Study of Race and Ethnicity at Ohio State University. Here is a website with an implicit bias test: http://implicit.harvard.edu.

The test takes only about ten to fifteen minutes. It is well worth the time for what you can learn. The test results are kept private and are meant to be a learning device.

Here is the description of the implicit racial bias test that I took:

> [The test] assesses how long it takes participants to categorize Black and White faces respectively with "good words" (e.g., happiness, joy, etc.) versus "bad words" (e.g., terrible, angry, etc.). The racial group that individuals most quickly associate with the positive terms reflects a positive implicit bias towards that group. Extensive research has uncovered an implicit pro-White/anti-Black bias in most Americans.[18]

The Kirwan Institute is a great place to get valuable implicit bias information. Cheryl Staats of the institute wrote "State of the Science: Implicit Bias Review 2014," in which she says:

> Implicit bias refers to the attitudes or stereotypes that affect our understanding, actions, and decisions in an unconscious manner. These biases, which encompass both favorable and unfavorable assessments, are activated involuntarily and without an individual's awareness or intentional control. . . . Residing deep in the subconscious, these biases are different from known biases that individuals may choose to conceal for the purposes of social and/or political correctness. Rather, implicit biases are not accessible through introspection.[19]

Staats quotes social scientist David R. Williams, who states, "This is the frightening point: Because [implicit bias is] an automatic and unconscious process, people who engage in this unthinking discrimination are not aware of the fact that they do it."[20] According to Staats, research suggests that our conscious mind can handle no more than 40 to 50 of the 11 million bits of information our brains process every second—so most of the information we process is unconscious.[21]

18. Cheryl Staats, "State of the Science: Implicit Bias Review 2014," Kirwan Institute for the Study of Race and Ethnicity, Ohio State University, March 2014, http://kirwaninstitute.osu .edu/wp-content/uploads/2014/03/2014-implicit-bias.pdf, 72.
    19. Ibid., 16.
    20. Ibid.
    21. Ibid., 73.

Staats explains that "implicit biases are robust and pervasive. . . . Everyone is susceptible to them, even people who believe themselves to be impartial or objective, such as judges."[22]

Implicit and explicit biases are obviously related and can even reinforce one another, but the critical thing is that one is conscious and the other is not. An implicit bias might not always align with someone's stated beliefs, even his or her sincerely felt beliefs and openly held public stances. And on the subject of race, multiple studies have shown that "most Americans, regardless of race, display a pro-White/anti-Black bias on the Implicit Association Test."[23] Anecdotally, I've found that a person who tests completely or mostly free of *implicit* (subconscious) racial bias in one direction or another is very rare; usually only people who have lived significant portions of their lives in proximity, dialogue, fellowship, and friendship with many people of other races are likely to fit this description.

The body of research in this field suggests that most Americans have various implicit biases about race, ethnicity, age, sexuality, and even different physical appearances. Those can come early in life, even in children as young as six, because of the messages we receive, both direct and indirect. And many of those received messages are quite subtle, especially in our early experiences, our family life, the neighborhoods we live in, the media we see, or the news coverage we read and watch.[24]

Biases are *taught* to us (as the *South Pacific* song suggests) both explicitly and implicitly. Our biases cause our attitudes, behaviors, and reactions in response to any number of things—both people and circumstances. The test results discussed above also show that implicit racial bias even exists among some black people against their own racial group. In other words, negative stereotypes taught about black people in white society can be internalized within the black community.

But the good news is that our implicit biases are not fixed or permanent, and they can be changed over time, but only by being aware and attentive to them and deliberately focusing on trying to change them.[25] Such training can be very helpful, especially to professional people such as law enforcement officers who need to be aware of their implicit biases.

22. Ibid., 70–73.
23. Ibid., 73.
24. Ibid., 70–71.
25. Ibid., 73.

What changes biases is exposure to different facts, realities, and situations, and, especially, getting to know and understand real people who
can change our stereotypes and biases about them. Living in the same
community, being alongside one another in the workplace, going to school
with different kinds of students and parents, and worshiping in open
congregations of racially and ethnically diverse believers can help change
both hearts and minds.

As far as race is concerned, we have indeed made progress from the
explicit, ugly, and even violent biases that made life so dangerous for
black Americans in our history—but, of course, such incidents still occur,
with Charleston being a recent horrifying example. But even though overt
racism has declined, implicit racial bias remains strong and pervasive in
our society, a fact demonstrated by a growing body of research. Even
when we say we disagree with certain racial stereotypes, for example,
we can still unconsciously hold them and act on them—the implicit can
turn into the explicit, as we have painfully seen. Even implicit racial biases can make life more difficult for black Americans, and dangerous, as
biases can explode in situations of tension and conflict, reaping violent
and tragic consequences.

From the research, here is a description of how implicit biases can
explode into explicit behavior:

> In a video game that simulates what police officers experience, research subjects
> were instructed to "shoot" when an armed individual appeared on the screen
> and refrain from doing so when the target was instead holding an innocuous
> object such as a camera or wallet. Time constraints were built into the study
> so that participants were forced to make nearly instantaneous decisions, much
> like police officers often must do in real life. Findings indicated that participants
> tended to "shoot" armed targets more quickly when they were African American
> as opposed to White, and when participants refrained from "shooting" an
> armed target, these characters in the simulation tended to be White rather than
> African American. Research such as this highlights how implicit racial biases
> can influence decisions that have life or death consequences.[26]

We must get to the place where racism and our response to it are not identified as liberal or conservative issues. We need leaders across the political
spectrum to stand up to racism, to address both explicit and implicit

26. Ibid., 72.

biases in order to keep moving our nation to "a more perfect union" where freedom and opportunity exist equally for everyone. In one of his pieces for *The New York Times* titled "Beware of Stubby Glasses," conservative columnist David Brooks says:

> Sometimes the behavioral research leads us to completely change how we think about an issue. For example, many of our anti-discrimination policies focus on finding the bad apples who are explicitly prejudiced. In fact, the serious discrimination is implicit, subtle and nearly universal. Both blacks and whites subtly try to get a white partner when asked to team up to do an intellectually difficult task. . . . In emergency rooms, whites are pervasively given stronger painkillers than blacks or Hispanics. Clearly, we should spend more effort rigging situations to reduce universal, unconscious racism.[27]

Sociologist Allen Johnson, whom I cited earlier on the history of white supremacy, also discusses the implicit nature of our biases from that history. He says:

> Most of the choices we make are unconscious, it being in the nature of paths of least resistance to appear to us as the logical, normal thing to do without our having to think about it. This means, of course, that we can participate in systems in ways we're not aware of and help produce consequences without knowing it and be involved in other people's lives, both historically and in the present, without any intention to do so. . . .
>
> I could say this history has nothing personally to do with me, that it was all a long time ago and done by someone else, that my ancestors were all good, moral, and decent people who never killed or enslaved anyone or drove anyone from their land. Even if that were true (I'll never know for sure), the only way to let it go at that is to ignore the fact that if someone was willing to take the time to follow the money, they would find that some portion of the house and land that we now call home can be traced directly back through my family history to the laws and practices that whites have collectively imposed through their government and other institutions. Back to the industrial capitalist revolution and the exploitation of people of color that made it possible. And back to the conquest, forced expulsion, and genocide through which the land that is now the United States was first acquired by Europeans. In other words, some portion of this house is our share of the benefits of white privilege passed on and accumulated from one generation to the next.[28]

27. David Brooks, "Beware of Stubby Glasses," *New York Times*, January 11, 2013, http://www.nytimes.com/2013/01/11/opinion/brooks-beware-stubby-glasses.html?hp.

28. Johnson, "White Privilege."

I Am a Beneficiary of Affirmative Action

An important issue in America's conversation about race is how we talk about individual achievement in the context of our historical and still-current racial disparities. Controversy continues around the concept of "affirmative action." Many people assume affirmative action only applies to preferential measures on behalf of black Americans in education and employment, for example, to make up for the unfair start African Americans had in this country—as former slaves and their descendants who experienced systematic discrimination in the United States. We didn't all begin at the same starting line in our run for success, the argument goes; whites got a big head start, and it's only fair that blacks receive some affirmative action to make up for the further distance they have needed to come.

But let me turn that discussion around a bit. My white family was a direct beneficiary of affirmative action as I was growing up. Most of those in my huge, white, baby boomer generation were too, and, if they were honest, they would have to admit the same thing. Here is what happened in the US government's biggest affirmative action program so far.

After World War II, the veterans of that war received several major benefits under the GI Bill. One hugely successful provision of the GI Bill provided funding to veterans to continue their education. As a result, "in the peak year of 1947, Veterans accounted for 49 percent of college admissions. By the time the original GI Bill ended on July 25, 1956, 7.8 million of 16 million World War II Veterans had participated in an education or training program."[29] A second major provision of the GI Bill provided loan guarantees for veterans to buy their first homes, enabling them to enter the housing market where a home was your best and most secure asset. Nearly 2.4 million loans were issued to World War II veterans and their families under this program between 1944 and 1952.[30]

The rationale for these benefits was explained by President Franklin D. Roosevelt: "The members of the armed forces have been compelled to make greater economic sacrifice and every other kind of sacrifice than the rest of us, and they are entitled to definite action to help take care of

29. "History and Timeline," US Department of Veterans Affairs, http://www.benefits.va.gov /gibill/history.asp.
    30. Ibid.

their special problems."[31] If this sounds familiar, it's because it closely parallels the argument for affirmative action that I outlined above. Returning veterans were at a significant disadvantage regarding education, jobs, savings, and overall financial security compared to their peers who didn't fight in the war, many of whom were thus able to go to college, advance in their careers, establish their credit ratings, and even buy homes. After the negative experiences faced by veterans of World War I, it was felt that World War II veterans needed significant help from the government to catch up to their peers who didn't serve. Of course, the government was also concerned about the social and economic impacts that might have been caused by millions of unemployed veterans.[32]

But here is the significant historical fact that we often miss or fail to be honest about: black veterans benefited very little from the GI Bill compared to white veterans. Nick Kotz, in his review for *The New York Times* of Columbia professor Ira Katznelson's book *When Affirmative Action Was White*, summarizes how and why this happened:

African-American veterans received significantly less help from the GI Bill than their white counterparts. "Written under Southern auspices," [Katznelson] reports, "the law was deliberately designed to accommodate Jim Crow." . . . Southern Congressional leaders made certain that the programs were directed not by Washington but by local white officials, businessmen, bankers and college administrators who would honor past practices. As a result, thousands of black veterans in the South—and the North as well—were denied housing and business loans, as well as admission to whites-only colleges and universities. They were also excluded from job-training programs for careers in promising new fields like radio and electrical work, commercial photography and mechanics. Instead, most African-Americans were channeled toward traditional, low-paying "black jobs" and small black colleges, which were pitifully underfinanced and ill equipped to meet the needs of a surging enrollment of returning soldiers.

The statistics on disparate treatment are staggering. By October 1946, 6,500 former soldiers had been placed in nonfarm jobs by the employment service in Mississippi; 86 percent of the skilled and semiskilled jobs were filled by whites, 92 percent of the unskilled ones by blacks. In New York and northern New Jersey, "fewer than 100 of the 67,000 mortgages insured by the GI Bill supported home purchases by nonwhites." Discrimination continued as well in elite

31. Franklin D. Roosevelt, "Excerpt from Franklin Roosevelt's Fireside Chat on Progress of War and Plans for Peace," FDR Library, Marist College, July 28, 1943, http://docs.fdrlibrary .marist.edu/odgibfc.html.
    32. "History and Timeline."

Northern colleges. The University of Pennsylvania, along with Columbia the least discriminatory of the Ivy League colleges, enrolled only 46 black students in its student body of 9,000 in 1946. The traditional black colleges did not have places for an estimated 70,000 black veterans in 1947. At the same time, white universities were doubling their enrollments and prospering with the infusion of public and private funds, and of students with their GI benefits.[33]

This was affirmative action for white people, and these were the most important government benefits many families ever received in the United States. But they were reserved predominantly for white people and not black people—even black veterans who risked their lives in the same war as their white counterparts.

My family was one of those that benefited from the GI Bill. The government made possible the education and the housing that enabled my family to join the middle class and become financially secure. Our neighborhood was called Redford Township in the Detroit area, and it was almost entirely composed of nearly identical three-bedroom ranch houses on every street; the vast majority of these homes were built in the 1940s and 1950s. Most of our neighbors were other veteran dads, just like mine, and their young families—but only white families. Without that government help, our family and many of our neighbors couldn't have procured the loans that enabled them to buy their homes, or afforded their fathers' college educations. It's also the case that as increasing numbers of whites left Detroit to work at newly built factories in the suburbs (and to leave neighborhoods that had growing numbers of blacks), discriminatory housing practices and policies prevented blacks from getting mortgages in these newly built white suburban neighborhoods, a legacy that haunts Detroit to this day.[34] To refuse to admit that the white families of my generation were beneficiaries of affirmative action—and then for those same white people to complain about the affirmative action blacks would later receive—is nothing but complete and utter hypocrisy.

Robert Jensen, a professor at the University of Texas at Austin who contributes to a website called Beyond Whiteness, wrote an essay, "How

33. Nick Kotz, "'When Affirmative Action Was White': Uncivil Rights," *New York Times*, August 28, 2005, http://www.nytimes.com/2005/08/28/books/review/28KOTZL.html?page wanted=print&_r=0.
34. Sarah Hulett, "Racial, Regional Divide Still Haunt Detroit's Progress," NPR.org, September 11, 2012, http://www.npr.org/2012/09/11/160768981/racial-regional-divide-still-haunt -detroits-progress.

White Privilege Shapes the U.S.," in which he describes how to acknowledge and deal with the benefits of white privilege. Jensen wrote:

> Like anyone, I have overcome certain hardships in my life. I have worked hard to get where I am, and I work hard to stay there. But to feel good about myself and my work, I do not have to believe that "merit," as defined by white people in a white country, alone got me here. I can acknowledge that in addition to all that hard work, I got a significant boost from white privilege, which continues to protect me every day of my life from certain hardships.
>
> At one time in my life, I would not have been able to say that, because I needed to believe that my success in life was due solely to my individual talent and effort. I saw myself as the heroic American, the rugged individualist. I was so deeply seduced by the culture's mythology that I couldn't see the fear that was binding me to those myths. Like all white Americans, I was living with the fear that maybe I didn't really deserve my success, that maybe luck and privilege had more to do with it than brains and hard work. I was afraid I wasn't heroic or rugged, that I wasn't special.
>
> I let go of some of that fear when I realized that, indeed, I wasn't special, but that I was still me. What I do well, I still can take pride in, even when I know that the rules under which I work in [sic] are stacked in my benefit. I believe that until we let go of the fiction that people have complete control over their fate—that we can will ourselves to be anything we choose—then we will live with that fear. Yes, we should all dream big and pursue our dreams and not let anyone or anything stop us. But we all are the product both of what we will ourselves to be and what the society in which we live lets us be. . . .
>
> A first step for white people, I think, is to not be afraid to admit that we have benefited from white privilege. It doesn't mean we are frauds who have no claim to our success. It means we face a choice about what we do with our success.[35]

"White Fragility"

One of the biggest obstacles to honest, open communication between white people and people of color on the difficult issues of race is the reality that due to the structural forces of racism and white privilege, the *experience* of people of color is *very different* from the experience of white people. White people tend to see racism as an individual issue, about good and bad behavior by moral or immoral people. And because

35. Robert Jensen, "How White Privilege Shapes the U.S.," Beyond Whiteness, http://www .beyondwhiteness.com/2012/02/23/robert-jensen-how-white-privilege-shapes-the-u-s/#sthash .XXCrRk7y.dpuf.

most white people don't think we are "bad" or "immoral" and certainly
not deliberately "racist," racism can't be applied to us. As I said above,
"I am not a racist" is a regular response in the white community, either
expressed or at least strongly felt. And defensiveness is a common reaction, as opposed to trying to really hear what black coworkers or fellow
citizens are saying. For many whites, it's all about me, or us, and we don't
believe we are responsible for racist behavior, even if we believe that some
other white people—the bad or immoral ones—are.

Sam Adler-Bell, who is a journalist and policy associate at the Century
Foundation, a New York–based think tank, did a fascinating interview
about how difficult it is for white people, such as him, to "check" their
privilege. His piece is provocatively titled "Why White People Freak Out
When They're Called Out about Race."[36]

Adler-Bell describes how defensiveness and indignation are common
responses when issues of racism and white privilege come up. He lifts up
language used by Robin DiAngelo, professor of multicultural education
at Westfield State University and author of *What Does It Mean to Be
White? Developing White Racial Literacy*. After more than two decades
of workshops on race, DiAngelo has come up with a term describing what
she has seen and heard "hundreds of times." She calls it "white fragility"
and defines it in a 2011 journal article as "a state in which even a minimum
amount of racial stress becomes intolerable, triggering a range of defensive
moves. These moves include outward display of emotions such as anger,
fear, and guilt, and behaviors such as argumentation, silence, and leaving
the stress-inducing situation."[37]

Adler-Bell says that when the Black Lives Matter movement started
marching in the streets, holding up traffic, disrupting commerce in business centers and malls, and otherwise "refusing to allow 'normal life' to
resume," white people got very nervous and stressed and often had very
difficult conversations online, on social media, or with friends. As a result
of all the national discussion after Ferguson, Adler-Bell reflects, "You could
say white fragility was at an all-time high."[38]

36. Sam Adler-Bell, "Why White People Freak Out When They're Called Out about Race,"
AlterNet, March 12, 2015, http://www.alternet.org/culture/why-white-people-freak-out-when
-theyre-called-out-about-race.

37. Robin DiAngelo, "White Fragility," *International Journal of Critical Pedagogy* 3, no.
3 (2011): 54.

38. Adler-Bell, "Why White People Freak Out."

Adler-Bell asked DiAngelo how to deal with "fragile white people." Her reflections can tell us a lot about the kind of conversations we need to construct and the issues we have to deal with—how white people can "shut down" or "lash out" when any "challenge to our racial reality" is raised. How do we help people get past their "resistance" and move to deeper reflection?

Sam Adler-Bell: What causes white fragility to set in?

Robin DiAngelo: For white people, their identities rest on the idea of racism as about good or bad people, about moral or immoral singular acts, and if we're good, moral people we can't be racist—we don't engage in those acts. This is one of the most effective adaptations of racism over time—that we can think of racism as only something that individuals either are or are not "doing." . . . If you call someone out, they think to themselves, "What you just said was that I am a bad person, and that is intolerable to me." It's a deep challenge to the core of our identity as good, moral people.

And white fragility also comes from a deep sense of entitlement. Think about it like this: from the time I opened my eyes, I have been told that as a white person, I am superior to people of color. . . . We are born into a racial hierarchy, and every interaction with media and culture confirms it—our sense that, at a fundamental level, we are superior.

And, the thing is, it feels good. Even though it contradicts our most basic principles and values. So we know it, but we can never admit it. It creates this kind of dangerous internal stew that gets enacted externally in our interactions with people of color, and is crazy-making for people of color. We have set the world up to preserve that internal sense of superiority and also resist challenges to it. All while denying that anything is going on and insisting that race is meaningless to us.

SAB: Something that amazes me is the sophistication of some white people's defensive maneuvers. What do you see going on there?

RD: Whites often confuse comfort with safety. We say we don't feel safe, when what we mean is that we don't feel comfortable. Secondly, no white person looks at a person of color through objective eyes. There's been a lot of research in this area. Cross-racially, we do not see with objective eyes.

SAB: There's also the issue of "tone-policing" here, right?

RD: Yes. One of the things I try to work with white people on is letting go of our criteria about how people of color give us feedback. We have to build our stamina to just be humble and bear witness to the pain we've caused.

In my workshops, one of the things I like to ask white people is, "What are the rules for how people of color should give us feedback about our racism? What are the rules, where did you get them, and whom do they serve?" Usually those questions alone make the point.

If people of color went around showing the pain they feel in every moment that they feel it, they could be killed. It is dangerous. They cannot always share their outrage about the injustice of racism. White people can't tolerate it. And we punish it severely—from job loss, to violence, to murder. For them to take that risk and show us, that is a moment of trust.

When I'm doing a workshop, I'll often ask the people of color in the room, somewhat facetiously, "How often have you given white people feedback about our inevitable and often unconscious racist patterns and had that gone well for you?" And they laugh.

Because it just doesn't go well. And so one time I asked, "What would your daily life be like if you could just simply give us feedback, have us receive it graciously, reflect on it and work to change the behavior? What would your life be like?" And this one man of color looked at me and said, "It would be revolutionary."[39]

Those reflections match my own in the hundreds of conversations I've also had over the years with white people on race, and with black men and women about how hard it is for whites to admit or take responsibility for their privilege. All of this information can guide us in ways to allow the honest feedback that alone creates trust between black and white people.

What Color Are the Children of God?

For people of faith and conscience, these issues about implicit racial bias and the realities of white privilege in our society are not just political matters; they are moral and religious questions. I am especially hopeful about how a new generation of leaders, including within the churches, is rising up to challenge the false ideology of white privilege and even "whiteness." In an article by Paul Alexander in *Prism Magazine* titled "Raced as White," the president of Evangelicals for Social Action explores the history and theology of white privilege and "whiteness." He uses the phrase "people raced-as-White" and describes how that socialization has occurred in "white" society. This is how we were raised and "raced" as white people—to expect, demand, and depend upon white privilege. We are raced for "enfranchisement and disenfranchisement," he says. These are not just emotional or rhetorical issues, says Alexander. They are "historical and theological realities," and we need to "discover how the Spirit

39. Adler-Bell, "Why White People Freak Out."

can disempower us in our Whiteness and help us become different and better."[40] Alexander, also the Sider Professor of Religion at Palmer Seminary of Eastern University, says: "I'm theorizing Whiteness as a historical and spatial reality with entry routes and exit routes that are continually presented to us."[41]

Alexander also has an interesting take on the now-common accusation in our society of blacks "playing the race card":

> When raced-as-White people cry out defensively, "They're playing a race card!" they forget why there are just so many race cards out there. Raced-as-Whites have manufactured and distributed them by the millions. . . . We raced-as-White folk just about perfected the racializing system that produces race cards, but we really don't like it when one gets handed back to us. It feels a lot better to give them than to receive them.[42]

The children of God are of many colors, so the answer is not to become "color-blind," as many suggest. If God created us in all our human diversity, then that diversity must be important. Race, as a political construct, does matter, because it impacts how we are treated in our society; so the differences in the ways people are treated because of their skin tone and ethnic heritage must be directly addressed. But more deeply, our recognizing, acknowledging, embracing, and even celebrating humanity's ethnic diversity is the beginning of living in the new and real world that is coming.

White privilege becomes the ideology and the idol that must be debunked, cast away, and repented of if we are to move into that new world of respecting the image of God in all God's children. It means that "white" people need to refuse and renounce the assumptions and benefits of "whiteness," and that must be done in concrete and practical ways. Paul Alexander says it should even mean no longer referring to yourself as "white" and even filling out identification forms with "other" instead. "European American" must take its place alongside "African American" and all the other adjectives that define the "places" we have come from rather than the "colors" that we are.[43] It certainly means no longer accepting the decisions

40. Paul Alexander, "Raced as White," *Prism Magazine*, July 1, 2013, http://prismmagazine .org/raced-as-white/.
41. Ibid.
42. Ibid.
43. Ibid.

and systems that perpetuate white privilege. That becomes our political, economic, and spiritual task.

Redefining ourselves as the children of God, who reject racial privileging and stand alongside one another as equals, is the beginning of social and political change. It is not only a question of language; even more, *it's a commitment to action* against racialized systems and structures, which means both to dismantle them and to create more equitable and fairer systems and processes—which we can and must build together.

Paul Alexander puts forward his vision of the future:

> I hope that future generations can inhabit a world in which no human being refers to herself or himself as White and that privilege no longer attaches to skin tone. Whiteness must become history, a construct that folks in the future study as a construct of the past. Perhaps in a few centuries people will be amazed when they learn that for several hundred years of human history some people called themselves "White." Let's start building that world, now.[44]

We can no longer "indulge in the luxury of obliviousness"[45] to implicit bias and the embedded history of white privilege. And we cannot take "the path of least resistance"[46] to racialized systems or act as if the behavior they sanction is normal. We can no longer plead that we are unaware of the systems around us and what their consequences are for our fellow citizens and brothers and sisters of color. The way things are must no longer be accepted—especially by the dominant racial group that most benefits from that unfairness. Things must change, and a new generation must take up that task. White privilege is a sin of which we must repent, and the best way to show that is by changing practices and policies—and by helping to create new communities that provide for another way.

44. Ibid.
45. Johnson, "White Privilege."
46. Ibid.

6 | A Segregated Church or a Beloved Community?

One of my favorite descriptions of the people of God, and the New Testament's call for the body of Christ, is the evocative language of "the beloved community," used by Martin Luther King Jr. during the civil rights movement. Representative John Lewis of Georgia, once a young activist beside Dr. King, still keeps that language alive today.

A *beloved community* is a most powerful vision of a new coming together, a new community that welcomes all peoples in all their diverse ethnicities and nationalities. *Every* group, clan, and tribe is included and invited in. That dream and vision undergirded King's movement for civil and voting rights, both spiritually and philosophically, and deeply reflected his own underlying moral belief and hope as a Christian minister. Mere political histories often overlook King's Christian base and the theological roots of the civil rights movement, which changed the social and racial framework of the nation.

The Most Segregated Hour of the Week

In one of his most famous quotations, King sadly said, "I am [ashamed] and appalled that eleven o'clock on Sunday morning is the most segregated hour in Christian America." He said this in one of his early sermons while he was associate pastor at his father's Ebenezer Baptist Church in Atlanta.[1] But obviously, and most painfully, that quote is still true today. This chapter will explore the biblical call to multiracial communities of faith, how we're doing in regard to that call, and what practical steps can be taken to make real progress toward that wonderful but difficult goal of a beloved community. When King said those stinging and prophetic words in 1953, there was no reliable data on the level of segregation in US churches. In fact, until 1998, there was no real information on how many US churches were "multiracial." However, most scholars on these questions agree that since the Civil War, multiracial churches in America have been very rare.

If we look at what the Bible says about who God's people are and what the body of Christ is supposed to be (and *was* during the earliest days of the church), the racial segregation of US churches is nothing short of scandalous and sinful. The life of the church was indeed appalling when King uttered those words in the 1950s; and the reality of churches separated by race is still appalling today in the first quarter of the twenty-first century.

Let's look at how much has changed in fifty years.

The most definitive scholar on multiracial congregations is Michael O. Emerson, the Allyn and Gladys Cline Professor of Sociology and codirector of the Institute for Urban Research at Rice University in Houston. In the opening lines of his article "The Persistent Problem," Emerson writes: "While whites tend to focus on creating good-intentioned, right thinking people, people of color tend to focus on group equality and justice. Both are important, so they need not be at war. But the focus must be on working together to undo the racialized society, and that is by definition not just about individuals."[2]

I have already discussed how whites and blacks often have different definitions of the meaning of racism, one more individually focused and one more systemic. Emerson documents this in his research: "Race relations are fraught with land mines. One is that racial groups, on average, do not define racism the same way. This means not only the potential for more group conflict, but also reduced potential for overcoming it."[3]

1. "Martin Luther King, Jr. Questioned Issues of Faith, New Volume Reveals," King Encyclopedia, Stanford University, http://mlk-kpp01.stanford.edu/kingweb/news/vol6announcement.htm.

2. Michael O. Emerson, "The Persistent Problem," Center for Christian Ethics at Baylor University, 2010, http://www.baylor.edu/content/services/document.php/110974.pdf.

3. Ibid.

Emerson's work supplies the best and most succinct data on what we know about multiracial congregations. He points to what he calls "the 20 percent rule":

> Research on a variety of organizations has shown that it takes 20 percent or more of another group to have their voices heard and effect cultural change on an organization. Short of that percentage, people are largely tokens. Part of this 20 percent or more rule is mathematics. At 20 percent of another group, the probability of contact across the groups is 99 percent.[4]

Let's agree with Emerson and define a "multiracial congregation" as one that has less than 80 percent of any single race. There is no data on the number of those churches that existed from the Civil War to 1998, but most scholarship and common sense concludes that there were extremely few Christian communities that included substantial numbers of both blacks and whites in the century after slavery.

Racial separation was institutionalized by slavery, of course, and continued afterward when it came to blacks and whites worshiping together. That reality should still be "appalling" to us—it should break our hearts and awaken our Christian conscience. King's prophetic words about the segregation of Christian worship are still one of the greatest moral indictments of US society and of the white church in particular. This is clearly a sin of which we need to repent. But what would that repentance mean?

The exceptions to American racial segregation in the churches were rare and notable. Let's look at a few.

The story of Koinonia Farm in Americus, Georgia, founded in 1948 by an extraordinary farmer/theologian named Clarence Jordan, showed how dramatic and even dangerous those exceptions could be. Jordan decided to take the gospel seriously when he was a student at Southern Baptist Seminary in Louisville, Kentucky. After his theological training, he went directly back to rural Georgia, his home state, to form a Christian community farm where blacks and whites could live, work, and worship together. The stories of Koinonia, one of the first interracial farms in the country, are inspirational even today, and Jordan's "Cotton Patch" versions of the New Testament are some of the best translations and paraphrases some of us have ever read.

4. Michael O. Emerson, "A New Day for Multiracial Congregations," *Reflections*, Yale University, Spring 2013, http://reflections.yale.edu/article/future-race/new-day-multiracial-congregations.

Clarence's son, Lenny Jordan, says that his father talked about how we relate to everyone and that being a follower of Christ meant not being a racist. Lenny tells the story of a group of Klansmen confronting his father on the farm, not long after his family first arrived, saying, "We don't allow the sun to set on anybody who eats with niggers." Clarence just smiled and said, "I'm a Baptist preacher, and I just graduated from the Southern Baptist Seminary. I've heard about people who had power over the sun, but I never hoped to meet one."[5] Jordan would often mix his southern humor and his prophetic utterings.

Some whites who lived around Koinonia, including members of the Ku Klux Klan, would shoot their guns into the farm, especially at night, hoping to frighten or even strike the black and white Christians who were trying to create an interracial community. In order to protect themselves, and especially their children, some of the white adults on the farm would take turns as unarmed sentries at night, stationing themselves out by the road under bright lights. The idea was that the potential shooters would see them first and hopefully not choose to directly shoot at an unarmed person in plain sight—and especially not shoot into the farm where the children were sleeping.[6] Such visible and dramatic risk taking, especially during times of crisis, made the choices more clear and dramatic for the Christians trying to live by the gospel, as they understood it, and for their white assailants.

Many powerful things came out of the Koinonia community, including the now-international ministry of Habitat for Humanity, founded by Millard Fuller, which has built more than 1 million homes for low-income families around the world. My first visit to Koinonia in the 1970s showed me how, even in the midst of violent opposition from the surrounding community, the gospel of Jesus Christ could still be lived out in very practical ways. Koinonia has inspired millions of people like me around the world. I didn't get to meet Clarence Jordan before he died at the age of fifty-seven, but his picture is on my home office wall as I write this book about racism. Jordan was a visionary and a courageous prophet, and the

5. Casey N. Cep, "Christ in the Cotton Patch: Clarence Jordan and Koinonia Farm," *Huffington Post*, October 19, 2012, http://www.huffingtonpost.com/casey-n-cep/clarence-jordan-and-koinonia-farm_b_1967749.html.

6. Tracy Elaine K'Meyer, *Interracialism and Christian Community in the Postwar South: The Story of Koinonia Farm* (Charlottesville: University of Virginia Press, 2000), 86–89.

Koinonia community was an exemplary experiment in the gospel whose members deliberately were not conformed to the racially segregated world around them.

Similarly, East Harlem Protestant Parish in New York City was another such gospel experiment. It was started in 1948 by Rev. Bill Webber and others, including another of my mentors and wall heroes named William Stringfellow, a Christian lawyer who went directly from Harvard Law School to Harlem to practice on the streets. Stringfellow's book *My People Is the Enemy*, published in 1964, was one of the earliest books on racism by a white Christian, and one that shaped me early in my life.

For Stringfellow, the problem of racism was not just economic and political; it was theological. Using language from the New Testament, he referred to racism as a "principality" or a "power." As a white Christian living in Harlem, he once said, "To no principality . . . have American churches been more notoriously and scandalously and complacently accommodating than to the principality of racism."[7] Speaking at the first National Conference on Religion and Race, in 1963, Stringfellow called racism a "demonic power" and, to the astonishment of the ecumenical and interfaith audience, linked the problem to a bad theology of baptism. In this first major meeting of mainline religion on race, the lawyer/theologian Stringfellow said,

> [Racism] is the power with which Jesus Christ was confronted and which, at great and sufficient cost, he overcame. In other words, the issue here is not equality among human beings, but unity among human beings. . . . The issue is baptism. The issue is the unity of all humanity wrought by God in the life and work of Christ. Baptism is the sacrament of that unity.[8]

Another exception to the segregated norm in the church was The Church for the Fellowship of All Peoples in San Francisco. This church was founded in 1944 and is billed as "the nation's first interracial, interfaith congregation." It was founded with a mission to "create a religious fellowship that transcended artificial barriers of race, nation, culture, gender, and social distinctions." The church began when Dr. Alfred G. Fisk, a Presbyterian clergyman and professor of philosophy, sought out Dr. Howard Thurman,

---

7. William Stringfellow, *Free in Obedience* (Eugene, OR: Wipf & Stock, 2006), 77.

8. William Stringfellow, quoted in "Exorcising an American Demon," by Bill Wylie Kellermann, *Christians and Racial Justice* (Washington, DC: Sojourners), http://sojo.net/sites/default /files/Christians%20and%20Racial%20Justice.pdf, 10–11.

who then left his position as Dean of the Chapel at Howard University to join Dr. Fisk in a team ministry and cofound this exemplary church.[9]

The church's foundational principles are articulated in its membership statement, "The Commitment":

> I affirm my need for a growing understanding of all people as children of God and I seek after a vital experience of God as revealed through Jesus of Nazareth and other great religious spirits whose fellowship with God was the foundation of their fellowship with all people.
>
> I desire to share in the spiritual growth and ethical awareness of men and women of varied national, cultural, racial, and creedal heritage united in a religious fellowship.
>
> I desire the strength of corporate worship through membership in The Church for the Fellowship of All Peoples with the imperative of personal dedication to the working out of God's purpose here and in all places.[10]

Howard Thurman, who led the church until 1953, was an extraordinary and influential figure. The church to this day credits its diversity to "the extraordinary heritage of Dr. Thurman's penetrating theology, articulated in over a dozen books." Some of those books include *The Growing Edge*, *The Search for Common Ground*, *The Inward Journey*, and *Jesus and the Disinherited*. In 1936, Thurman and his wife were the first black Americans to meet with Gandhi. It was during their conversation that Gandhi predicted that "it could be through the African American that nonviolence would exert its greatest global impact."[11] This prediction was, of course, fulfilled by the midcentury civil rights movement—and Martin Luther King Jr. considered Howard Thurman one of his most important influences. King reportedly carried Thurman's *Jesus and the Disinherited* with him whenever he traveled.[12]

What has happened since? Emerson confirms that the first scientifically systematic surveys about multiracial congregations weren't done until 1998, and that first data showed that only 7.4 percent of all congregations in the United States were "multiracial." He comments:

> These types of congregations were rarer among Christian congregations than, for example, Muslim congregations. Within Christianity, multiracial congregations

9. "Fellowship Church History," The Church for the Fellowship of All Peoples, http://www.fellowshipsf.org/history.html.

10. Ibid.

11. Ibid.

12. Ibid.

were rarer among Protestants than Catholics. The key factor to understanding the level of racial segregation across religious traditions, I have found, is quite simple. The more choices people have—for instance, a larger number of congregations within a religious tradition to consider—the more people choose to worship with people who are racially like themselves.[13]

Emerson's conclusion is perhaps the most disappointing of all: that, given a choice, people mostly choose to worship with their own race. For people in black churches, which became places of protection, survival, and sustenance for African Americans, who were never allowed to worship with whites, the choice to stay with one's black congregation was certainly understandable. However, the many black churches that I have visited have always been very warm and welcoming to white visitors. It's still a painful reality, even five decades after the great victories of the civil rights movement, that few white Christians choose to come to black churches and worship with black Christians.

But there seems to be some multiracial church movement since 1998. Emerson says:

> Our latest data suggests the overall movement is having an impact. The 2010 Faith Communities Today Survey, which randomly sampled over 11,000 U.S. congregations across all faith traditions, found significant growth in multiracial congregations since our first nationally representative survey in 1998. . . . Whereas 7.4 percent of U.S. congregations were multiracial in 1998, in 2010 that figure had grown to 13.7 percent. Admittedly, this recent figure is still a tiny fraction of all congregations, but at the same time, it represents significant change in but a little over a decade.[14]

We will return later in this chapter to the things that scholars such as Emerson and pastors who are trying to lead new multiracial churches have been learning about *how* congregations can successfully become multiracial. But first, let's turn to the biblical narrative about race.

The Biblical Narrative: From Genesis to Revelation

There is a biblical pilgrimage on the questions of race that runs from Genesis, to the tower of Babel, to the identity of the children of Israel, to

13. Emerson, "New Day."
14. Ibid.

the Hebrew prophets, to the beginning of the church at Pentecost, to the establishment of the "body of Christ" and the early church in the world, and to the end of history as foretold in Revelation by John the apostle.

The movement toward inclusion starts at the beginning of biblical history. In the beginning, on issues we would later speak of as "race," God addresses the most basic and root matter by creating human beings "in the image of God"—not some human beings, but all of them. In the last chapter we quoted Genesis 1, in which God created humankind "in the image of God," both "male and female," then "blessed" us all and gave us the human vocation to "be fruitful and multiply," to "fill the earth and subdue it" with the task of having "dominion," meaning care and stewardship, over the earth and all its creatures.

Most scholars believe that human civilization began in Africa or in the Middle East and that human migration moved out from there. Skin color would develop in different climates and cultures over the many years of human existence. But to suggest that differences in skin color would or should change the created reality of all human beings, made in the image of God, is both preposterous and profoundly evil. Together, humankind was to oversee the rest of creation—to have dominion or "stewardship" over the planet and all its creatures. But sin entered (in what the Christian tradition calls "the Fall") when humans sought to have dominion—or domination—over one another, and even over creation itself. Choosing not to trust God, we decided to trust ourselves instead.

And *sin* is the right word to use for racism, as we've been suggesting, because it's something that seeks to undermine the very creation of human beings as being equally valued, loved, and cared for in the eyes of God. Our worth as men and women comes from *all* of us being the children of God, and all other political affirmations of our equality derive not just from governments but directly from our identity as God's equally valued children. Many conversations about racism and economic policies and criminal justice would benefit by going back to the beginning of the human story.

Then, in the stories of the garden of Eden and the tower of Babel, we see human dispersal—both geographically and linguistically. The cultural mandate given to God's human creatures in Genesis 1:28 to go and "fill the earth" kept moving forward. In Genesis 12, God calls Abraham to enter into a covenant as a people that would be a "blessing" to others and to all nations, with their temple as a "house of prayer for all peoples" (Isa. 56:7).

The Old Testament Hebrew prophets were always calling the children and nation of Israel to, in particular, be *welcoming* of "the stranger."

The recent campaign for comprehensive immigration reform in the United States has drawn many Christians and other people of faith. The presence and influence of people of faith in that struggle has altered the political landscape of the issue, but it has also taught many Christians more about the central role of "the stranger" in biblical history. The biblical word for stranger or immigrant is *ger*, which occurs ninety-two times in the Old Testament.

What has been most eye-opening for many of us in those Hebrew Scriptures is God calling the children of Israel to love *three things*: first, love the Lord your God; second, love your neighbor; and third, love *the stranger* (Lev. 19:18, 34; Deut. 6:5; 10:12, 19). This biblical command to love the stranger comes before even the love of our own families and children. That is the clear instruction. It comes after loving our God and loving our neighbor, and singles out the neighbor who is "a stranger," an outsider—a person who is seen as a different kind of human being than those already in our in-groups. This is an unmistakable command to welcome the stranger and invite the outsider into the community, and, as such, it is an absolute repudiation of racism. Throughout the Old and the New Testaments, caring for the outsiders, the sojourners, is central to the call of the people of God.

The beginning of the church happened at the first Pentecost with a dramatic outpouring of the Holy Spirit, an exciting expression of many tongues and languages, and the call to spread this multicultural gospel throughout the world (Acts 2).

The origin of the church occasioned a glorious multicultural display of unity and evangelism with three thousand converts that first day—clearly including many ethnicities and races. All this made the early churches quite radical in their historical context, and the message of inclusion was extended to every cultural context that Christians entered going forward. The welcoming diversity of the early church attracted great attention and made the new community even *more* evangelistic.

Unity in Christ was meant to be one of the most important pillars of the church. The apostle Paul's epistle to the Galatians perhaps says it best: "There is no longer Jew or Greek, there is no longer slave or free, there is no longer male and female; for all of you are one in Christ Jesus" (Gal.

3:28). This text powerfully asserts that the three most divisive barriers between human beings—race, class, and gender—are meant to be overcome in the new human community that had formed around Jesus. This was a declaration of the meaning of "the body of Christ," and Galatians 3 was used as a baptismal formula for Christian converts to the early church.[15]

The Galatians passage became the baptismal text, telling both converts and the world about the new kind of community that people were joining. These divisive and oppressive factors were used to fuel human conflicts, but now there was a new human community that would deliberately and publically work to reconcile and unite human beings—from different races, classes, and genders.

One of the ongoing missions and struggles of the early church was offering the salvation of Christ to both Jews and Gentiles, and the missionary journeys of the early Christians took the message out across the Middle East and to the far-flung corners of the known world. This breaking down of cultural and racial barriers became a prime characteristic of the early church, pulling a divided humanity together.

Many Christians today don't fully realize that racial and cultural integration was an original mission of the first disciples of Jesus. Galatians, and similar passages in the epistles of Ephesians and Colossians, were a culmination of earlier biblical commands about how the children of God should always be welcoming to "outsiders."

The early church was making a public statement, because baptism was a public and not a private event: In this community we will overcome the divisions between Jews and Greeks, men and women, slaves and free. If you don't want to be part of the kind of community whose purpose is to bring people together, don't join this community! Imagine churches in America making that kind of strong statement today. We need to reimagine that reality into being again.

Other changes threaten when churches become conformed to their culture, as Paul would later warn the Christians in Rome. "Do not be conformed to this world, but be transformed by the renewing of your minds, so that you may discern what is the will of God—what is good and acceptable and perfect" (Rom. 12:2). My favorite paraphrase of this Romans

15. Nicholas Taylor, "Liturgy and Identity: Conversion-Initiation in Galatians 3:26–29," Academia.edu, http://www.academia.edu/4583251/Liturgy_and_Identity_Conversion-Initiation _in_Galatians_3_26-29TAYLOR.

text is from the English Bible translator and commentator J. B. Phillips: "Don't let the world around you squeeze you into its own mold." As the Scriptures make clear, racial exclusion and cultural uniformity are not "the will of God" and are not what "is good and acceptable and perfect."

Back to Michael Emerson on this. "Whites typically lack a racial consciousness," Emerson writes. "Most whites are unaware that they are 'raced,' and that their race has real consequences for their lives. Whites often believe they are cultureless."[16] But whites are not "cultureless" as we sometimes think. As I described in the last chapter, "Dying to Whiteness," whites lost their European ethnicities and were very much "raced" when they came to America as "white people" with the assumption of white privilege.

Paul Alexander comments on Galatians 3:

> When I reflect on Paul's claim that there is "neither Jew nor Greek" in Christ Jesus, I think Paul was trying to protest the exclusion of Gentiles, women, and slaves in the people of God and testifying and arguing that they should be included. But perhaps Paul's "neither Jew nor Greek" was like a person raced-as-White saying we should all be colorblind, which I occasionally hear from raced-as-White people. They're saying: "Color shouldn't matter; we should all just get along." But color does matter. We are not supposed to be colorblind, because there are colors and shades and complexities within the shades, so we should see the colors, and injustices, and oppressions, and exploitation clearly and work for liberation. . . .
>
> So rather than saying "there is neither Jew nor Greek" or calling for colorblindness, perhaps Paul could have written that "there are both Jews and Greeks . . . for you are all many in Christ Jesus." This is a call for a recognition of diversity and particularity, a valuing of one's own and the other's bodily and culturally inscribed differences. Not blindness, but seeing as clearly as possible and valuing highly the differences as well as the similarities. This does not essentialize race, which is a social construct, but recognizes that human beings are diverse.[17]

Contrary to the assumptions of white privilege and supremacy, scriptures reflecting the drive toward racial inclusion culminate in the book of Revelation, with John the apostle foretelling the future. There, at the end of time, all the peoples of the world are worshiping God together. The most compelling thing is how they do so in their native languages as different

16. Emerson, "Persistent Problem."
17. Paul Alexander, "Raced as White," *Prism Magazine*, July 1, 2013, http://prismmagazine.org/raced-as-white/.

races, ethnicities, and nations—perhaps the most powerful biblical expression of diversity as a natural human gift and strength. As human history comes to an end, there is no homogenous language or single identity but rather the most magnificent gathering of all of God's multicultural children coming together to worship and praise the God who created them all in God's own image—with equal love and dignity in *unity*.

There is no otherworldly heavenly culture and certainly no superior human cultural identity in God's reign. Rather, we see the collective and common response of every ethnicity, race, and nation, giving praise to God in all their glorious human diversity. Human diversity is not abolished but rather celebrated and ultimately reconciled in praise of the Creator. Revelation 7:9–10 says,

> After this I looked, and there was a great multitude that no one could count, from every nation, from all tribes and peoples and languages, standing before the throne and before the Lamb, robed in white, with palm branches in their hands. They cried out in a loud voice, saying, "Salvation belongs to our God who is seated on the throne, and to the Lamb!"

A Microcosm of Society

In a sermon delivered on his last Christmas Eve, Dr. King expressed the vision in his heart and behind the movement that he led: "Our loyalties must transcend our race, our tribe, our class, and our nation." It was the inclusive biblical theology of the church King loved so much that formed a foundation for his commitment to racial integration in a pluralistic society. For King, the church was a "microcosm" of what the society was supposed to be. The campaigns of the movement were always around specific and concrete demands—such as civil rights and voting rights—but the spiritual and philosophical vision that inspired and drove King was that of "the beloved community." As King said in the mission statement for his organization, the Southern Christian Leadership Conference (SCLC), "The ultimate aim . . . is to foster and create the 'beloved community' in America where brotherhood is a reality. . . . Our ultimate goal is genuine intergroup and interpersonal living—*integration*."[18] As Kenneth Smith and Ira Zepp

18. "This Is SCLC," National Humanities Center, http://nationalhumanitiescenter.org/pds/maai3/protest/text2/thisissclc.pdf (emphasis original).

put it in "Martin Luther King's Vision of the Beloved Community," "King's was a vision of a completely integrated society, a community of love and justice wherein brotherhood would be an actuality in all of social life. In his mind, such a community would be the ideal corporate expression of the Christian faith."[19]

Historian Charles Marsh shows how King's theology changed his sociology. That is the opposite of what happens in many white American churches—their sociology changes their theology. The sociology of many white communities shapes the theology of their churches, making them "conformed to the world" and disobedient to the gospel. So white churches become sociologically predictable, based on their race and geography.

Although the theological commitments of black churches "radiated"[20] into the society during the civil rights movement, the sociology of white churches turned many of them against the movement for racial justice, against the black churches, and against Dr. King, putting them on the wrong side of history and, more important, on the wrong side of God's purposes in the world.

King was, in fact, making a democratic argument that was based in the theological meaning of Galatians 3:28. The white pastors who opposed the civil rights movement, and even those who ignored it, were indeed disobeying Paul's theological proclamation that, in Christ, there is no Jew or Gentile, slave or free, male or female; but all are one in Christ Jesus. So the difference between most black and most white churches concerning civil rights was not just a political disagreement but a theological one. Therefore, theological obedience on the part of Dr. King and the black churches, and theological disobedience on the part of white churches who opposed them, was the real issue at play in that time and in ours—it went much deeper than politics.

"Letter from Birmingham Jail"

One of the most important letters in American history, and in the history of the church in America, was written in a jail cell in Birmingham,

19. Kenneth L. Smith and Ira G. Zepp Jr., "Martin Luther King's Vision of the Beloved Community," http://www.nathanielturner.com/belovedcommunity.htm.
20. Charles Marsh, *The Beloved Community: How Faith Shapes Social Justice from the Civil Rights Movement to Today* (New York: Basic Books, 2004), 50.

Alabama, in 1963, by a young Martin Luther King Jr. King had been locked up for leading marches in the city for freedom. King's letter is now classic, dealing with movements and their strategy, but it was written as a specific response to local white clergy who had criticized him and other black ministers for causing such disruption in their city. They claimed to be "moderate" white clergy, and they accused King of going too fast.

Shortly after he'd been arrested, King read their letter in jail. It was signed by eight of Alabama's most prominent clergy—including Methodist, Episcopal, and Catholic bishops, mainline Protestant and evangelical ministers, and a rabbi—and published in the *Birmingham News*. The religious leaders' letter was, ironically, titled "A Call for Unity," and it attacked the civil rights campaign as "unwise and untimely" and accused the nonviolent protesters of "provoking hatred and violence." It appealed "to both our white and Negro citizenry to observe the principles of law and order and common sense."[21]

King crafted his letter in reply on the margins of the newspaper where the letter against him appeared and on other paper smuggled into his cell. The letter was written during King's eight days in jail and was quietly smuggled out in pieces by visitors to King. The content of King's "Letter from Birmingham Jail" feels as relevant today as it was then, more than fifty years ago, when the letter was published in America and around the world. In this now-famous letter, King spoke of the global connections between injustices in different places. "Injustice anywhere is a threat to justice everywhere. We are caught in an inescapable network of mutuality; tied in a single garment of destiny."[22]

Obedience to the law, even unjust laws, had become one of the most egregious ways that ministers and their churches had become conformed to their culture. King's response to the cultural conformity of the white churches was more theological than just political when he wrote: "There are two types of laws: just and unjust. I would be the first to advocate obeying just laws. One has not only a legal but a moral responsibility to

21. C. C. J. Carpenter et al., "A Call for Unity," in *Letter from Birmingham Jail*, Newseum, http://www.newseum.org/wp-content/uploads/2014/08/education_resources_letterfrom birminghamjail.pdf.
22. Martin Luther King Jr., "Letter from a Birmingham Jail," African Studies Center, University of Pennsylvania, April 16, 1963, http://www.africa.upenn.edu/Articles_Gen/Letter _Birmingham.html.

obey just laws. Conversely, one has a moral responsibility to disobey unjust laws. I would agree with St. Augustine that 'an unjust law is no law at all.'"[23] The Birmingham ministers didn't realize they would be dealing with St. Augustine, along with Martin Luther King Jr.

King had hoped for a better response from his fellow clergy in the white churches and synagogues. At first, he really expected that when they saw such racial and economic injustice exposed, as these clergy had seen in their city, they would also stand up to it. But that is not what King found in Birmingham:

> I had hoped that the white moderate would see this need. Perhaps I was too optimistic; perhaps I expected too much. I suppose I should have realized that few members of the oppressor race can understand the deep groans and passionate yearnings of the oppressed race, and still fewer have the vision to see that injustice must be rooted out by strong, persistent and determined action.[24]

King's disappointment in the churches, expressed throughout his letter from jail, was so painful because it was so personal. He loved the church so much, and he felt as loyal to it as to his own family:

> But despite these notable exceptions, I must honestly reiterate that I have been disappointed with the church. I do not say this as one of those negative critics who can always find something wrong with the church. I say this as a minister of the gospel, who loves the church; who was nurtured in its bosom; who has been sustained by its spiritual blessings and who will remain true to it as long as the cord of life shall lengthen.[25]

Even years earlier, at the beginning of the movement in Montgomery, Alabama, as the new minister at Dexter Avenue Baptist Church, King had thought other ministers in town might rally around their black brothers and sisters who were boycotting the buses and walking long distances in order to achieve fair, respectful, and equal seating on their city's transportation vehicles. But he was disappointed, not just by those who actively became the movement's opponents, but also by those who didn't have the courage to raise their voices and remained silent in the face of injustice, behind their "stained glass windows":

23. Ibid.
24. Ibid.
25. Ibid.

When I was suddenly catapulted into the leadership of the bus protest in Montgomery, Alabama, a few years ago, I felt we would be supported by the white
church. I felt that the white ministers, priests and rabbis of the South would be
among our strongest allies. Instead, some have been outright opponents, refusing to understand the freedom movement and misrepresenting its leaders; all
too many others have been more cautious than courageous and have remained
silent behind the anesthetizing security of stained glass windows.[26]

His hopes for a better response in Birmingham had now been disappointed again. The eight clergy who had written "A Call for Unity" spoke
more as white leaders than as faith leaders when they attacked King and
called upon him to stop the protests.

King's letter was so powerful because he wasn't a politician speaking
to other politicians but a member of the clergy offering a pained response
to his fellow clergy's moral failure in the face of clear issues of injustice
and faith. Instead of playing the critically needed role of intermediaries
between the people and the power holders, and between the black community and the white establishment, these clergy just played their role as
part of the white power structure.

The biblical narrative we have just reviewed, along with the powerful witness of the early church, must have been in King's mind as he looked at the
actions of the white churches, which he described as mere "thermometers"
that conformed to the status quo instead of acting as "thermostats" that
could have helped shape and change the temperature of society. Instead
of being "a colony of heaven," the white churches tolerated the racial hell
of Birmingham's black community and even of its black churches—their
brothers and sisters in Christ. King recalls to his own scholarly and passionate mind a time when the church was a powerful voice for social change,
recognizing that took a willingness to sacrifice and even suffer, and to
disturb the status quo, traits that a culturally conformed church had lost:

There was a time when the church was very powerful—in the time when the early
Christians rejoiced at being deemed worthy to suffer for what they believed. In
those days the church was not merely a thermometer that recorded the ideas and
principles of popular opinion; it was a thermostat that transformed the mores
of society. Whenever the early Christians entered a town, the people in power
became disturbed and immediately sought to convict the Christians for being

26. Ibid.

"disturbers of the peace" and "outside agitators." But the Christians pressed on, in the conviction that they were "a colony of heaven," called to obey God rather than man. Small in number, they were big in commitment. They were too God-intoxicated to be "astronomically intimidated." By their effort and example they brought an end to such ancient evils as infanticide and gladiatorial contests. Things are different now. So often the contemporary church is a weak, ineffectual voice with an uncertain sound. So often it is an archdefender of the status quo. Far from being disturbed by the presence of the church, the power structure of the average community is consoled by the church's silent—and often even vocal—sanction of things as they are.[27]

Again, King spoke as a pastor and not a politician by lamenting how such moral disobedience on the part of the white churches would turn people, and especially young people, away from an irrelevant church. The young people were with King, and are always with those who show courage, King said:

But the judgment of God is upon the church as never before. If today's church does not recapture the sacrificial spirit of the early church, it will lose its authenticity, forfeit the loyalty of millions, and be dismissed as an irrelevant social club with no meaning for the twentieth century. Every day I meet young people whose disappointment with the church has turned into outright disgust.[28]

King wondered if he had been too optimistic about the church and asked if religion still had the power to change the "status quo." But then he spoke of the hope he felt, particularly from those souls who had courageously left their moribund and conformed churches to walk the path of faith by joining them as partners in the freedom struggle. The time had come for decisive action in what King would later call the "fierce urgency of now."

Perhaps I have once again been too optimistic. Is organized religion too inextricably bound to the status quo to save our nation and the world? Perhaps I must turn my faith to the inner spiritual church, the church within the church, as the true ekklesia and the hope of the world. But again I am thankful to God that some noble souls from the ranks of organized religion have broken loose from the paralyzing chains of conformity and joined us as active partners in the struggle for freedom. They have left their secure congregations and walked the streets of Albany, Georgia, with us. They have gone down the highways of

27. Ibid.
28. Ibid.

the South on tortuous rides for freedom. Yes, they have gone to jail with us. Some have been dismissed from their churches, have lost the support of their bishops and fellow ministers. But they have acted in the faith that right defeated is stronger than evil triumphant. Their witness has been the spiritual salt that has preserved the true meaning of the gospel in these troubled times. They have carved a tunnel of hope through the dark mountain of disappointment. I hope the church as a whole will meet the challenge of this decisive hour.[29]

Fifty Years Later

Unbelievably, for five decades there was no clergy or church leader response to the "Letter from Birmingham Jail." But on the fiftieth anniversary of the letter, a broad coalition of church leaders that I was honored to be among came together back in Birmingham. The participants were from Christian Churches Together in the U.S.A. (CCT), and they chose Birmingham for their annual meeting to issue a long-overdue response to King's classic letter from jail.

CCT says this about itself: "Formed in 2006, Christian Churches Together in the U.S.A. is a fellowship of 36 national communions, including African American, Catholic, Evangelical/Pentecostal, Historic Protestant, and Orthodox; and seven national organizations, including American Bible Society, Bread for the World, Evangelicals for Social Action, Habitat for Humanity, National Hispanic Christian Leadership Conference, Sojourners, and World Vision."[30]

The CCT church leaders joined together in Birmingham from January 11 to 14, 2011, to examine the issue of domestic poverty through the lens of racism. It was stunning to many of us that, apparently, no one had ever issued a clergy response to King's famous letter. Now it was a half century later. We committed to drafting an initial response at our January meeting and releasing a more expansive response in 2013 for the fiftieth anniversary.[31]

In our letter of response, the church leaders remembered with gratitude the sacrifices of the leaders of the civil rights movement, who demonstrated

29. Ibid.
30. "A Response to Dr. Martin Luther King Jr.'s 'Letter from Birmingham Jail,'" Christian Churches Together in the U.S.A., April 16, 2013, http://christianchurchestogether.org/wp-content /uploads/2013/08/CCT-Response-Letter-Birmingham-Jail.pdf, 2.
31. "CCT Response to Dr. King's Letter from Birmingham Jail," Christian Churches Together in the U.S.A., January 14, 2011, http://christianchurchestogether.org/letter-from-birmingham-jail/.

the power of Christian nonviolent action. We also expressed repentance that "some of us have not progressed far enough beyond the initial message from the Birmingham clergy."[32]

> Too often our follow-through has been far less than our spoken commitments. Too often we have chosen to be comfortable rather than prophetic. Too often we have chosen not to see the evidence of a racism that is less overt but still permeates our national life in corrosive ways.[33]

These twenty-first-century church leaders visited both the Civil Rights Institute in Birmingham and Sixteenth Street Baptist Church; we were of multiple races and represented a wide range of church backgrounds. Our Birmingham meeting became a time of "inspiration and renewed commitment."[34]

Many of us were struck by the two windows at the Sixteenth Street Baptist Church where we were meeting—one where the face of Jesus had been blown out by the bombing in 1963 that killed four little girls, and the other that depicts a Christ figure who with one hand rejects the injustice of the world and with the other extends forgiveness. Together we said, "In the spirit of this loving Jesus, and in the spirit of those who committed their very lives to that love, we renew our commitment to ending racism in all forms."[35] Together, we began by rereading the "Letter from Birmingham Jail" and the message from the eight Birmingham clergy that prompted it, and reflecting on their meaning for us today. After drafting an initial response during our time together in 2011, we worked closely together over the following two years to write a more expansive document that would include a common response on behalf of all our members, as well as additional reflections and confessions from the five "families" that make up CCT (African American, Catholic, Evangelical/Pentecostal, Historic Protestant, and Orthodox). Then, in April 2013, we reconvened in Birmingham to release our official response on the fiftieth anniversary of King's letter.[36]

I helped open the event by starting a conversation with Rep. John Lewis, a man almost beaten to death in Selma nearly a half century earlier as he tried to march for voting rights two years after Birmingham.

32. Ibid.
33. Ibid.
34. Ibid.
35. Ibid.
36. "Response to Dr. Martin Luther King."

Lewis, of course, was also in Birmingham, and he reminded us of what happened near the church in which we were meeting, events that were commemorated in the civil rights museum we had visited earlier in the day. He described the everyday grievances of brutal racial discrimination in Birmingham, and the violent attacks by Sheriff Bull Connor's Birmingham police—including fire hoses and dogs unleashed against children—when the people of Birmingham began demonstrating for change. Lewis shared his feelings about the group of "moderate" white clergy writing their open letter accusing the civil rights movement of causing all the trouble. He told us his humorous personal story of how his parents would always tell him to "be quiet and stay out of trouble," and how he had spoken out and made trouble ever since he was a young man.

Lewis reminded us how, while sitting in jail, King wrote his historic letter full of civility, reason, clear analysis of the situation, and a moral response—one of real mutual respect and great love, even for his critics. Lewis spoke powerfully about how important love is as the response to injustice—and it still is today, he said.

I listened to this still-very-passionate elder from the civil rights movement, and now a member of Congress (whom some call the "conscience of the Congress") speak so strongly about love. And it struck me how those eight clergy leaders who attacked Martin Luther King and John Lewis are now long forgotten. But the memory and power of King's letter, and his comrades in the civil rights struggle, such as John Lewis, are remembered and regarded with such honor and respect, fifty years later.

Bernice King, Martin Luther King's youngest child, was there, and she watched, transfixed, as one by one the heads of denominations from across the nation bent down to sign the Christian Churches Together statement called "A Response to Dr. Martin Luther King Jr.'s 'Letter from Birmingham Jail.'" She sat with us in the first row of a church one block from Kelly Ingram Park, where fifty years earlier children had run scared from German shepherds and fire hoses.[37]

As they signed, the presidents of CCT's five church "families" stepped to the podium. Each read his or her church family's confession of complicity with the demons of racism and injustice during and since the civil rights era.[38]

37. Lisa Sharon Harper, "A Passing of the Baton," *Sojourners*, July 2013, http://sojo.net /magazine/2013/07/passing-baton.
38. Ibid.

After every denomination had added its "amen" and every confession had been read aloud, Martin Luther King Jr.'s daughter walked forward to receive a signed copy of Christian Churches Together's response to her father's letter from jail. Lisa Sharon Harper called it "a heavy and a beautiful moment. A baton was passed."[39]

Then Bernice King went to the podium and "spoke of the fact that she was born early—19 days before the Birmingham march. If she had been born on time, her daddy might not have been able to join the protest and his letter might never have been written."[40] Then the now-Reverend Bernice King spoke of the clergy's particular calling to face down the demons of racism and injustice in our world and within the church. The CCT response was specific in regard to the legacy of racism still in the economy, the criminal justice system, the popular culture, and the churches, with our tendency to prefer charity to justice, attending to symptoms and not the causes of injustice. The signers recalled King's words, "The question is not whether we will be extremists, but what kind of extremists will we be. Will we be extremists for hate or for love? Will we be extremists for the preservation of injustice or for the extension of justice?"[41] King reminds us, the church leaders said, "that [although] we may pursue the illusion of moderation, in reality, we cannot avoid taking a stand."[42]

In order to take that stand together, the response letter used these words: "self-examination . . . communicating . . . action . . . equipping . . . collaboration . . . relationship . . . and God working among us."[43] The CCT letter concluded: "Inspired and ennobled by Dr. King's vision, may the fruit of our Christian unity be justice. And may the fruit of justice be to draw all people to know and glorify the God of justice."[44]

Reverend King ended her response to the CCT confession and commitment with a reference to John's Gospel: "May these words become flesh and live among us."[45] The congregation replied, "Amen."

39. Ibid.
40. Ibid.
41. "Response to Dr. Martin Luther King."
42. Ibid.
43. Ibid.
44. Ibid.
45. Harper, "Passing of the Baton."

A Future Multiracial Church

Something new, real, and potentially very important is happening among some groups of white Christians, including some evangelicals. A new conviction and growing passion about racial reconciliation is taking root in the unexpected soil of the white, conservative Christian world.

For a very long time, white evangelicalism has been simply wrong on the issue of race. Indeed, conservative white Christians have served as a bastion of racial segregation and a bulwark against racial justice efforts for decades, in the South and throughout the country. During the civil rights struggle, the vast majority of white evangelicals and their churches were on the wrong side—the wrong side of the truth, the Bible, and the gospel.

Ever since, when evangelical Christians gathered to draw up their theological concerns, the sin of white racism was nowhere to be found. In recent years, when conservative white Christians began to construct their political agendas, a recognition of racism's reality was absent from the issues list of abortion, homosexuality, tax cuts for the middle class, and, yes, opposition to affirmative action.

Fortunately, some of that appears to be changing. One of the first signs was in the National Association of Evangelicals (NAE), the country's largest group of evangelical denominations and organizations. In 1995, NAE president Don Argue called together white, black, and brown evangelical leaders and, in a dramatic moment, personally confessed the sin of racism by white evangelicals, asked forgiveness of the black and brown evangelicals in the room, and committed the NAE to forge new multiracial relationships to change evangelical institutions.[46] Even initially skeptical evangelical leaders of color became convinced that the new direction was sincere. Similar declarations of repentance have been made by the Southern Baptist Convention and by Pentecostals at a historic gathering in 1994 that was dubbed the "Memphis Miracle."[47]

One visible white evangelical men's group, the Promise Keepers, began to use the language of "racial reconciliation." In their large stadium rallies and in their list of "promises," a commitment to build relationships

46. Kathleen Garces-Foley, *Crossing the Ethnic Divide: The Multiethnic Church on a Mission* (Oxford: Oxford University Press, 2007), Google eBook edition, 43.

47. Vinson Synan, "Memphis 1994: Miracle and Mandate," Pentecostal/Charismatic Churches of North America, http://www.pccna.org/about_history.htm.

between white, black, and brown men became more central to the Promise Keepers' mission. When the new language began, black staff and board members of Promise Keepers told me they thought the initial efforts to be sincere, but the real tests were yet to come. Several Promise Keepers leaders came to Washington, DC, and to Sojourners to discuss their hopes and plans for advancing the agenda of racial reconciliation.

Clearly, they said, this new pilgrimage toward "racial reconciliation" must lead to concrete commitments to racial justice if the journey was to be truly authentic. Sitting around the campfire together and at stadiums singing "Kumbaya" and holding hands will not suffice, they said. But those commitments to racial justice never came to the Promise Keepers. Outside the church meeting rooms and stadium rallies where white and black Christians were hugging one another was a nation where racial polarization was on the rise, where the legacy of slavery and discrimination was still brutally present, and where the majority white population was signaling its weariness with the "issue" of race by opposing long-standing affirmative action policies and accusing black people of "playing the race card."

One black evangelical leader privately wondered to me whether his white evangelical colleagues "who still hold the trump cards will ever be willing to give them up—purse strings and the decision-making power." Will "racial reconciliation" just be "another fad," others asked, or will white evangelicals let that commitment take them to places they have never been before? Will they allow racial reconciliation to transform the evangelical world, or will they stop short of any real changes? "The crowd still looks pretty much the same," observed one black leader closely involved in the process.

Lisa Sharon Harper of Sojourners took a critical view of the Promise Keepers' efforts at "racial reconciliation":

> "Reconciliation" is a very controversial word. In the mid-1990s the Promise Keepers movement focused a great deal of its energy attempting to move Christian men forward in their value and practice of racial reconciliation, but they ultimately failed. They focused exclusively on interpersonal reconciliation with no mention of systemic and structural justice. The omission of justice ultimately created a deep divide between participants of color and whites. The white Promise Keepers thought they were doing well to have a black friend (or even two). It was great to go out for coffee and share each other's stories and maybe even swap pulpits on a special Sunday. But those white men shut down when their black or brown or Asian or Native American "friends" began to

call on their friends to advocate against laws, policies, and structures in the church and society that oppressed or impoverished their people. This dynamic was pervasive and caused deep disillusionment within the African American community. As a result, many evangelical African Americans now push back against the use of the words "racial reconciliation." They explain that it presupposes a time when we were in right relationship with one another. They argue that there has never been a time when we have been in right relationship. The language of racial reconciliation has become a mental barrier for many African Americans. It's nothing new in our eyes. Just more of the same. The Evangelical Covenant Church has adopted the language "racial healing" instead of "racial reconciliation"—which I prefer. I believe that deeper language speaks to both justice and reconciliation.[48]

But in contrast to definitions of "reconciliation" that come up short, faith is greatly needed on the *front lines* of the struggle for justice, and it is a new generation that best understands that. Ferguson leader Brittany Packnett and many others are trying to square their life experiences and their involvement in this new movement for justice with their faith, even when many churches haven't engaged them or the issues they are dealing with every day. Having grown up in a religious family, Packnett spoke of how she turned back to faith in situations of doubt, fear, and uncertainty, often on those front lines of the struggle for justice.

[My leadership in the movement] has made me more reliant [on my faith] in a way that I never have been before. . . . I've gone through my own situations of doubt and confusion because of how I often felt that those things didn't line up, and yet I then find myself in a position where there were some days we didn't know what was going to happen to us . . . where the next steps just didn't always seem clear, and so there was nowhere to turn but God—and in that necessity I really started to understand that God is strong when we are weak, clear where we are confused, and brings peace where there is none. And so [there's] this idea that [God's] peace surpasses all understanding, [even] when you are standing in the middle of the street and getting teargassed.[49]

Lessons to Be Learned

How does the clear and hopeful biblical narrative translate into reality, particularly in the United States, with its legacy of racism and white privilege?

48. Lisa Sharon Harper, conversation with the author, April 24, 2015.
49. Brittany Packnett, interview with the author, March 27, 2015.

How can multiracial churches come into being when racial conformity is the norm in most religious congregations?

Michael Emerson describes the "lessons" we have learned so far in creating successful multiracial congregations. From a variety of sources, he describes "an emerging agreement on the core ingredients of successful multiracial congregations."[50] Here are the five key ingredients, according to Emerson, who has done the best work on this critical subject:

- Intentionality. Although congregations do become multiracial without intentionality, they don't stay diverse without focused intentionality. For congregations to remain diverse, they must desire to do so.
- Diversity as a necessary means to a larger goal. Diversity cannot be an end in itself—this is not sufficient motivation to sustain the difficulties of being diverse. Instead, diversity must be a path to a larger goal.
- Spirit of inclusion. This can be done in many ways, including through worship, small groups, diversity in who is seen "up front," structures that encourage cross-racial relationships, and mission statements.
- Empowered leadership. Leaders of multiracial congregations need to be diverse, be truly empowered (not "token" leaders), and be experienced in managing diversity.
- Adaptability. Leaders and parishioners must develop skills of adapting to change, to each other's racial and ethnic cultures, and to each other's religious traditions and histories. Grace is essential.[51]

An article in *USA Today* tells the story of a successful multiracial church:

Lena Hampton felt at home from the first time she walked into Rural Hill Church of Christ in Antioch, Tenn., in 1975. She says it didn't matter that she was the only African American in a congregation of about 200. The people were friendly and loved God, and that was good enough for her. "I've been to churches where they didn't even talk to you," she said.

Soon, Hampton joined the church and invited some friends and family to come with her. Then they invited some friends as well and on it went. Now, Rural Hill is one of the most diverse churches in the Nashville area. Its 600-member congregation is 40% African-American, 40% white and 20% Hispanic. It is

50. Emerson, "New Day."
51. Ibid.

one of a small but growing number of churches in the country where Sunday service is no longer the most segregated hour of the week.[52]

The *USA Today* piece, by Bob Smietana, offers different perspectives from a number of leaders of multiracial churches, as well as experts in this emerging field who attended the Mosaix conference, a regular gathering for people working on building such churches. For example, Mark DeYmaz, who is the pastor of Mosaic Church, a diverse nondenominational church in Little Rock, Arkansas, and the convener of this annual gathering, says he believes the number of multiracial churches across the country will continue to grow over time. His congregation of six hundred "is about 40 percent white, 33 percent African-American, 15 percent Hispanic, with the rest from a variety of backgrounds."[53] DeYmaz points out: "When we get to heaven, the kingdom of God isn't going to be segregated. So why should the local church be segregated?"[54] Gary McIntosh, professor of Christian Ministry and Leadership at Biola University in La Mirada, California, has a somewhat different perspective. He doubts that multiracial churches will ever become the norm. He says that it's human nature for churches to attract people from similar backgrounds and cultures—an observation very much in line with Emerson's research. However, in McIntosh's view, that doesn't mean that churches that are predominantly made up of people from the same racial background are intentionally segregated. McIntosh says: "Churches gather around to worship Jesus Christ—but there are always secondary factors that draw people together."[55]

Efrem Smith, president and CEO of World Impact and author of *The Post-Black and Post-White Church*, is more hopeful. Smith, who was also the founding pastor of Sanctuary Covenant Church, a multiracial church of one thousand in Minneapolis, says that churches should be diverse precisely *because* Jesus told his followers to spread his message "to all nations." Diverse churches also can be filled with unexpected graces, Smith testifies, where people from different races, ethnicities, and cultures learn from one another. He believes America is now ready for multiracial churches. As

52. Bob Smietana, "Churches Open Doors to All," *USA Today*, September 18, 2012, http://usatoday30.usatoday.com/news/nation/story/2012/09/18/churches-open-doors-to-all/57798200/1.
53. Ibid.
54. Ibid.
55. Ibid.

Smith puts it, these leaders are "black people who [aren't] just leaders of other black people. They are leaders of all people."[56]

Rural Hill Church of Christ, the Tennessee church referenced above, is a great example of the cross-cultural learning Efrem Smith is talking about and demonstrates Emerson's "key ingredients" for a successful multiracial church. As Smietana describes it:

> When Hispanic members joined the church, the English-speaking members ran English classes for them. Now Hispanic members are organizing Spanish classes for people who speak English. "It reinforces the idea that we are all one church and we need to learn from each other," said Ramiro Alvarez, Rural Hill's Hispanic minister. The church also has a diverse set of leaders from different races. That's helped bind the congregation together despite their differences, says Rex Barker, an elder at Rural Hill. "If one segment of the church says, 'We are going to tell all of you how it's going to be,' that's not healthy," Barker said.[57]

Indeed, the fact that Rural Hill has a commitment to leadership that is both multiracial and shared is critical to its success. For multiracial churches to succeed, they need this commitment to diversity in both their leadership and their liturgy. Soong-Chan Rah, professor of church growth and evangelism at North Park University in Chicago and author of *Many Colors: Cultural Intelligence for a Changing Church*, summarizes this notion very well: "Churches have to move from welcoming diverse newcomers to sharing life with them. It's not just getting people sitting in the same room on Sundays."[58]

Rah also points to the need for the white church to broaden its theological horizons. For the most part, when we talk about theology in America, we're usually talking specifically about Western theology. As Rah puts it:

> Theologies that speak of a corporate responsibility or call for a social responsibility are given special names like: liberation theology, black theology, *minjung* theology, feminist theology, etc. In other words, Western theology with its individual focus is considered normative theology, while non-Western theology is theology on the fringes and must be explained as being a theology applicable only in a particular context and to a particular people group. . . . Because theology emerging from a Western, white context is considered normative, it

56. Ibid.
57. Ibid.
58. Ibid.

places non-Western theology in an inferior position. . . . This bias stifles the theological dialogue between various cultures.[59]

Rah's observations here have implications far beyond theological education. If white Christians hope to build multiracial and multicultural communities of faith, they must be prepared to listen to and include the worldviews and theologies of nonwhites and non-Westerners. That process can begin by recognizing that many non-Western expressions of Christian theology have just as much to teach us about God as Calvin, Luther, or German popes do.

David Drury, a Wesleyan Methodist, also reported on some of the most important moments of the 2013 Mosaix conference:

> Speaker Noemi Chavez noted, "My upbringing in the church didn't equip me to love people who weren't just like me." . . . Ed Stetzer also cautioned that in our multi-cultural communication we tend to think people hear what we are trying to communicate, but our cultural context impacts how we encode our message. He added, "Talking is not the same thing as being heard."
>
> At a crucial moment at the conference, John Perkins, founder of the Christian Community Development Association, displayed deep emotion as he spoke to the crowd. As Perkins spoke, the participants got the sense he was seeing a long-held dream beginning to come true in the Church as he looked on the multi-ethnic crowd of Church leaders assembled. After saying that he "could die now," Perkins then called the crowd to a selfless sacrificial vision of serving others, saying, "Most people don't have a vision about God, they have a vision about themselves."[60]

A hopeful example of a growing multiracial church is Bridgeway Church in Columbia, Maryland. The church, led by a black pastor, provides perhaps a stronger model than white-led churches trying to become multiracial. Bridgeway, founded on Easter Sunday, 1992, by Pastor David Anderson and his team, began with very few members, often meeting in people's homes. Today, it has more than three thousand members and is still growing. The vision of the church is "to become a multicultural body of fully devoted followers of Christ, moving forward in unity and love, to

59. Soong-Chan Rah, *The Next Evangelicalism: Freeing the Church from Western Cultural Captivity* (Downers Grove, IL: InterVarsity, 2009), 77–78.

60. David Drury, "Multi-ethnic for the Sake of the Gospel: Mosaix 2013 Conference," The Wesleyan Church, November 6, 2013, https://www.wesleyan.org/1202/multi-ethnic-for-the -sake-of-the-gospel-mosaix-2013-conference.

reach our community, our culture, and our world for Jesus Christ."[61] The key to Bridgeway's success as a multiracial church is that its desire to be so is right there in its mission statement. When I visited Bridgeway, that mission statement was right out front, the first thing I saw when I entered the church. And every part of the church service deliberately reflected that commitment to be a multicultural worshiping community—as does their ministry to the world outside their church walls. It's both intentional and foundational. *Sojourners* magazine recently profiled three other multiracial churches in the Washington, DC, area—one Catholic, one Methodist, and one nondenominational—that are enjoying similar success.[62]

"Multi-ethnic ministry must not become a fad or a church-growth strategy," Rah told the Mosaix conference audience, "but instead, a response to the call of scripture to unity."[63] Unity is indeed the issue, as William Stringfellow told Christians fifty years ago. And our commitment to pursue congregations that reflect the grand diversity of the people of God will be the twenty-first-century test of how much Christians really do care about their "unity in Christ." A segregated church or a beloved community—you can't have both, and we must make a choice.

It's Our Calling

Who will lead in our racially polarized time? Who will help America navigate its changing demographics? Who will help a new generation create a diverse, multiracial society?

The church has a prophetic role to play. Perhaps a community of faith that is intentionally multiracial and becoming more so will lead in this area. The churches in this country are becoming a wonderful medley of European Americans, African Americans, Latinos, Asian Americans, Native Americans, and other people from all over the world. This diversity within Christianity in the United States holds enormous potential for helping to build a multiracial American future.

When racism is tolerated, the reconciling work of Christ on the cross is contradicted. And when the church remains silent on the issue, we deny

61. "Our History," Bridgeway Community Church, http://bridgeway.cc/about/our-history/.
62. Maria-Pia Negro, "One in the Lord," *Sojourners*, November 2014, http://sojo.net/magazine/login?nid=60101.
63. Ibid.

our calling to display "the wisdom of God in its rich variety" (Eph. 3:10) through our unity and reconciliation.

In the fall of 2013, Sojourners and more than seventy Christian leaders signed a pledge called "One Church, One Body." It invited the community of faith to engage in three commitments—first, to help build a multiracial faith community; second, to help fix an unjust criminal justice system; and third, to protect voting rights for minority citizens.

The pledge begins with these words:

> In Christ there is no Jew or Gentile, slave or free, male or female (Galatians 3:28). There is no difference between races, classes, or genders in the salvation that Christ brings to us all. This is essential to the work of Jesus Christ, and the early apostles made a clear choice to create a multiracial Christian community. Therefore, a multiracial body of Christ is not only admirable—it is intrinsic, mandated, and expected by God."[64]

The church is meant to be "a royal priesthood, a holy nation, God's special possession," so that we would "declare the praises of [God] who called [us] out of darkness into [God's] wonderful light. Once [we] were not a people, but now [we] are the people of God; once [we] had not received mercy, but now [we] have received mercy" (1 Pet. 2:9–10 NIV).

The apostle Paul goes even further and describes how in Christ we are one body (1 Cor. 12:12–26). Paul compares the church to the human body, saying when "one part suffers, all parts suffer with it" (v. 26 TLB). What does that mean when brothers and sisters in black churches suffer the pain of economic discrimination, disproportional negative experiences with the criminal justice system, and the police-shooting deaths of black young men? Do all the parts of the body in white churches suffer with parts of the body in black churches when such things happen? If we did, that would change the whole conversation about race in America.

It's not easy to face the deep wounds of racism in our country and in our church. It will require self-examination and repentance. But just as Christ reconciled us to God, let us show one another the forgiveness, grace, peace, and mercy we have received. The church must be at the forefront of racial reconciliation and justice and healing in this country. It is nothing less than our calling.

64. "The One Church, One Body Pledge," *Sojourners*, http://sojo.net/sites/default/files/One%20Church%20One%20Body-HeaderFooter.pdf.

7 | From Warriors to Guardians

When it comes to improving the ways we do policing in America and reforming our criminal justice system in general, I want to turn first to Plato and then to Rev. Darren Ferguson.

In *The Republic*, Plato identifies the types of people essential to the ideal state. The most important of these is the "guardian." Whoever else makes up a society, it cannot function without guardians. This is as true today as it was twenty-four hundred years ago. That should be the goal, even the vocation, of our police officers and all those involved in our criminal justice system. Being our guardians is a vocation that many law enforcement officials could and do aspire to. But "the guardian" is not the first image that comes to many minds today when thinking about the police or the courts. So how do we reclaim the ancient idea and restore the rightful vocation of those whose mission is to "serve and protect"?

The problem comes when those who have been chosen to be our guardians behave instead like warriors or soldiers—a crucial difference. As Sue Rahr, one of the members of the President's Task Force on 21st Century Policing, explains:

> Although police officers wear uniforms and carry weapons, the similarity [to soldiers] ends there. The missions and rules of engagement are completely different. The soldier's mission is that of a warrior: to conquer. The rules of

engagement are decided before the battle. The police officer's mission is that of
a guardian: to protect. The rules of engagement evolve as the incident unfolds.
Soldiers must follow orders. Police officers must make independent decisions.
Soldiers come into communities as an outside, occupying force. Guardians are
members of the community, protecting from within.[1]

Another member of the task force, Bryan Stevenson of the Equal Justice Initiative, agrees with Rahr, summarizing the task of reforming US
law enforcement as "transforming the warrior model into the guardian
model."[2] Stevenson is a compelling lawyer who has won national acclaim
for challenging bias against the poor and people of color and has been
called "America's young Nelson Mandela" by South African archbishop
Desmond Tutu.[3] He himself has become a guardian of young black men,
who, he says, are regularly assumed to be guilty and dangerous.

When I met Stevenson at the release of the task force's interim report,
I told him that the mission to transform our nation's police forces from
warriors to guardians is one that many of us, including in the faith community, would be eager to support, offering to be partners, connecters,
and intermediaries between the police and our communities. Stevenson
and many of the other task force members were eager for that partnership.

Of course, it will not be easy to reform police practices and make the
shift from warriors to guardians. Doing so requires that we take a deeper
look at the criminal justice system and a deeper look into our very society.
As we will see in this chapter, the criminal justice system in its current
form is racialized at *every level*, from stops and arrests to sentencing,
incarceration, and recidivism.

Stopping the Train

Reverend Ferguson spent nine years in federal prison, first at Rikers Island
and then at Sing Sing in New York, where he and I first met. I had received

---

1. Sue Rahr, "Transforming the Culture of Policing from Warriors to Guardians in Washington State," *International Association of Directors of Law Enforcement Standards and Training
Newsletter* 25, no. 4 (2014): 3–4.

2. Jim Wallis, "Police: From Warriors to Guardians," *God's Politics* (blog), *Sojourners*, March
5, 2015, http://sojo.net/blogs/2015/03/05/police-warriors-guardians.

3. Nicholas Kristof, "When Whites Just Don't Get It, Part 3," *New York Times*, October
11, 2014, http://www.nytimes.com/2014/10/12/opinion/sunday/nicholas-kristof-when-whites
-just-dont-get-it-part-3.html?_r=0.

an invitation from another inmate to come to Sing Sing and discuss my book *The Soul of Politics*, which he and other inmates had been reading. When I asked when the prisoners wanted me to come, the answer came back in a second letter from the young man: "Well, we're free most nights. We're kind of a captive audience here!"

So I went to Sing Sing one night and spent several hours with fifty men in a room deep inside the bowels of that tough and infamous prison. We had rigorous discussion about the book and how faith must be applied to the fundamental issues of injustice in our time. I will never forget the comment of one of those young inmates. "Reverend, almost all of us in this prison are from about four or five neighborhoods in New York City. It's like a train that begins in your neighborhood. You get on when you are nine or ten years old, and the train ends up here—at Sing Sing." I remember the compelling testimony and clear promise of a young prisoner that night, who told me this: "But I have been converted now, and when I get out of here, I am going to go back to those neighborhoods and stop that train."

Two years later, I was again in New York City to speak at a big town meeting on overcoming poverty. And there, up front, was that same young man whom I had met on that unforgettable night at Sing Sing: Darren Ferguson. He had been released from prison and was now back home trying to stop that train. Ferguson has become an ally, partner, brother, and dear friend. I want people to hear his whole story. It's one of mass incarceration and the broken criminal justice system, but also a story of hope—and it has the power to both inform and change minds and hearts. I hope people will talk about Darren Ferguson's story and what it means for all of us in relation to criminal justice.

In June 2014, Sojourners hosted a gathering called "The Summit: World Change through Faith and Justice" in Washington, DC. One of our key areas of focus was mass incarceration and America's racialized criminal justice system. I remember how moving the discussion was with the three hundred leaders who had come.

The Summit laid out the facts. The United States contains 5 percent of the world's population, and 25 percent of the world's prisoners. Statistics on mass incarceration and our criminal justice system reveal a startling racial disparity: 1 out of every 15 African American men and 1 in 36 Latino men in the United States are currently incarcerated. Meanwhile, only 1

in every 106 white men are behind bars.[4] Black men have a 1 in 3 chance
of being incarcerated at some point in their lives.[5] The Summit featured
experts in this field and leaders in the movement. But perhaps the most
powerful speaker on this topic was Rev. Darren Ferguson, who shared his
testimony of how he came to his faith in prison and issued a powerful call
for Christians to get involved in reforming our brutal and terribly flawed
criminal justice system.

From pastors and church leaders all over the country, I hear a desire for
tools to talk about issues of racism, mass incarceration, and the criminal
justice system. Just like immigration reform, mass incarceration and the
need to change our criminal justice system are sparking another movement—especially after the events in Ferguson, Missouri, woke up many
people around the country.

Listening to stories such as Darren Ferguson's is a good place to start.
Personal stories are what most stir new conversations in our churches
and beyond. We will need a solid beginning with both strong moral and
theological foundations and a framework of facts and critical information
that can undergird new ministries and movements. Ferguson's dynamic
and moving testimony is such a compelling message that it can be used
in reaching out to many more people.

On a panel, then standing up and beginning to preach, Ferguson touched
so many in the audience that day that we have made an animated video
of his remarks. Here are some of his comments (you can watch the full
video at http://summitforchange.com/portfolio-item/elevating-the-issues
-mass-incarceration/):

> So I'm saying to you today: Yeah, there's racism. Yeah, there's problems. Yeah,
> there's issues. Yes, there's legislation, and there's grassroots things that we
> must address and we must do. But the first thing that we must address is the
> human element of humanizing men and women who will be suffering for the
> rest of their lives for *one mistake*. Who will be suffering for the rest of their
> lives because they had no other recourse. Because they knew no better, they
> saw no better, they experienced no better, so they did no better! They won't

4. Sophia Kerby, "The Top 10 Most Startling Facts about People of Color and Criminal
Justice in the United States," Center for American Progress, March 13, 2012, https://www
.americanprogress.org/issues/race/news/2012/03/13/11351/the-top-10-most-startling-facts
-about-people-of-color-and-criminal-justice-in-the-united-states/.

5. Kelly Welch, "Black Criminal Stereotypes and Racial Profiling," *Journal of Contemporary
Criminal Justice* 23 (2007): 280, doi: 10.1177/1043986207306870.

do better until we teach them better, until we show them better, until we love them better, until we preach for them better, until we understand them better, until we understand that today is the day that we have to say, "This must come to an end!" It's *our* job! It's no one else's job! If you call yourself a Christian, read Matthew 25:31–46 ["just as you did it to one of the least of these who are members of my family, you did it to me" (v. 40)], and if you *still* choose to sit on your behind, burn the Bible, stop going to church, and stop calling yourself a Christian. Because we can't serve a man and we can't talk about a man [Jesus] who was a victim of capital punishment unless we do something about all forms of punishment, to make them humane, to make them right, and to solve this problem in our country today. Amen.[6]

The Service of Police

In the wake of the national attention and outrage generated by the events in Ferguson, Baltimore, Cleveland, and too many other places, in December 2014 President Obama established the President's Task Force on 21st Century Policing. The task force was formed to "examine how to foster strong, collaborative relationships between local law enforcement and the communities they protect; and to make recommendations to the President on how policing practices can promote effective crime reduction while building public trust."[7]

The need for such a task force was obvious, coming at a time when decades of mistrust between law enforcement officers and the communities they serve have repeatedly boiled over, creating situations such as those we witnessed in Ferguson and elsewhere. The mistrust on the part of community members for those who are pledged to protect and serve them is born of serious mistreatment and bias by police officers toward communities of color in particular.

Incidents such as the shooting of Michael Brown in Ferguson, the choking death of Eric Garner on Staten Island in New York, the shooting death of twelve-year-old Tamir Rice in Cleveland, and so many other painful examples suggest that the killing of civilians by police, especially men of color, is a major problem in our country. As we saw in chapter 2, there is

6. Rev. Darren Ferguson, "From Prison to Pulpit," Summit for Change, 2014, http://summit forchange.com/portfolio-item/elevating-the-issues-mass-incarceration/.

7. President's Task Force on 21st Century Policing, *Interim Report of the President's Task Force on 21st Century Policing* (Washington, DC: Office of Community Oriented Policing Services, 2015), http://www.cops.usdoj.gov/pdf/taskforce/interim_tf_report.pdf, 1.

no good national data on how many people are shot by police each year, so the full extent of the problem cannot be known. The good news is that people in positions of power are now aware of this problem, and some want to fix it. FBI director James Comey spoke eloquently and insightfully in February 2015 about the tension between law enforcement and communities of color:

> We are at a crossroads. As a society, we can choose to live our everyday lives, raising our families and going to work, hoping that someone, somewhere, will do something to ease the tension—to smooth over the conflict. We can roll up our car windows, turn up the radio and drive around these problems, or we can choose to have an open and honest discussion about what our relationship is today—what it should be, what it could be, and what it needs to be—if we took more time to better understand one another. . . . All of us in law enforcement must be honest enough to acknowledge that much of our history is not pretty. At many points in American history, law enforcement enforced the status quo, a status quo that was often brutally unfair to disfavored groups. . . . Little compares to the experience on our soil of black Americans. That experience should be part of every American's consciousness, and law enforcement's role in that experience—including in recent times—must be remembered. It is our cultural inheritance. . . . We must better understand the people we serve and protect—by trying to know, deep in our gut, what it feels like to be a law-abiding young black man walking on the street and encountering law enforcement.[8]

Representative Steve Cohen of Tennessee has introduced a bill to mandate that statistics on shootings of civilians by law enforcement officers be tracked nationally. As Congressman Cohen has said:

> It is ridiculous that we can't tell the American people how many lives were ended by police officers this year, or any year. Before we can truly address the problem of excessive force used by law enforcement we have to understand the nature of the problem and that begins with accurate data. That is why I introduced the National Statistics on Deadly Force Act; so that our country can do a better job of honestly assessing racial disparities and other problems in our justice system and begin to fix them.[9]

8. James B. Comey, "Hard Truths: Law Enforcement and Race," Federal Bureau of Investigation, February 12, 2015, http://www.fbi.gov/news/speeches/hard-truths-law-enforcement-and-race.

9. Steve Cohen, "FBI Director Is Right, Police Departments Should Have to Report Police Shootings," Office of Rep. Steve Cohen, February 12, 2015, http://cohen.house.gov/press-release/congressman-cohen-fbi-director-right-police-departments-should-have-report-police.

But the crisis of racialized policing in this country goes far beyond police shootings of civilians and is not just a crisis for the communities affected— it's a crisis for all of us. President Obama said it very well in announcing the new task force:

> When any part of the American family does not feel like it is being treated fairly, that's a problem for all of us. It's not just a problem for some. It's not just a problem for a particular community or a particular demographic. It means that we are not as strong as a country as we can be. And when applied to the criminal justice system, it means we're not as effective in fighting crime as we could be.[10]

The task force itself is made up of an impressive group of law enforcement professionals and civil rights and community leaders. It held listening sessions all over the country, gathering important feedback from "government officials; law enforcement officers; academic experts; technical advisors; leaders from established nongovernmental organizations, including grass-roots movements; and any other members of the public who wished to comment."[11] In March 2015, the task force released its interim report, a document of remarkable depth and breadth, which does an excellent job of identifying the challenges of the law enforcement system today and offering many concrete recommendations for how these challenges could be overcome.

I was fortunate enough to be invited to both the launching and the official release of the interim report and given the opportunity to suggest some input to the commission. At the report's release, I was encouraged by what the task force members said about how this tragic moment in time could and should lead to a historic turning point for change. Their recommendations respond to the legitimate issues that people have in their communities with the opportunity to fix these systems. I agreed with what one member said, "We have a moment in time." That reflected the challenge of Rasheen Aldridge, a twenty-year-old from Ferguson who was among the young leaders who met with President Obama in the Oval Office just before the announcement of the new policing commission. Aldridge looked squarely at the law enforcement officials, city mayors,

10. President's Task Force, *Interim Report*, 1.
11. Ibid., 2.

and faith leaders sitting around the table and said, "This is a moment in history, and we have to respond."[12]

A 2015 article in *The New York Times* reported on a fray between the police and the public in Philadelphia, where Police Commissioner Charles Ramsay, who also served as cochair of the president's national task force, was trying to ease the tensions. The central problem was summarized by Jonathan Simon, director of the Center for the Study of Law and Society at the University of California, Berkeley:

> The mission we've adopted for the police in recent years has been that police need to be aggressively deployed and confronting people who are deemed suspects in high crime neighborhoods, which invariably means young people of color. . . . That is the 800 pound gorilla in the room.[13]

By understanding what is wrong with the system as it currently exists, we can then act to make it right.

Black Lives Matter, Blue Lives Matter

I have been a supporter of the "Black Lives Matter" movement since its beginning after the shooting of Michael Brown in Ferguson. But along with many other supporters of "Black Lives Matter," I also believe that "blue" lives matter.

Before we get into examining the problems with our nation's law enforcement systems and how to fix them, it's vital to acknowledge the many good police in our communities and to recognize that our police officers do a very difficult and dangerous job. Their safety and well-being—physical, mental, emotional, and spiritual—is central to solving the problems that have been revealed.

Being a police officer is indeed dangerous. The Bureau of Labor Statistics estimates that "more than 100,000 law enforcement professionals are injured in the line of duty each year. Many are the result of assaults . . . but most are due to vehicular accidents."[14] In 2014, 126 officers died in the

12. Author was present at this meeting.
13. Timothy Williams, "Philadelphia Commissioner Steps into Fray between Police and Public," *New York Times*, March 20, 2015, http://www.nytimes.com/2015/03/21/us/philadelphia -commissioner-steps-into-fray-between-police-and-public.html.
14. President's Task Force, *Interim Report*, 62.

line of duty—50 from firearms-related incidents, 49 from traffic-related incidents, and 27 from other causes, of which 24 were from job-related illnesses such as heart attacks.[15]

In December 2014, not long after grand juries declined to indict Darren Wilson for the death of Michael Brown and Daniel Pantaleo for the death of Eric Garner, an unstable man named Ismaaiyl Brinsley murdered two New York City police officers, Wenjian Liu and Rafael Ramos, claiming on Instagram that it was revenge for Brown and Garner.[16] The reaction from those who had been protesting police treatment and tactics was swift and strongly supportive of the slain officers, calling for the safety of the police. For example, Marc Morial of the National Urban League said, "The brutal shooting of Officers Wenjian Liu and Rafael Ramos in Brooklyn, N.Y. is heinous and reprehensible. . . . In Dr. Martin Luther King Jr.'s ever-relevant words, 'If we do an eye for an eye and a tooth for a tooth, we will be a blind and toothless nation.'"[17] Other national leaders echoed those sentiments—with President Obama stating that officers who serve their communities "deserve our respect and gratitude every single day."[18]

Reactions were similar in March 2015, after the release of the Department of Justice's damning report on the Ferguson Police Department, when two police officers were wounded by gunfire during a protest outside the Ferguson police station. Protesters were heartsick that someone would use the cover of their legitimate nonviolent protests of police violence to shoot police officers. In fact, when the police made an arrest in the case a few days later, they credited information received from the public for helping them track down the alleged shooter.[19] The protesters reportedly helped the police find the suspect in the officer shootings. Vocal critics of the Ferguson Police Department were equally strong in condemning

15. "Preliminary 2014 Law Enforcement Officer Fatalities Report" (Washington, DC: National Law Enforcement Officers Memorial Fund, 2015), http://www.nleomf.org/assets/pdfs /reports/Preliminary-2014-Officer-Fatalities-Report.pdf, 1.

16. Benjamin Mueller and Al Baker, "2 N.Y.P.D. Officers Killed in Brooklyn Ambush; Suspect Commits Suicide," New York Times, December 20, 2014, http://www.nytimes.com/2014/12/21 /nyregion/two-police-officers-shot-in-their-patrol-car-in-brooklyn.html?_r=0.

17. Jo-Carolyn Goode, "From the President's Desk—National Urban League President Marc Morial," Houston Style Magazine, December 23, 2014, http://stylemagazine.com/news/2014 /dec/23/presidents-desk-national-urban-league-president-ma/.

18. Mueller and Baker, "2 N.Y.P.D. Officers Killed."

19. Eliott C. McLaughlin, "Ferguson Police: Public Info Led to Arrest of Man in Shootings of Two Officers," CNN.com, March 15, 2015, http://www.cnn.com/2015/03/15/us/ferguson -police-shot-arrest/.

the shooting of police. Attorney General Eric Holder's statement was particularly powerful:

> This heinous assault on two brave law enforcement officers was inexcusable and repugnant. I condemn violence against any public safety officials in the strongest terms, and the Department of Justice will never accept any threats or violence directed at those who serve and protect our communities—from this cowardly action, to the killing of an officer in Philadelphia last week while he was buying a game for his son, to the tragic loss of a Deputy U.S. Marshal in the line of duty in Louisiana earlier this week. Such senseless acts of violence threaten the very reforms that nonviolent protesters in Ferguson and around the country have been working towards for the past several months. We wish these injured officers a full and speedy recovery. We stand ready to offer any possible aid to an investigation into this incident, including the department's full range of investigative resources. And we will continue to stand unequivocally against all acts of violence against cops whenever and wherever they occur.[20]

United States Representatives Emanuel Cleaver and William Lacy Clay, both Democrats representing Missouri, offered a $3,000 reward for information leading to the arrest of the shooter, and stated, "The path of violence does not lead to justice."[21]

Another major challenge faced by law enforcement is officer suicide. According to the President's Task Force on 21st Century Policing, "police [die] from suicide 2.4 times as often as from homicides. And though depression resulting from traumatic experiences is often the cause, routine work and life stressors—serving hostile communities, working long shifts, lack of family or departmental support—are frequent motivators too."[22]

So it's important to acknowledge legitimate grievances and protests directed toward our broken law enforcement system while also recognizing that police do a very dangerous and stressful job in trying to protect our communities. Black lives matter, and blue lives matter, too. It's precisely *because* we want police to behave like guardians and not soldiers that we

20. Eric Holder, "Attorney General Holder Statement on the Overnight Shooting of Two Officers in Ferguson, Missouri," Department of Justice Office of Public Affairs, March 12, 2015, http://www.justice.gov/opa/pr/attorney-general-holder-statement-overnight-shooting -two-officers-ferguson-missouri.

21. "Police Search for Those Who Shot 2 Officers in Ferguson 'Ambush,'" *St. Louis Post-Dispatch*, March 12, 2015, http://www.stltoday.com/news/local/crime-and-courts/police-search-for -those-who-shot-officers-in-ferguson-ambush/article_eda6589f-d0fc-5420-8489-787a218a6d83 .html.

22. President's Task Force, *Interim Report*, 61.

should want our law enforcement officers to feel as safe and supported as possible. Police officers who do not feel supported or safe are more likely to lash out at the community they are assigned to protect, engaging in verbal abuse, excessive force, and other destructive behavior.

The policing task force was very clear on this point, making "Officer Wellness and Safety" one of the six key "pillars" or areas that are needed to reform the law enforcement system. As the commission put it:

> The wellness and safety of law enforcement officers is critical not only to themselves, their colleagues, and their agencies but also to public safety. An officer whose capabilities, judgment, and behavior are adversely affected by poor physical or psychological health may not only be of little use to the community he or she serves but also a danger to it and to other officers. As task force member Tracey Meares observed, "Hurt people can hurt people."[23]

Some of the key recommendations for improving officer safety and wellness include establishing a task force to study mental health issues unique to officers, passing federal funding for all police officers to be equipped with tactical first-aid kits and bulletproof vests, and the implementation of scientifically supported shift lengths for all officers.[24]

The Clear Data on Racialized Stops, Arrests, Sentences, Incarceration, and Recidivism

The biggest reasons we need to reform our criminal justice system come down not to politics but to the *data* that overwhelmingly shows that we have a serious problem in America. The data regarding how the criminal justice system interacts with Americans of color at every step of the way is incredibly clear: the system as it exists today is intrinsically biased against African Americans and Latinos. The research in this field shows clear and disturbing disparities in how people are treated in terms of who gets stopped by the police, who gets arrested, who gets charged or indicted, what sentences people receive, and what happens to them after they complete their sentences. Here are just a few of these facts that are important to understand.

23. Ibid.
24. Ibid., 100–101.

Vehicle Stops

According to a 2013 Justice Department report, as reported by *The Washington Post*, "Black drivers are 31 percent more likely to be pulled over than whites; they are more than twice as likely to be subject to police searches as white drivers; and they are nearly twice as likely to not be given any reason for the traffic stop, period."[25] As Bryan Stevenson notes, "There is no evidence out there that says young men of color drive faster than young white men."[26] So why are black people pulled over so much more often than white people? These numbers suggest that racial profiling has a lot to do with it.

Arrests

According to a recent study of FBI statistics, African Americans are about three times more likely to be arrested than are whites.[27] In some cities, this number is even more lopsided. For example, in Dearborn, Michigan, blacks make up only 4 percent of the population, yet they made up more than half the arrests in 2011 and 2012 (the caveat here being that many of those arrested don't live in Dearborn but are arrested while driving through—yet it still points to a staggering disparity).[28] Although the cause is a matter of much debate, and probably goes beyond simple police bias/profiling (economic and educational inequality always account for some level of difference in the crime rates), the racial disparities in arrests are so extreme that they cannot simply be ignored or written off. Arrest rates are particularly dramatic when it comes to drug offenses. The Center for American Progress reports that "African Americans comprise 14 percent of regular drug users but are 37 percent of those arrested for drug offenses. From 1980 to 2007 about one in three of the 25.4 million adults arrested for drugs was African American."[29]

25. Christopher Ingraham, "You Really Can Get Pulled Over for Driving While Black, Federal Statistics Show," *Washington Post*, September 9, 2014, http://www.washingtonpost.com/blogs/wonkblog/wp/2014/09/09/you-really-can-get-pulled-over-for-driving-while-black-federal-statistics-show/.
26. Tim Funk, "Bryan Stevenson Talks about Black Men, Police, Obama, the South," *Charlotte Observer*, April 25, 2015, http://www.charlotteobserver.com/news/politics-government/article19549932.html.
27. "Racial Disparities in Arrests Are Prevalent, but Cause Isn't Clear," NPR.org, November 23, 2014, http://www.npr.org/blogs/codeswitch/2014/11/23/366159956/racial-disparities-in-arrests-are-prevalent-but-cause-isnt-clear.
28. Ibid.
29. Kerby, "Top 10 Most Startling Facts."

Sentencing

The US Sentencing Commission reported in 2010 that in the federal system, black offenders receive sentences that are 10 percent longer than those for white offenders for the same crimes.[30] Furthermore, according to the Sentencing Project, African Americans are "21 percent more likely to receive a mandatory minimum sentence than white defendants facing an eligible charge."[31] Finally, African American drug defendants are 20 percent more likely to be sentenced to prison than white drug defendants.[32]

Incarceration

According to the Sentencing Project, which has extensively analyzed the data compiled by the government's Bureau of Justice Statistics, "More than 60% of the people in prison today are people of color. Black men are six times more likely to be incarcerated than white men, and Hispanic men are 2.5 times more likely. For black men in their thirties, 1 in every 10 is in prison or jail on any given day."[33] Perhaps even more shocking is the fact that 1 in 3 African American men will be imprisoned at some point in his lifetime. This compares to 1 in 6 Latino men and 1 in 17 white men.[34] Women are imprisoned at much lower rates for all races, but the racial disparities in imprisonment rates are virtually the same for women as they are for men.[35]

In reporting on the disparity in incarceration rates for drug crimes, *The Washington Post* notes the following:

> Nowhere are racial disparities in criminal justice more evident than in drug law enforcement. In 2003, black men were nearly 12 times more likely to be sent to prison for a drug offense than white men. Yet, national household surveys show that whites and African Americans use and sell drugs at roughly the same rates. African Americans, who are 12 percent of the population and about 14 percent of drug users, make up 34 percent of those arrested

30. Ibid.
31. Marc Mauer, "Testimony of Marc Mauer" (Washington, DC: The Sentencing Project), April 29, 2009, http://www.sentencingproject.org/doc/dp_crack_testimony.pdf, 6.
32. Ibid., 7.
33. "Fact Sheet: Trends in U.S. Corrections" (Washington, DC: The Sentencing Project), updated April 2015, http://sentencingproject.org/doc/publications/inc_Trends_in_Corrections _Fact_sheet.pdf, 5.
34. Ibid.
35. Ibid.

for drug offenses and 45 percent of those serving time for such offenses in state prisons. Why?[36]

Recidivism

Recidivism is the rate at which people who have formerly been incarcerated have further contact with the criminal justice system, ranging from being arrested again at some point after release to being reimprisoned. A study by the Bureau of Justice Statistics, using data from thirty states over five years (2005–2010), found the following about racial disparities:

> From at least 6 months after release from prison through the end of the 5-year follow-up period, black offenders had higher rates of recidivism than white offenders. This pattern generally held, regardless of the type of offense for which the inmate was imprisoned. Three years after release, 55.6% of white inmates who were imprisoned for a violent crime had been arrested for a new offense, compared to 66.4% of black inmates. By the end of the fifth year after release, these proportions for inmates who were imprisoned for a violent crime increased to 65.1% for white and 76.9% for black inmates. [Overall], by the end of the fifth year after release from prison, white (73.1%) and Hispanic (75.3%) offenders had lower recidivism rates than black offenders (80.8%).[37]

It's a major problem that so many of our citizens of *all* races are being rearrested for new offenses and in many cases returning to prison. It speaks to a broken justice and mass incarceration system that is not "reforming" or "correcting" those whom it imprisons, much less empowering them with the basic life skills they need to succeed when they return to society. This is made much worse by the revocation of so many of the basic rights of being an American citizen that accompanies being convicted of a felony. Yet even though the numbers are high for all groups, they are highest for African Americans, which combined with the data on arrest rates suggests that it is even more difficult for a black American to succeed in society after he or she has been incarcerated and released for the first time.

36. Marc Mauer and David Cole, "Five Myths about Incarceration," *Washington Post*, June 17, 2011, http://www.washingtonpost.com/opinions/five-myths-about-incarceration/2011/06/13 /AGfIWvYH_story.html.

37. Matthew R. Durose, Alexia D. Cooper, and Howard N. Snyder, "Recidivism of Prisoners Released in 30 States in 2005: Patterns from 2005 to 2010" (Washington, DC: Bureau of Justice Statistics, US Department of Justice, April 2014), http://www.bjs.gov/content/pub/pdf /rprts05p0510.pdf, 13–14.

Establishing Trust

The President's Task Force on 21st Century Policing focused on many areas crucial for law enforcement reform. The first, and perhaps most important, of its six key pillars is focused on "Building Trust and Legitimacy." As the task force's report states, "building trust and nurturing legitimacy on both sides of the police/citizen divide is . . . the foundational principle underlying this inquiry into the nature of relations between law enforcement and the communities they serve."[38]

As we have seen in the data on racial disparities in the criminal justice system, there is an enormous trust deficit between communities of color and the law enforcement professionals assigned to protect and serve them. Gallup has documented this, noting that for at least the last thirty years nonwhites feel less confidence in police to protect them from violent crime than do whites, by an average of 14 percentage points.[39] For example, in 2014, 60 percent of white survey respondents said they felt "a great deal" or "quite a lot" of confidence in the ability of police to protect them from violent crime, as opposed to just 49 percent of nonwhites who expressed the same sentiment.[40]

One of the best things we can do to improve the relationship between law enforcement and communities of color is to improve and build feelings of trust and legitimacy between the two. As the task force states: "Decades of research and practice support the premise that people are more likely to obey the law when they believe that those who are enforcing it have the legitimate authority to tell them what to do. But the public confers legitimacy only on those whom they believe are acting in procedurally just ways."[41]

But what does "procedurally just" behavior mean, and what does it look like? According to some of the prominent research on this topic, procedurally just behavior is based on four main principles:

1. Treating people with dignity and respect
2. Giving individuals "voice" during encounters

---

38. President's Task Force, *Interim Report*, 7.
39. Justin McCarthy, "Nonwhites Less Likely to Feel Police Protect and Serve Them," Gallup, November 17, 2014, http://www.gallup.com/poll/179468/nonwhites-less-likely-feel-police -protect-serve.aspx.
40. Ibid.
41. President's Task Force, *Interim Report*, 7.

3. Being neutral and transparent in decision making

4. Conveying trustworthy motives[42]

If law enforcement officers consistently followed these precepts in the communities they serve (and there are many who do), trust and legitimacy would be significantly improved.

Of course, it is easier said than done to transform police culture across the country to one that values procedural justice first and foremost. The task force noted that there are important internal and external elements to procedural justice. Internal procedural justice means that officers feel respected, listened to, and treated fairly within their own police departments. It should come as no surprise that officers who feel they are treated fairly by their superiors and coworkers are more likely to manifest fair and impartial behavior in dealing with the communities they serve.[43]

But the external aspect of procedural justice—in other words, how officers treat members of the community—is more complicated than that. One of the primary reasons for this is bias, both explicit and implicit. It should go without saying that explicit bias has no place in any police department in the country. But as we discussed in chapter 5, implicit bias is also extremely harmful and deeply ingrained in much of society, and police officers are sadly no exception. In order for officers to be able to behave in ways that truly model procedural justice, efforts must be taken in police departments at all levels to help officers recognize and mitigate their implicit bias.[44] That will generally take outside training and education.

Community Policing

It may be that the best way for police departments and the communities they serve to increase the trust and sense of legitimacy between them is to embrace a model for their relationship called *community policing*. Community policing, another of the key pillars that the President's Task Force identified, is "a philosophy that promotes organizational strategies that

42. Lorraine Mazerolle, Sarah Bennett, Jacqueline Davis, Elise Sargeant, and Matthew Manning, "Legitimacy in Policing: A Systematic Review," *Campbell Collection Library of Systematic Reviews* 9 (Oslo, Norway: The Campbell Collaboration, 2013), 8.

43. President's Task Force, *Interim Report*, 8.

44. Ibid.

support the systematic use of partnerships and problem-solving techniques to proactively address the immediate conditions that give rise to public safety issues such as crime, social disorder, and fear of crime."[45]

What this means in lay terms is that police need to form relationships with the people and communities they serve, and vice versa. By developing rapport and relationships based on mutual respect and trust when there *isn't* an emergency or a crime taking place, an officer is more likely to receive help, support, and information from the community when crimes do happen. As the task force puts it:

> By combining a focus on intervention and prevention through problem solving with building collaborative partnerships with schools, social services, and other stakeholders, community policing not only improves public safety but also enhances social connectivity and economic strength, which increases community resilience to crime. And, as noted by one speaker, it improves job satisfaction for line officers, too. . . . Community policing starts on the street corner, with respectful interaction between a police officer and a local resident, a discussion that need not be related to a criminal matter. In fact, it is important that not all interactions be based on emergency calls or crime investigations.[46]

The task force's report goes on to give several examples of practices that can help foster the community policing model, such as "assigning officers to geographic areas on a consistent basis, so that through the continuity of assignment they have the opportunity to know the members of the community," as well as encouraging officers' "participation in community organizations, local meetings and public service activities."[47]

These are useful and important suggestions that could really make a difference in building better relationships between police officers and low-income communities of color. Of course, another important step that police departments should take is to go the extra mile to recruit quality officers of color. As we saw in Ferguson, it is much more difficult to build lasting trust between law enforcement and the community when the racial mix of the police force is so different from that of the community it is assigned to protect and serve.

45. US Department of Justice, "Community Policing Defined" (Washington, DC: Office of Community Oriented Policing Services, 2014), http://ric-zai-inc.com/Publications/cops-p157 -pub.pdf, 1.
46. President's Task Force, *Interim Report*, 41.
47. Ibid., 42.

The President's Task Force report ends its section on community policing on a powerful and enlightening note:

> It must also be stressed that the absence of crime is not the final goal of law
> enforcement. Rather, it is the promotion and protection of public safety while
> respecting the dignity and rights of all. And public safety and well-being cannot
> be attained without the community's belief that their well-being is at the heart
> of all law enforcement activities. It is critical to help community members see
> police as allies rather than as an occupying force and to work in concert with
> other community stakeholders to create more economically and socially stable
> neighborhoods.[48]

Establishing trust is more foundational than just crime statistics and,
in the end, will lead to greater public safety and security. This is indeed
the vision that we should seek as we look to the future of law enforcement
and a new America where communities of color and law enforcement are
true partners in promoting public safety and well-being for all. The necessary shift from a "warrior" model of policing to a "guardian" model can
best be accomplished by embracing the concept of community policing.

School-to-Prison Pipeline

When I lived in Washington, DC's Columbia Heights neighborhood,
which was primarily low-income and African American at the time, many
of the parents in the neighborhood had attended the same schools where
their children were now going. These parents had bad experiences as
kids because the schools weren't good then—and were still not good for
their children. These parents' past experiences as children made them
reluctant to approach the school administration when their own kids
were having problems in school. The lack of trust there is similar to the
lack of trust that exists between low-income communities of color and
law enforcement.

Of course, there's also a broader problem with the educational system,
and it ties directly into the broken and racialized nature of the criminal
justice system that has led to the mass incarceration of low-income African Americans and Latinos. This phenomenon is commonly called the

48. Ibid., 43.

"school-to-prison pipeline." Tavis Smiley, in a report for PBS, explained it as follows:

> Far too often, students are suspended, expelled or even arrested for minor offenses that leave visits to the principal's office a thing of the past. Statistics reflect that these policies disproportionately target students of color and those with a history of abuse, neglect, poverty or learning disabilities.
>
> Students who are forced out of school for disruptive behavior are usually sent back to the origin of their angst and unhappiness—their home environments or their neighborhoods, which are filled with negative influence. Those who are forced out for smaller offenses become hardened, confused, embittered. Those who are unnecessarily forced out of school become stigmatized and fall behind in their studies; many eventually decide to drop out of school altogether, and many others commit crimes in their communities.[49]

The statistics on this phenomenon are beyond troubling. According to the Department of Education, black students, despite making up only 16 percent of enrollees in public school, account for 31 percent of students subjected to a school-related arrest. Black students are also suspended and expelled at a rate three times higher than white students.[50] In Washington, DC, there's a disturbing trend in which students who get in to DC's more exclusive charter schools are expelled at rates well above the national average and sent back to the traditional public schools, which do not have the right to expel them.[51]

Although the causes of the school-to-prison pipeline are complex, the results are clearly unjust and have a disproportionate effect on people of color. Some of the blame for this phenomenon can be placed on so-called "zero-tolerance" policies that many schools have adopted. According to the American Civil Liberties Union:

> Lacking resources, facing incentives to push out low-performing students, and responding to a handful of highly-publicized school shootings, schools have

49. Carla Amurao, "Fact Sheet: How Bad Is the School-to-Prison Pipeline?," *Tavis Smiley Reports*, PBS, http://www.pbs.org/wnet/tavissmiley/tsr/education-under-arrest/school-to-prison-pipeline-fact-sheet/.

50. Civil Rights Data Collection, "Data Snapshot: School Discipline" (Washington, DC: US Department of Education Office for Civil Rights, March 2014), https://www2.ed.gov/about/offices/list/ocr/docs/crdc-discipline-snapshot.pdf, 1.

51. Emma Brown, "D.C. Charter Schools Expel Students at Far Higher Rates Than Traditional Public Schools," *Washington Post*, January 5, 2013, http://www.washingtonpost.com/local/education/dc-charter-schools-expel-students-at-far-higher-rates-than-traditional-public-schools/2013/01/05/e155e4bc-44a9-11e2-8061-253bccfc7532_story.html.

embraced *zero-tolerance policies* that automatically impose severe punishment regardless of circumstances. Under these policies, students have been expelled for bringing nail clippers or scissors to school.[52]

And although much of the traditional scholarship and advocacy in this area has focused on black boys in particular, recent research shows that black girls are also at significant risk in schools with zero-tolerance policies. In fact, zero-tolerance environments may even exacerbate the problems of sexual harassment and bullying against girls because it penalizes them when they defend themselves from such behavior.[53]

One of the most outrageous and heartbreaking stories I've heard that embodies the problems with zero-tolerance policies and the racialized school-to-prison pipeline came from testimony given to the President's Task Force on 21st Century Policing. A young man named Michael Reynolds told the following story about something that happened to him during his freshman year of high school:

> As I walked down the hall, one of the police officers employed in the school noticed I did not have my identification badge with me. Before I could explain why I did not have my badge, I was escorted to the office and suspended for an entire week. I had to leave the school premises immediately. Walking to the bus stop, a different police officer pulled me over and demanded to know why I was not in school. As I tried to explain, I was thrown into the back of the police car. They drove back to my school to see if I was telling the truth, and I was left waiting in the car for over two hours. When they came back, they told me I was in fact suspended, but because the school did not provide me with the proper forms, my guardian and I both had to pay tickets for me being off of school property. The tickets together were 600 dollars, and I had a court date for each one. Was forgetting my ID worth missing school? Me being kicked out of school did not solve or help anything. I was at home alone watching Jerry Springer, doing nothing.[54]

52. "What Is the School-to-Prison Pipeline?," American Civil Liberties Union, https://www.aclu.org/racial-justice/what-school-prison-pipeline.
53. Kimberlé Williams Crenshaw with Priscilla Ocen and Jyoti Nanda, "Black Girls Matter: Pushed Out, Overpoliced and Underprotected" (New York: Center for Intersectionality and Social Policy Studies; African American Policy Forum, 2015), http://static1.squarespace.com/static/53f20d90e4b0b80451158d8c/t/54d23be0e4b0bb6a8002fb97/14, 10.
54. Listening Session on Community Policing and Crime Prevention (oral testimony of Michael Reynolds for the President's Task Force on 21st Century Policing, Phoenix, AZ, February 13, 2015).

Lessons and Solutions

The task force's report is not just an analysis of the things that are wrong with current policing, law enforcement, and the criminal justice system more broadly. It's mostly focused on lessons and solutions that could begin to change these systems for the better.

When I attended the release of the interim report of the President's Task Force, the task force members shared their personal insights and recommendations. Those comments were very helpful, as they reflected the expertise, experience, and passion of the diverse commission members. Though the list of recommendations contained in the report is too exhaustive to reprint here, I have combined the task force members' personal priorities with my own thoughts and experiences, and I offer these recommendations for how our broken system can be transformed.

1. Realize that this is more than a police problem; it is also a criminal justice system and societal problem.

Dramatic examples of inappropriate and excessive uses of force have created highly public incidents that focused the nation's attention on policing issues. But this is not just, or mostly, a problem with the police. What the incidents reveal is a broken criminal justice system more broadly and systemically. But that doesn't go far enough: the criminal justice system takes place in a *society* with great economic inequalities that reflect our racial divisions in key areas such as education and employment. History tells us that poverty leads to crime. Where there is poverty, there will be crime, and when poverty is also reflective of racial discrimination, crime will be racially disproportionate. And policing will normally reflect these racial divisions and realities. So if we want to change crime, we obviously have to change society.

2. Acknowledge past mistakes and damage on all sides—and signal the need for change.

There is nothing quite like an honest admission of having made a mistake or doing wrong to build trust in those who have experienced those mistakes or wrongdoings. And expressing a willingness and even a commitment to change those behaviors goes even further in restoring trust in broken relationships. Traditionally, police and police departments haven't always been so good about admitting mistakes—and that will have to change. The forthright, honest, and self-critical comments quoted earlier in this book by FBI director James Comey and New York City police commissioner Bill Bratton are good examples of law enforcement leaders telling the truth and admitting past mistakes.

3. Implement training that sets a new culture and is constitutionally grounded.

We all need training, instruction, and education to help us improve, which teaches us things that we likely couldn't have easily learned on our own. But training can't just be in the techniques and technologies of police work; it should also help us understand the *cultures* in which police need to work and things about the cultures of police departments that need changing too. Changes in the cultures of police departments where officers often cover-up rather than challenge the mistakes of their fellow officers (even across racial lines) is part of the cultural change the police departments will need. And the Constitution is not an enemy that must be worked around when police are making arrests; it is, rather, the foundation for law enforcement that protects us all and prevents us from becoming a police state.

4. Change the dynamic between the community and the police with engagement, not only during crisis but also in everyday life— moving from a reactive stance to a proactive one.

This point is absolutely key. Police need to be members of the communities they serve. And they can't just be there when things go wrong, when there is a crime or a crisis. If fact, they will be more helpful in reacting to a crisis or solving a crime if they are also regular members of the community. They should know the families and the kids, understand their wants and needs, and learn to see and appreciate the good things going on in their neighborhoods and not just the bad. They can get involved in the community.

5. Establish a community presence aimed at slowly building trust to replace long-standing mistrust.

My best recommendation is for cops to volunteer to coach or umpire in Little League baseball! In my experience, that's a great way to come to know the community and the families in it. Of course, they could coach soccer and join other neighborhood organizations as well. When families know police officers and law enforcement officials as members of their communities, they will much more easily go to them in a crime situation, giving police the information they need and the help they can always use.

6. *Treat both the police and those they relate to with dignity and fairness with both internal and external procedural justice.*

Or do unto others as you would have them do unto you. That "golden rule" is still the best way to proceed in life, and certainly in a neighborhood. Everyone wants to be treated with dignity and reacts when they don't feel like they are—police included. And fairness may be the most important principle in a law enforcement system. The report talks wisely about the need for both "internal" procedural justice, which police themselves are rightly very sensitive to, and "external" justice procedures in how the people whom the police relate to are treated. And one seems to affect the other. Who's fair and not and what's fair and not are very central to how the people in a community, and a police force, will feel about the relationship between the police and the community. And cops quickly get a reputation for being fair or unfair.

7. *Change aggressive and provocative behavior during demonstrations.*

As we noted in chapter 2, Martin Luther King once said that "a riot is the language of the unheard." Peaceful demonstrations that are rooted in a commitment to nonviolence are the best alternative to the violence of "the riot." But demonstrators want to be heard too, and that's why they are demonstrating. The role of police officers during a demonstration is to help make sure that the voices of the demonstrators can be heard *and* to protect public order and property in the midst of a protest demonstration. The whole strategy of police in response to demonstrations is to try and *defuse* conflict, not accelerate it. To be aggressive toward demonstrators is counterproductive, and trying to provoke demonstrators is the best way to turn a disciplined nonviolent demonstration into a violent riot. Protecting public safety is always the vocation of law enforcement officers, but that also means making safe and effective space for public protest when citizens believe that is called for. Police themselves should have a strong preference for nonviolent demonstrations over riots. People need to be heard, one way or another, and police should support the constructive alternatives to avoid the more destructive ones. Being arrested in protest demonstrations and partnering with police officials and officers in demonstrations and nonviolent civil disobedience have shown me the great differences between effective collaboration and senseless confrontation. Even after going to jail, being able to represent the protesters to the prison authorities has often been a helpful practice for all involved.

8. Process and investigate shooting deaths by the police externally and independently.

The data is extremely clear that police officers are almost never indicted or brought to trial for using lethal force in a confrontation with suspects and citizens. That's because such decisions are usually made by county prosecutors who are very involved with the police in their communities and are dependent upon them for doing their job of prosecuting crime. The commission makes one of its most important recommendations when it calls for independent and outside prosecutors to be used in all investigations of situations that involved the lethal use of force. In the end, those more independent prosecutors will not only better protect the victims of excessive force but also the police themselves and the reputation of their police forces. As the report says, "Strong systems and policies that encourage use of an independent prosecutor for reviewing police uses of force and for prosecution in cases of inappropriate deadly force and in-custody death will demonstrate the transparency to the public that can lead to mutual trust between community and law enforcement."[55]

9. Aim for more than crime reduction and understand the potential costs of overly aggressive law enforcement.

This was one of the most important and creative recommendations from the commission—to focus not solely on the prevention of crime as the only measure of success. Too-aggressive policing might reduce the

---

55. President's Task Force, *Interim Report*, 22.

overall crime rate, but it may have other unintended consequences for public safety and undermine the constructive relationships between the police and their communities. As the task force observed, "Crime reduction is not self-justifying."[56] In the end, relationships are most important to public safety, for abundant reasons, and good trusting relationships are often disrupted by quick and aggressive police behavior—even if it sometimes does help reduce the metrics of crime in the moment. Police should trust and rely on their relationships more than their tactics.

10. Smartly implement audiovisual technologies, including cameras.

Every police officer in the country now knows that everything he or she does can be caught on somebody's cell phone camera, and likely will be. The courageous actions of a citizen, Feidin Santana—who took the video of the Charleston, South Carolina, police officer shooting a fleeing black man after a traffic violation—led to the officer being charged with murder, likely only because the terrible action was recorded. This case was another example of the need to record such lethal interactions to protect everyone involved. Such video recordings are more common now, and they have already made a difference in police behavior around the country. Police officers now know their actions are more likely to be filmed. So why not build effective audio and visual technology for the police to use themselves? That will not only protect citizens from hidden police abuse but will also protect the police themselves from unwarranted accusations and attacks. There is nothing like the light of day to protect everyone. The task force cited important research released in 2014 that found that "the officers wearing the cameras had 87.5 percent fewer incidents of use of force and 59 percent fewer complaints than the officers not wearing the cameras."[57]

11. Demilitarize local police departments.

This was a big topic of conversation on the commission and in the discussion on the report's release day. It goes back to the very important difference between "warriors" and "guardians" described at the beginning

56. Ibid., 15.
57. Ibid., 32.

of this chapter. "The soldier's mission is that of a warrior: to conquer. . . . The police officer's mission is that of a guardian: to protect."[58] The militarization of our nation's police forces, especially in big-city departments targeting urban high-crime areas, has been an overreaction and the wrong reaction to crime. It's also been a major problem at demonstrations, as testimony to the task force made clear: "When officers line up in a military formation while wearing full protective gear, their visual appearance may have a dramatic influence on how the crowd perceives them and how the event ends."[59] Our militarized police forces look more like armies now than police and, with all that military equipment, often act more like armies than cops on the street. Perhaps nothing has worked against the old idea of community policing—which we are hopefully getting back to—more than the police being militarized, which removes them from the community both physically and emotionally.

12. Redevelop community and neighborhood policing.

The alternative, as we have already said, is community policing. The cop who walks the street, talks to the people, knows the kids, and watches them grow up can best protect the people of a neighborhood. That cop is intelligent about the context in which he or she serves and is well informed about the events in a community that lead to communal peace or disruptive crime. That cop knows the people and the people know him or her—and that is what makes all the difference because it leads to both information and trust. And as we noted above, community policing "improves job satisfaction for line officers, too."[60] Policing used to be this way, as Vice President Joe Biden has noted: "Being able to see each other was the whole theory behind the notion of community policing. . . . Growing up . . . you knew the cop on the block when you were kids, in the 50s and 60s."[61] And it can and should be this way again.

58. Rahr, "Transforming the Culture of Policing," 3–4.

59. Listening Session on Policy and Oversight (written testimony of Edward MacGuire, American University, for the President's Task Force on 21st Century Policing, Cincinnati, OH, January 30, 2015).

60. President's Task Force, *Interim Report*, 41.

61. Joe Biden, "Biden: Police Relations with Communities 'Not as Bad as It Has Been,' 'Press Exaggerates,'" *Real Clear Politics*, January 27, 2015, http://www.realclearpolitics.com /video/2015/01/27/biden_police_relations_with_communities_not_as_bad_as_it_has_been _press_exaggerates.html.

13. End the school-to-prison pipeline.

The train I heard about at Sing Sing Prison does lead from only certain inner-city neighborhoods and zip codes to places such as Sing Sing, and it has a lot to do with schools. There is a "pipeline" that starts with aggressive "zero-tolerance" policies in schools that are mostly directed toward children of color and often leads eventually to jail, and we have to stop that train. My nephew, who taught in a tough Oklahoma City neighborhood with Teach for America, could tell in his first month which kids in his fourth-grade class were already likely to be headed to prison. That is a train we have to stop, and we need to reevaluate and reform educational school policies to do that. As the task force recommends: "In order to keep youth in school and to keep them from criminal and violent behavior, law enforcement agencies should work with schools to encourage the creation of alternatives to student suspensions and expulsion through restorative justice, diversion, counseling, and family interventions."[62]

14. Learn and adapt the principles and practices of restorative justice.

The most fundamental shift we need to make in our criminal justice system is from retributive to restorative justice, and I was pleased to see that powerful language used in the commission report. Restorative justice is a process that engages "those who are harmed, wrongdoers and their affected communities in search of solutions that promote repair, reconciliation and the rebuilding of relationships. . . . Restorative approaches seek a balanced approach to the needs of the victim, wrongdoer and community through processes that preserve the safety and dignity of all."[63] The transformation from retributive to restorative justice is the most important work that we need to do in order to reform—and even transform—our criminal justice system. Other places such as New Zealand, Australia, and Canada are already doing so. We will discuss restorative justice in the next chapter.

---

62. President's Task Force, *Interim Report*, 48.
63. "What Is Restorative Justice?," Center for Restorative Justice, Suffolk University, https://www.suffolk.edu/college/centers/15970.php.

8 | The New Jim Crow and Restorative Justice

A stunning thing has happened in the last several decades to dramatically set back the civil rights of millions of black and Latino Americans. And this fundamental injustice has been carried out through our criminal justice system. As a result of our profoundly unequal law enforcement system, we have seen much of the progress of the civil rights movement stalled, and in many cases rolled back, in a number of insidious ways. And the worst parts of this process have happened under the very noses of those of us who have fought for civil rights since the 1960s.

The New Jim Crow

Michelle Alexander, a civil rights lawyer and legal scholar, shed light on this phenomenon perhaps better than anyone else in her landmark book *The New Jim Crow: Mass Incarceration in the Age of Colorblindness*. As the title of her book suggests, the creation of a new system of segregation and disenfranchisement—more subtle than the Jim Crow laws in the post-Reconstruction period but in some ways no less destructive—is directly dependent on the United States' status as the world's leader in imprisoning its own citizens, and is systematically racialized in its implementation.

Although the United States has 5 percent of the world's population, it contains nearly 25 percent of the world's known prisoners.[1] This represents a 500 percent increase in total number of prisoners over the last forty years. Nearly 7 million people were under some form of "correctional supervision" (prison, jail, parole, or probation) in 2013.[2] This increase is not due to rising crime rates but rather was caused mainly by *changes in sentencing law and policy*.[3]

Michelle Alexander reminds us that this surge in mass incarceration has had a strongly racial character. For example, she notes the shocking fact that "there are more African-American adults under correctional control today—in prison or jail, on probation or parole—than were enslaved in 1850, a decade before the Civil War began."[4]

In a 2011 article for *Sojourners* magazine, Alexander succinctly explains the link between the dramatic rise in incarceration rates, US drug policy, and the racial dimension of these developments:

We're told black culture, bad schools, poverty, and broken homes are to blame [for the high rates of incarceration of people of color]. Almost no one admits: We declared war. We declared a war on the most vulnerable people in our society and then blamed them for the wreckage. . . . The so-called War on Drugs has driven the quintupling of our prison population in a few short decades. The vast majority of the startling increase in incarceration in America is traceable to the arrest and imprisonment of poor people of color for nonviolent, drug-related offenses. . . . Politicians claim that the enemy in this war is a thing—drugs—not a group of people. The facts prove otherwise. Studies consistently show that people of all colors use and sell drugs at remarkably similar rates, yet in some states African-American men have been admitted to prison on drug charges at a rate up to 57 times higher than white men. In some states, 80 to 90 percent of all drug offenders sent to prison have been African Americans. The rate of Latino imprisonment has been staggering as well. Although the majority of illegal drug users and dealers

1. Oliver Roeder, "The Imprisoner's Dilemma," FiveThirtyEight.com, February 12, 2015, http://fivethirtyeight.com/features/the-imprisoners-dilemma/.

2. Lauren E. Glaze and Danielle Kaeble, "Correctional Populations in the United States, 2013" (Washington, DC: Bureau of Justice Statistics, US Department of Justice, December 2014), http://www.bjs.gov/content/pub/pdf/cpus13.pdf, 1.

3. "Fact Sheet: Trends In U.S. Corrections" (Washington, DC: The Sentencing Project), updated April 2015, http://sentencingproject.org/doc/publications/inc_Trends_in_Corrections_Fact_sheet.pdf, 2.

4. Michelle Alexander, "Cruel and Unequal," *Sojourners*, February 2011, http://www.sojo.net/magazine/2011/02/cruel-and-unequal.

are white, three-fourths of all people imprisoned for drug offenses have been black and Latino.[5]

The racial disparities in drug-law convictions and sentencing are blatant and extraordinary. The reason that the disproportionate policing and incarceration of people of color leads to a "new Jim Crow," according to Alexander, is connected to what happens to people when they return to society after having served their sentences. Those convicted of felonies—even if the felony in question was a nonviolent offense such as possession of an illegal drug—find themselves stripped of many of the rights that most American citizens take for granted. The tragic irony here is that many of the rights they forfeit are precisely those that people of color fought for during the civil rights movement, such as "the right to vote, the right to serve on juries, and the right to be free from legal discrimination in employment, housing, and access to education and public benefits."[6]

America has become a prison state for low-income people of color. That system has effectively created a new form of segregation, where those convicted of felonies are forever relegated to the status of second-class citizens—unable to vote, get a good job, or even use the public safety net to get back on their feet.

Alexander's historic work has caused many of us to wake up to this twenty-first-century caste system. As she said to our Sojourners social justice constituency:

God knows we've slept too long.

Many of us—myself included—slept through a revolution. Actually, it was a counterrevolution that has blown back much of the progress that so many racial justice advocates risked their lives for. This counterrevolution occurred with barely a whimper of protest, even as a war was declared, one that purported to be aimed at "drugs." . . .

A penal system unprecedented in world history emerged in a few short decades; by the year 2000, 2 million people found themselves behind bars, and 60 million were saddled with criminal records that would condemn them for life—staggering statistics, given that in the 1970s there were only about 350,000 people in prison.[7]

5. Ibid.
6. Michelle Alexander, "How to Dismantle the 'New Jim Crow,'" *Sojourners*, July 2014, http://sojo.net/magazine/2014/07/how-dismantle-new-jim-crow.
7. Ibid.

Alexander documents how the "drug war" has not been focused on those actually running the drug traffic, the drug "kingpins," or the bankers laundering tremendous amounts of money. No, this drug war has been waged mostly in poor communities of color:

> Federal funding flows to those state and local law enforcement agencies that dramatically boost the sheer volume of drug arrests; it's a numbers game. Agencies don't get rewarded for bringing down drug bosses or arresting violent offenders. They're rewarded in cash for arresting people en masse. Ghetto communities are swept for the low-hanging fruit—which generally means young people hanging out [on] the street corner, walking to school or the subway, or driving around with friends. They're stopped and searched for any reason or no reason at all.[8]

When drug arrests show a 5 to 1 ratio for possession over sales, something is wrong. And when most of those arrests are in poor communities of color—despite the fact that drug use is the same or higher in white middle-class communities or campuses—something is clearly wrong.

One of the most drastic examples of the racial disparity in our criminal justice system is the sharp contrast between our response to crack cocaine users and drunk drivers. Because of the tireless efforts of grassroots groups such as Mothers Against Drunk Drivers (MADD) a change in the national conversation about "drunk drivers" and "designated drivers" has occurred. The movement to crack down on drunk drivers was a broad-based, bottom-up movement. In contrast, the so-called war on drugs was initiated by political elites, and only much later did ordinary people identify drug crime as an issue of such extraordinary concern.

Alexander points out what happened next. The civil rights lawyer's detailed narrative of the political choices being made here by those political elites in the criminal justice system is worth a careful read.

> At the close of the decade (1970's), drunk drivers were responsible for approximately 22,000 deaths annually, and overall alcohol-related deaths were close to 100,000 a year. By contrast, during the same time period, there were no prevalence statistics at all on crack, much less crack-related deaths. . . . The total of all drug-related deaths, whether from AIDS, drug overdose, or the violence associated with the illegal drug trade, was estimated at 21,000

8. Alexander, "Cruel and Unequal."

annually—less than the number of deaths directly caused by drunk drivers, and a small fraction of the number of alcohol-related deaths that occur every year.[9]

She points out that the response to the growing concern about drunk-driving deaths by groups such as MADD fueled a movement for change. The media began to cover the problem, and states adopted new and tougher laws to punish drunk driving, with many states now having mandatory sentencing for this offense, including some days in jail. But the contrast and hypocrisy then emerged. Alexander writes:

> New laws governing crack cocaine were passed at the same time legislatures were "getting tough" on drunk drivers. But notice the contrast: While drunk driving results in a few days in prison, possession of a tiny amount of crack carries a mandatory minimum sentence of five years in federal prison. In fact, some people are serving life sentences for minor drug offenses. In Harmelin vs. Michigan, the U.S. Supreme Court upheld a sentence of life imprisonment for a defendant with no prior convictions who tried to sell 23 ounces of crack cocaine. The court concluded that life imprisonment was not "cruel and un-usual punishment" in violation of the Eighth Amendment, despite the fact that no other developed country in the world imposes life imprisonment for a first-time drug offense.[10]

Why such a different response? Again, many of the differences in policy and practice in our criminal justice system come down to race.

> The vastly different sentences afforded drunk drivers and drug offenders speaks volumes regarding who is viewed as disposable—someone to be purged from the body politic—and who is not. Drunk drivers are predominately white and male. White men comprised 78 percent of the arrests for drunk driving when the new mandatory minimums for the offense were being adopted. They are generally charged with misdemeanors and typically receive sentences involving fines, license suspension, and community service.[11]

The consequences of those "vastly different sentences" play out in how people of different races and socioeconomic status are treated both before they go to prison and after they come out.

9. Ibid.
10. Ibid.
11. Ibid.

Although drunk driving carries a far greater risk of violent death than the use or sale of illegal drugs, the societal response to drunk drivers has generally emphasized keeping the person functional and in society, while attempting to respond to the dangerous behavior through treatment and counseling. People charged with drug offenses, though, are disproportionately poor people of color. They are typically charged with felonies and sentenced to prison. If and when they're released, they become members of the undercaste, no longer locked up, but locked out—for the rest of their lives.[12]

The vivid contrast between what has disappeared in those poor neighborhoods of color and what has come to dominate them is morally striking and deeply alarming. "But it is in the poverty-stricken, racially segregated ghettos," Alexander writes, "where the War on Poverty has been abandoned and factory jobs have disappeared, that the drug war has been waged with ferocity."[13] That is the reality of life in the nation's poorest and most racially segregated places that we now must see, acknowledge, and morally confront:

SWAT teams are deployed here; buy-bust operations are concentrated here; drug raids of schools and housing projects occur here; stop-and-frisk operations are conducted on these streets. If such tactics were employed in middle-class white neighborhoods or on college campuses, there would be public outrage; the war would end overnight. But here in the ghetto, the stops, searches, sweeps, and mass arrests are treated as an accepted fact of life, like the separate water fountains of an earlier era.[14]

This is, indeed, the new Jim Crow. Millions of black and brown people have been affected now—both in terms of arrests and imprisonment and also in terms of being stripped of their most cherished democratic rights when they return to society. They are arrested, sent to jail, and then deprived of their citizenship and ability to politically influence the direction of their nation. To say that this is not deliberate is to be naïve and to ignore that the use of race to deny citizenship is a long-standing characteristic of American society. Voting rights were won in 1965, but the tripartite strategy of denying the vote to returning prisoners, suppressing minority voting through new ID requirements, and the partisan gerrymandering

12. Ibid.
13. Ibid.
14. Ibid.

of districts to "bleach" them white are all working together to deny black and brown Americans their voting rights as American citizens.

Such a system of systematic disenfranchisement would never be accepted in America if it were being directed at white people. Disenfranchising African American and Latino voters is one way to delay the political consequences of the demographic changes now coming in America. It is an attempt to politically veto a new American future where there is no longer a majority white culture but a majority of minorities.

Reforming Our Criminal Justice System

Now that we've seen what's needed to reform the law enforcement and broader criminal justice system, let's talk a bit about *who* can and should be on the front lines of making that happen. The good news is that many in the faith community have come alive to this issue in recent years and have been doing excellent work to push for the changes the system needs.

The Samuel DeWitt Proctor Conference (SDPC), a network of several thousand black churches, has been very involved in the issue of mass incarceration. Dr. Iva Carruthers, general secretary of SDPC, believes that "faith communities should facilitate the institutionalized development of citizen advocates and oversight systems to ensure a more equitable and humane criminal justice system—in the courts, in prisons, and in rehabilitation and restorative justice for people who have been incarcerated."[15] PICO, a national faith-based community organizing network, has made mass incarceration and changes in our policing system a core commitment of its "Live Free" campaign. Michael McBride, who leads this campaign, says: "This is a moment in time, we should not let it slip by. We have mass movements of social justice and social awareness in the streets—people agree that something is wrong in our country. . . . [This is] the civil rights issue of our generation—the human rights issue of our generation."[16] CCDA, the Christian Community Development Association, has also focused on

15. Iva E. Carruthers, "International Human Rights Day: African American Faith Leaders Call for End to War on Drugs and Mass Incarceration," *World Post*, December 9, 2013, http://www.huffingtonpost.com/iva-e-carruthers/international-human-rights-day-call-for-end_b_4414483.html.
16. Stephanie Condon, "Is It Time to End the War on Crime?," CBSnews.com, April 3, 2015, http://www.cbsnews.com/news/is-it-time-to-end-the-war-on-crime/.

mass incarceration at its national conferences and made this a core goal for its nearly one thousand local parachurch organizations.

As CCDA CEO Noel Castellanos says in his 2015 book, *Where the Cross Meets the Street: What Happens to the Neighborhood When God Is at the Center*: "Instead of simply continuing to minister to inmates in prison or providing aftercare once men are out of the penitentiary, we are now convinced that working to confront and reform the unjust mass incarceration system in our country is a component of kingdom ministry we must engage."[17]

Sojourners has also become deeply involved in this issue, making mass incarceration one of the core themes of our annual Summit in Washington, DC, which gathers together three hundred of the most promising young faith-inspired leaders each year to learn from one another and strengthen the national movement for social justice. Lisa Sharon Harper, who served as the program director for the 2015 Summit, has shared with me her hopes for our gathering relating to race:

> Through the racial justice Summit conversations we aim to go deeper on the question of implicit [unconscious] bias and its impact on the church and society. Within the church we'll examine the outcomes of unconscious bias from several angles: race, gender, immigrant status, and age status. In society, we'll discern the outcomes and remedies of the unconscious criminalization of blackness, poverty, and youth. Several Ferguson and Black Lives Matter movement leaders will participate.[18]

But it's not just in the faith community where we're finally starting to see some momentum. In 2014, in what is perhaps the quintessential US Senate "odd couple," Sen. Cory Booker (D-N.J.) and Sen. Rand Paul (R-Ky.) teamed up to introduce the REDEEM Act. Harper explains its purpose:

> This measure aims to cut recidivism rates by helping restore people who serve time to right relationship with their communities upon return. REDEEM would redirect minors away from adult courts and into the juvenile court system, automatically seal or expunge juvenile records upon release, and create a path for adults to have their records sealed upon release. The measure would

17. Noel Castellanos, *Where the Cross Meets the Street: What Happens to the Neighborhood When God Is at the Center* (Downers Grove, IL: Intervarsity, 2015), Google eBook edition, 147.
18. Lisa Sharon Harper, conversation with the author, April 24, 2015.

also restore access to SNAP and welfare for low-level non-violent offenders upon release.[19]

"I will work with anyone, from any party, to make a difference for the people of New Jersey, and this bipartisan legislation does just that," says Sen. Booker. "The REDEEM Act will ensure that our tax dollars are being used in smarter, more productive ways. It will also establish much-needed sensible reforms that keep kids out of the adult correctional system, protect their privacy so a youthful mistake can remain a youthful mistake, and help make it less likely that low-level adult offenders reoffend."[20] Booker's partner in this legislation, Republican senator Rand Paul, said this: "Our current system is broken and has trapped tens of thousands of young men and women in a cycle of poverty and incarceration. Many of these young people could escape this trap if criminal justice were reformed."[21]

The year 2014 also saw the introduction of the bipartisan "Smarter Sentencing Act," sponsored by Senators Richard Durbin (D-Ill.) and Mike Lee (R-Utah) in the Senate and Representatives Raul Labrador (R-Idaho) and Bobby Scott (D-Va.) in the House of Representatives. The bill "does not repeal any federal mandatory minimum sentences, but instead reduces prison costs and populations by creating fairer, less costly minimum terms for nonviolent drug offenders."[22]

Reforming the criminal justice system should be by definition a bipartisan issue, as both parties have much to gain by significant reforms to this broken system. So it is heartening to see some bipartisan action in Congress that recognizes this fact and tries to make at least modest and incremental reforms.

Ultimately, modest and incremental reforms will not be enough to fix a system that is so fundamentally broken. The system must instead be *transformed*, and that will only happen when a groundswell of grassroots supporters demands that their elected leaders do so. I believe that people of faith can and will help lead that charge.

19. Lisa Sharon Harper, "Cory Booker, Rand Paul Shine Light on Shadow Side of U.S. Justice System," *God's Politics* (blog), *Sojourners*, July 10, 2014, http://sojo.net/blogs/2014/07/10/cory-booker-rand-paul-shine-light-shadow-side-us-justice-system.

20. Ibid.

21. Ibid.

22. "S. 502/H.R. 920, The Smarter Sentencing Act," Families Against Mandatory Minimums, http://famm.org/s-502-the-smarter-sentencing-act/.

Restorative Justice

In order to truly transform the system, we also need to think about it under a completely different paradigm than we do now. Just as we discussed in the last chapter in saying that law enforcement must move from a "warrior" model to a "guardian" model, the broader criminal justice system needs to move from *retributive* justice to *restorative* justice. Rather than focusing on merely punishing the perpetrator of a crime for what he or she has done (retributive justice), restorative justice focuses instead on "repairing the harm caused by crime."[23] According to a story in *The New York Times*, restorative justice "considers harm done and strives for agreement from all concerned—the victims, the offender and the community—on making amends. And it allows victims, who often feel shut out of the prosecutorial process, a way to be heard and participate."[24] New Zealand is one of the foremost practitioners of restorative justice, as it aligns closely with the indigenous Maori concepts of reconciliation and reciprocity.[25] It's also an important concept in the Mennonite Church.[26]

Howard Zehr is widely known as "the grandfather of restorative justice."[27] Zehr is a Mennonite from Illinois, and in 1966 he was the first white student to graduate from Morehouse College.[28] He has probably done more than any single person in the United States to develop and further the cause of restorative justice. In 2002, he published *The Little Book of Restorative Justice*, a wonderful primer for anyone who wants to know more about or begin learning how to practice restorative justice. In this book, he gives an excellent summary of what restorative justice is about:

23. "Home Page," Restorative Justice Online, Prison Fellowship International, http://www.restorativejustice.org/.

24. Paul Tullis, "Can Forgiveness Play a Role in Criminal Justice?," *New York Times Magazine*, January 4, 2013, http://www.nytimes.com/2013/01/06/magazine/can-forgiveness-play-a-role-in-criminal-justice.html?pagewanted=all.

25. "Restorative Justice in New Zealand Best Practice," New Zealand Ministry of Justice, http://www.justice.govt.nz/publications/global-publications/r/restorative-justice-in-new-zealand-best-practice.

26. "Restorative Justice," Mennonite Central Committee, http://mcc.org/learn/what/restorative-justice.

27. "Howard Zehr," Eastern Mennonite University, https://www.emu.edu/personnel/people/show/zehrh.

28. "Famous Alumni of Morehouse College," Morehouse College Alumni Association, December 10, 2012, http://www.morehousecollegealumni.com/2012/12/10/famous-alumni-of-morehouse-college/.

Restorative justice is based upon an old, commonsense understanding of wrong-doing. Although it would be expressed differently in different cultures, this approach is probably common to most traditional societies. For those of us from European background, it is the way many of our ancestors (and perhaps even our parents) understood wrongdoing.

- Crime is a violation of people and of interpersonal relationships.
- Violations create obligations.
- The central obligation is to put right the wrongs.

Even more fundamentally, this view of wrongdoing implies a concern for healing of those involved: victims, but also offenders and communities.[29]

Howard Zehr explains the primary differences between the typical criminal justice approach and the restorative justice approach. In the traditional criminal justice system:

- Crime is a violation of the law and the state.
- Violations create guilt.
- Justice requires the state to determine blame (guilt) and impose pain (punishment).
- Central focus: offenders getting what they deserve.[30]

By contrast, in the restorative justice view:

- Crime is a violation of people and obligations.
- Violations create obligations.
- Justice involves victims, offenders and community members in an effort to put things right.
- Central focus: victim needs and offender responsibility for repairing harm.[31]

Restorative justice is not a concept unique to a particular political or religious ideology. Indeed, one of the foremost online resources on restorative justice, Restorative Justice Online, is run by Chuck Colson's Prison Fellowship International Centre for Justice and Reconciliation.[32] Colson

29. Howard Zehr with Ali Gohar, *The Little Book of Restorative Justice* (Uni-Graphics Peshawar, 2003), revised edition for Pakistan/Afghanistan, http://www.unicef.org/tdad/little bookrjpakaf.pdf, 17–18.
30. Ibid., 19.
31. Ibid.
32. "About RJ Online," Restorative Justice Online, Prison Fellowship International, http://www.restorativejustice.org/about-rj-online.

became an advocate for restorative justice as part of his more than thirty years of ministry to prisoners after his own imprisonment for his role in the Watergate scandal and his personal conversion experience.[33] Colson said this about restorative justice in 2011: "Our current criminal justice system is failing. However, there is an alternative, and it is literally as old as the Bible itself. It's called restorative justice, a biblical conception of justice that seeks to repair the damage that crime brings to victims and the community, and that the offender brings upon himself as well."[34] Undertaking such a dramatic paradigm shift in our criminal justice system will not be easy, but it is absolutely vital if we are to solve our nation's mass incarceration crisis and the racial injustice that it perpetuates.

Reform mostly based on the growing fiscal costs of a bad system won't be enough, and merely minimizing some of the most egregious aspects of the present system will not suffice. A mostly retributive system cannot just be tweaked for changes in some of its most negative aspects. And the racialized character of the system can't just be reduced; it must be removed. The vision of restorative justice is both powerful and transformational. It says some core moral values must be "restored" to the way we process the inevitable human need for a criminal justice system: the system needs to be fair and help to "restore" right behavior. But as we have learned again and again, change is never inevitable, and injustice doesn't just sort itself out. Both in pressuring for real change and in ensuring that the changes are fundamental and not just minimal, we will need people of faith, along with others who try to bring moral principles to public life.

This isn't just a matter of policy changes. It will be a test of our moral conscience and philosophy and, for people of faith, a test of our theology—whether we really believe that *all* of God's children are made in the image of God and must be treated with human dignity and respect.

33. David Plotz, "Charles Colson," Slate.com, March 10, 2000, http://www.slate.com/articles/news_and_politics/assessment/2000/03/charles_colson.html.

34. Chuck Colson, "Restorative Justice: A Win-Win-Win," ChristianHeadlines.com, November 10, 2011, http://www.christianheadlines.com/columnists/chuck-colson/restorative-justice-a-win-win-win.html.

9 | Welcoming the Stranger

The issue of race in America is not just one of black and white. The demographic changes in the United States will be a focus of the next chapter, on what a "new America" will look like. The growing Latino population in the United States, for example, is changing the culture and politics of the country. And the issue that has brought the powerful impact of the growing Latino community in the United States to the forefront is America's utterly broken immigration system.

I've always thought the best way to understand the immigration problem that the United States now faces is to imagine two invisible signs at the border between Mexico and the United States. One says "No Trespassing!" The other reads "Help Wanted." And 11 million vulnerable people are trapped between those two signs, and have been for many years. As with the reasons for the slavery of black Africans, the arrival of other immigrants to America (involuntarily, in the case of the slaves) has always had economic reasons.

For example, in the 1800s Chinese immigrants began arriving in California to seek their fortunes in the Gold Rush. When the gold ran out, many of them were employed as laborers in factories and, notably, in building the transcontinental railroad.[1] Japanese immigrants were lured

1. "Chinese Immigration and the Chinese Exclusion Acts," US Department of State, Office of the Historian, https://history.state.gov/milestones/1866-1898/chinese-immigration.

to Hawaii in large numbers by large US commercial interests, to work the sugar plantations under often-brutal conditions.[2] In these cases and others, white America has not always been ready to welcome the people whose labor they need as fully equal citizens and neighbors. And the failed immigration system we now have in America is an example of that.

A Broken System

We have been witnessing for decades a true *moral crisis* created by the failures of the immigration status quo. Most Americans never see pictures of vulnerable human beings hungrily searching for economic survival, frustrated with complicated and unresponsive immigration procedures and with legal protections or guest worker programs incredibly hard to access. These people take very risky and illegal journeys across borders, with some dying as they venture across vast desert expanses—all in an often-desperate attempt to find a better life.

Every day millions of immigrant families live in fear of their lives being irreparably disrupted or permanently dislocated because of one or more member's undocumented immigration status. Undocumented workers, many of whom are women, have their rights and dignity violated on a daily basis because they have little recourse against their employers. Young people who came here as small children live as "illegals," because they are undocumented, in the only country they have ever truly known as home.

Though this system has been broken for a long time, the excuses for that brokenness are disappearing. For the actual people who are living the consequences of this dysfunctional system, reform cannot come soon enough. And several key constituencies—faith communities, law enforcement officials, and corporations, in a new movement that some have described as "Bibles, Badges, and Business"—are waking up to the *moral and practical urgency* of fixing this system, which is inflicting untold pain upon millions of people, most of whom are people of color who came here from Latin America, Asia, the Caribbean, and Africa. One remarkable thing about the immigration reform movement of the past few years is that it has been supported by people of all racial backgrounds.

2. "Hawaii: Life in a Plantation Society," Library of Congress, http://www.loc.gov/teachers/classroommaterials/presentationsandactivities/presentations/immigration/japanese2.html.

Some have said that it will take a miracle for Congress to pass common-sense immigration reform. That may be true, but the "miracle" may already be in the making, helped along by faith communities who want to put their faith into action.

The Evangelical Immigration Table

These days, pictures often show the changing reality of America. And the picture in the front of the room at Washington's National Press Club on June 12, 2012, showed the face of the new America that is coming—Latinos, Anglos, Asians, and African Americans—all part of the Evangelical Immigration Table that was publicly announced that day. A very broad range of Evangelical organizations was represented: from groups such as the National Latino Evangelical Coalition, Esperanza, and the National Hispanic Christian Leadership Conference, to Sojourners and the Christian Community Development Association, to the National Association of Evangelicals and World Relief, to the Southern Baptist Convention and Focus on the Family.

That broad cross-section of evangelical leaders clearly and carefully laid out the principles of the Evangelical Immigration Table. The EIT has not supported any particular piece of legislation, but it holds all bills about immigration reform accountable to its six principles. The EIT supports any solution that:

- Respects the God-given dignity of every person
- Protects the unity of the immediate family
- Respects the rule of law
- Guarantees secure national borders
- Ensures fairness to taxpayers
- Establishes a path toward legal status and/or citizenship for those who qualify and who wish to become permanent residents[3]

I ended our press conference on that Tuesday by saying, "Together, we make a prophetic announcement today. Washington will change on this

3. Ibid.

issue. Washington will enact comprehensive immigration reform . . . because the people of God have come together to begin that change in our own lives and our own churches. And every Sunday we pray, 'Thy kingdom come, they will be done, on *earth* as it is in heaven.' We mean that. Amen."[4]

Big things don't first change in Washington, DC; they change in the nation's capital last. You'd think that with all the lobbyists on K Street and the billions of dollars being spent, that Washington is the most important place. But this is the place where things don't change, where politics maintains the status quo and the special interests maintain their own interests.

Things change when hearts and minds across the country change. Things change when social movements begin, when people's understandings change, when families rethink their values, when congregations examine their faith, when communities get mobilized, and when nations are moved by moral contradictions and imperatives.

Things change when people believe that more than politics is at stake; that human lives, human dignity, the well-being of moms and dads and kids, and even faith are at stake. And when the definitions of moral values change, culture changes, and eventually change comes to Washington, DC.

The immigration system in America is broken, and politics hasn't changed that. Both sides, Republicans and Democrats, are responsible for allowing this failed system for so long. The people who are now blocking reform are a Republican core of members of Congress and their leaders. Sadly, they are more concerned with their political bases and getting reelected than with the people and families whose lives are being crushed by a broken system.

The Bible says that these forgotten people fall into the category of "the stranger," and Jesus says how we welcome and treat them is how we welcome and treat him (see Matt. 25:40). That means they are no longer just the political pawns of Washington. And now Anglo Christians are coming to know Latino Christians as their brothers and sisters in the body of Christ. Because of worshiping together, they have come to know one another and even to love one another. White families have seen immigrant families in great danger, and seeing Latino families being torn apart is now tearing their hearts apart too. They have come to believe that families

4. Jim Wallis, "Immigration: Unity, Morality and Common Sense," *Huffington Post*, June 14, 2012, http://www.huffingtonpost.com/jim-wallis/immigration-unity-moralit_b_1597520.html.

being separated and even destroyed also breaks God's heart, and that has called them to action.

There have been many subsequent visits to Washington by the Evangelical Immigration Table. At one press conference, *Christianity Today* editor Andy Crouch, speaking as a journalist, said he had never seen such evangelical unity over any other issue.[5] Together, we are creating a national groundswell for immigration reform by reaching out to our fellow evangelicals, to students at Christian colleges and seminaries, and to our churches—both Anglo and Latino. Evangelicals have large constituencies across America, and they have been telling their political representatives that it is time to shed their partisan behavior and act instead on the moral and biblical imperative to fix a broken system. They say it is time to transcend politics and do what is right.

Just blocks away from the political centers of power, we would walk into churches packed with Christians from across the country who had traveled to meet and talk to their elected representatives. For many years, our Latino Christian brothers and sisters have led the way on the issue of immigration reform, but I remember speaking to one of those crowds and saying, "We are *all* here now." Again, the picture was the story. The pews and aisles were filled with worshipers from every racial and ethnic community, and across the generations—Latino, Anglo, African American, Asian American, pastors, and old and young people. You could sense the passion in the sanctuary.

I remember "closing" one of those services. After feeling the power of faith in the room, I said, "We are not closing worship today; we're just going to move it" to the United States Capitol. This movement is praying its way to changing the immigration system, and "Pray4Reform" has been our call.[6] And across the country, we have given feet to our prayers.

We had countless meetings with members of Congress and their top staff. Our delegations met with those Republican leaders who would be key in the decisions made about immigration reform. Most important, evangelical pastors and leaders met with *their* members of Congress, remembering that the most eloquent voice to a politician is one in his or her own constituency. One of those congressional leaders we met with, Rep. Paul Ryan, a

5. Jim Wallis, "The Moral Urgency of Immigration Reform," *God's Politics* (blog), *Sojourners*, July 25, 2013, http://sojo.net/blogs/2013/07/25/moral-urgency-immigration-reform.
6. "Pray4Reform," Evangelical Immigration Table, http://pray4reform.org/.

Republican from Wisconsin, said it well: "This is new—the new factor. In all the immigration votes I've been a part of, we didn't have evangelicals involved like this. You are a grassroots movement that has real influence on the Right, on Republicans, and you could make a crucial difference on this."

Many faith communities—Catholics and Protestants, Jews and Muslims, and now evangelical Christians—are asking for a moral and religious conversation about immigration reform, and not just a political one.

While many have pointed to the moral and political impact the faith community is having on the debate, the three reasons why evangelical Christians in particular have become increasingly involved in support of comprehensive immigration reform should be looked at very carefully. And all three reasons are related to churches becoming more multiracial, as I suggested they need to do in chapter 6.

The Bible Tells Me So

The first reason evangelicals have come around on this issue is biblical. Instead of just thumping their Bibles, Christians began reading them again.

It's very difficult to make a faith-based argument against immigration reform, at least if you're reading the Bible closely. God's passionate, abiding concern for immigrants and foreigners, strangers and travelers—for our neighbors—is obvious to anyone reading through Scripture. And the Bible's message is about welcoming strangers and outsiders, who are almost always from another ethnicity or race—that's what most "strangers" are in a new country.

In the Old Testament, the Lord commands: "When a foreigner resides among you in your land, do not mistreat them. The foreigner residing among you must be treated as your native-born. Love them as yourself" (Lev. 19:33–34 NIV). The stranger is not "native-born" but from another place or country and might often be from another racial or ethnic group. God also tells us, "You shall not oppress a stranger, for you know the heart of a stranger, because you were strangers in the land of Egypt" (Exod. 23:9 NKJV). The reference here is, of course, to when the Jews were themselves outsiders from a different race in a foreign land.

As I discussed earlier, the biblical word *ger* for "strangers" or "foreigners" in our midst occurs almost one hundred times in the Hebrew Scriptures, with the consistent instruction to protect them. We are commanded to love God, our neighbor, and the stranger. Jesus said to love your neighbors, which of course his listeners took to mean those around them—and those like them. But then Jesus extended the meaning of neighbors to include . . . well, even the Samaritans. The outsider, usually from a different ethnicity or race, is specifically lifted up to be loved. A very strong point is being made here. While it is assumed that we will love ourselves and our own families, we are commanded to love our neighbors as ourselves, and we are specifically told that the stranger is our neighbor. This is clearly a commandment to include people from other racial communities into our own.

In the New Testament, the stranger and all the vulnerable are at the very heart of the gospel. In the book of Matthew, Jesus offers a vision in which caring for them is the defining mark of God's kingdom:

> For I was hungry and you gave me something to eat, I was thirsty and you gave me something to drink, *I was a stranger and you invited me in*, I needed clothes and you clothed me, I was sick and you looked after me, I was in prison and you came to visit me. (Matt. 25:35–36, emphasis added)

The clear scriptural mandate to "welcome the stranger" has inspired many evangelical Christians to be at the forefront of the push to fix our broken immigration system. Evangelicals have long been considered an important political constituency, and their engagement on this issue has drawn significant attention for its breadth and depth. And what motivates us is the call of Jesus who audaciously proclaims that the way we treat the most vulnerable members of our society, including immigrants—the biblical "stranger"—reflects how we treat Christ himself (as stated above in Matt. 25). So we stand outside a broken political system, urging our leaders to prioritize the common good, believing that what is morally right should never be nakedly sacrificed for political gain.

Compassion is indeed all over the Bible. We hope and pray that it will also be found someday in the Congress. When it is, we will see the miracle we need.

You Deported Jose

The second reason many evangelicals have changed their hearts and minds on this issue is the personal relationships white Christians have formed with immigrants in their congregations and communities, and hearing the stories that have emerged from those relationships. I remember a conversation between President Obama's senior staff and evangelical pastors about the administration's deportation policies. While they were pushing for immigration reform, the Obama administration was still pursuing an aggressive deportation policy, likely to appease their conservative critics with tough law enforcement. Indeed, the Obama administration had deported more undocumented people than previous administrations had, a record number that averaged 1,100 per day.[7] The pastors were very concerned about those deportations and how they were literally breaking up families in their congregations—tearing fathers and mothers away from their sons and daughters.

I recall a top White House official telling the pastors that the administration's policy was to deport only criminals and those involved in drug cartels—which was the White House message at the time. But a pastor raised his hand to ask a question. I looked over at the older white clergyman from Orange County, California, and heard this Anglo megachurch pastor tell one of President Obama's highest and closest aides, "No, you deported Jose . . . and now his son Joaquin has joined a gang." There were tears in his eyes. But the White House official just repeated the line—we only deport drug dealers and those guilty of crimes. So then I raised my hand and said to the senior Obama adviser, who is also a friend, "Listen to the pastors."

And they did. Jose, who had become a member of this pastor's church, had broken no laws since coming to this country illegally many years ago. He had started a family and was a committed and involved Christian. When Jose was discovered one day to be undocumented, he was deported. Now without a father, his son Joaquin joined a violent street gang. The stories began to come out around the room, from both Latino and Anglo evangelical pastors who were losing their people to deportation and watching their families being destroyed. It was a powerful and emotional meeting for everyone. These stories go on and on in the faith community—one family after another broken apart by a broken system. And here were the pastors in relationship to those families who had become a part of their

7. David Nakamura, "Immigration Advocates Ask Obama to Suspend Some Deportations," *Washington Post*, May 13, 2013, http://www.washingtonpost.com/blogs/post-politics/wp/2013/05/13/immigration-advocates-ask-obama-to-suspend-some-deportations/.

churches, part of their lives, and part of their families now. And that is what made the big difference. The immigrants' stories were changing the pastors and eventually helped begin to change the Obama administration's immigration and deportation policies.

All this was because of new relationships. That evangelical Christians would finally act to reform the immigration system should surprise no one, and not just for theological reasons. Undocumented immigrants have joined our congregations; we understand the problem firsthand. They are our brothers and sisters in the body of Christ. We know that by reforming our immigration laws, we can create a system that also reflects the best values of our nation and the highest ideals of our faith. We act because, as James 2 reminds us, "faith without works is dead" (v. 26).

Beyond the witness of the Scriptures that speak to the experience of immigrants and the importance of "welcoming the stranger," the suffering that so many face involves *real people and real stories*. Every undocumented immigrant is someone's son or daughter, and many are spouses, siblings, or parents themselves.

I recall a father I met who had lived in nearby Maryland for many years. He had a steady job, and he had no infringements of the law in all the years he had been in America. But when he was stopped for a missing bolt on his license plate, the police discovered that he was undocumented. His wife had passed away, and now he was a single dad telling us that he was being deported away from his two young daughters who were right there too, hanging on to his legs with deep fear in their eyes, while there were tears in his.

Or there was the 2010 case of Bernard Pastor. Pastor exemplifies the best that immigrants bring to this country and the tragedy of our broken immigration system. He was an honors student, record-holding athlete, and active church member who was arrested in 2010 after a minor traffic accident (which was not even his fault) led police to uncover his undocumented status. He was threatened with deportation to his parents' native Guatemala, a country he left when he was three years old. When word spread about Pastor's detainment, his classmates and members of the local faith community rallied to support him. His story soon spread around Ohio and even received national media attention. An interfaith group of national religious leaders raised our voices in favor of his release. After a month of imprisonment, Pastor was released on "deferred action status" and has since been able to attend Xavier University thanks to the efforts of those who stood up for him.[8]

The good news is that the faces and stories of real people are, in fact, compelling many white Christians to come alive to the importance of this issue. Take, for example, the now very typical story of how Mike McClenahan, the senior pastor of Solana Beach Presbyterian Church in Southern California, became, as he puts it, "an accidental advocate for reform."[9] After baptizing children whose parents live in fear of deportation and building outreach ministries to immigrants in his community, he realized that the gospel's call to "love your neighbor as yourself" required advocating for immigration reform. As a result, this ordinary pastor found himself in the Oval Office with the president of the United States, telling the story of how he as a conservative white pastor had changed his mind. I got to know McClenahan in that meeting and afterward, and his response is typical of what I now see all over the country.

Who's Growing the Churches?

The third major reason evangelicals in particular and Christians more broadly have increasingly embraced immigration reform is that many national church leaders and local pastors now understand that immigrants are the future of their churches. Many outside the church don't realize that *growth in American churches is being driven largely by immigrants*,[10] while church membership among US-born whites is broadly declining. That's particularly true in relationship to the Catholic Church. Many new Latino immigrants, and those from other places, are drawn to their Catholic identity, the church they came from in their native countries. When they arrive in America, legally or illegally, they immediately go to a Catholic church, where they are accepted. Pew found that as of 2014, 55

8. Mark Curnutte, "Bernard Pastor—A Year Later," Cincinnati.com, November 17, 2011, http://archive.cincinnati.com/article/20111116/NEWS01/111170305/Bernard-Pastor-year-later.

9. Mike McClenahan, "Broken Immigration System Brings Real, Personal Problems," *U-T San Diego*, October 17, 2013, http://www.utsandiego.com/news/2013/Oct/17/broken-immigration-system-brings-real-personal/.

10. See especially Wesley Granberg-Michaelson, *From Times Square to Timbuktu: The Post-Christian West Meets the Non-Western Church* (Grand Rapids: Eerdmans, 2013), 82–83.

percent of Latinos identify as Catholic.[11] Wesley Granberg-Michaelson, in his book *From Times Square to Timbuktu: The Post-Christian West Meets the Non-Western Church* tells us:

> About 35 percent of the U.S. Catholic community is now Hispanic. That figure will continue to rise. Hispanics are dramatically reshaping the nature and texture of Catholicism in the United States, particularly in regions with high Hispanic populations. In Los Angeles, for example, an estimated 70 percent of Catholics are Hispanic. . . . *Hispanics have constituted 71 percent of the growth of U.S. Catholics since 1960.*[12]

Given these facts, it is quite clear that the growth of Catholicism in the United States has been and will continue to be dependent on Latino Catholics. And given that about 80 percent of our country's undocumented population is Latino,[13] it is natural that the Catholic Church in the United States has rightly been a leading voice for comprehensive immigration reform. The United States Conference of Catholic Bishops has spoken about the Catholic social teaching that undergirds its position on this issue:

> Persons have the right to immigrate and thus government must accommodate this right to the greatest extent possible, especially financially blessed nations: "The more prosperous nations are obliged, to the extent they are able, to welcome the foreigner in search of the security and the means of livelihood which he cannot find in his country of origin. Public authorities should see to it that the natural right is respected that places a guest under the protection of those who receive him." (Catholic Catechism, 2241)[14]

Pope Francis has spoken more broadly about the need for a change in mind-set regarding immigration:

> A change of attitude towards migrants and refugees is needed on the part of everyone, moving away from attitudes of defensiveness and fear, indifference and marginalization—all typical of a throwaway culture—towards attitudes

11. "The Shifting Religious Identity of Latinos in the United States," Pew Research Center, May 7, 2014, http://www.pewforum.org/2014/05/07/the-shifting-religious-identity-of-latinos -in-the-united-states/.

12. Granberg-Michaelson, *From Times Square to Timbuktu*, 92–94 (emphasis added).

13. Ibid., 92.

14. "Catholic Church's Position on Immigration Reform," United States Conference of Catholic Bishops, August 2013, http://www.usccb.org/issues-and-action/human-life-and-dignity /immigration/churchteachingonimmigrationreform.cfm.

based on a culture of encounter, the only culture capable of building a better, more just and fraternal world.[15]

But as people all over Latin America know, including the Catholic Church in Latin America, many Latin Americans have been joining evangelical and mostly Pentecostal churches for many years in their home countries. Although 80 percent of Latin Americans are Catholic, non-Catholic expressions of Christian faith are growing at *three times* the rate that Catholic churches are.[16] So when those non-Catholic Latinos come to the United States, they usually first go to Pentecostal and evangelical churches in America. There are about 9.3 million Protestant Latinos in the United States—more people than in the entire Episcopal Church—and 85 percent of them are Pentecostal or evangelical.[17] It is widely acknowledged that "immigrants are the fastest growing part of the evangelical church in America."[18]

The dramatic thing is that for both Protestants and Catholics, the primary driver of church growth is people who are foreign-born and/or nonwhite. And most American church leaders know that. In other words, *immigrants are the future of Christianity in America.*

Fasting for Families

In June 2013, the Senate passed a bipartisan bill to reform the immigration system, written and forged by an impressive coalition of Republican and Democratic Senate leaders. It was quickly clear that if a similar bill was put to a vote in the House of Representatives, it would also pass. However, months later, a minority of lawmakers—almost all white legislators from artificially gerrymandered white congressional districts—were blocking a vote on immigration reform.

The public debate over immigration reform has been won—by those who favor a commonsense agenda for reform. Nearly two out of every

15. "Pope Calls for Protection of Unaccompanied Child Migrants," Vatican Radio, July 15, 2014, http://en.radiovaticana.va/news/2014/07/15/pope_calls_for_protection_of_unaccompanied _child_migrants_/1102879.

16. Granberg-Michaelson, *From Times Square to Timbuktu*, 10.

17. Ibid., 93.

18. "Immigration Reform," National Association of Evangelicals, http://www.nae.net/govern ment-relations/for-the-health-of-the-nation/human-rights/immigration-reform.

three Americans favor fixing our broken immigration system with comprehensive reform—two out of three! According to a 2013 report by the Public Religion Research Institute, 65 percent of Americans said that the US immigration system is either completely or mostly broken. That same report found that 63 percent of Americans, across party and religious lines, favor immigration reform that creates a pathway to citizenship. A pathway to citizenship is also favored by 60 percent of Republicans, 57 percent of independents, and 73 percent of Democrats.[19] A March 2015 report from LifeWay Research shows that 68 percent of evangelicals support a balanced approach to immigration reform that includes a pathway to citizenship.[20]

These numbers show that this minority of white Republican members of the House of Representatives is blocking democracy in our nation, literally vetoing the will of the majority of the people in the United States—including those who form traditional constituencies within the Republican Party such as evangelical Christians, business leaders, and law enforcement officials.

There was no real substance behind the opposition to reforming what mostly everyone agrees is a broken and brutal system. Rather, it was politics: angry politics, fearful politics, and, sadly, racial politics, using institutional political practices and rules to avoid democratic accountability. Democracy was being vetoed by corrupt racial politics. It became clear to us that it was not just our immigration system that is broken; our politics are too.

The faith-based movement to fix and heal the brutal immigration system had preached and protested, mobilized and organized, repeatedly visited and written to our members of Congress and the White House, written letters to the editor and opinion pieces in our local newspapers, run ads on radio and television, marched, and even been arrested! We reached out with great compassion to immigrant families who live in such jeopardy and fear. In fact, we had done everything one is supposed to do to change hearts and minds in a democracy, and we had changed the hearts and minds of a significant majority of the people of the United States. But democracy had been obstructed again and again by dysfunctional politics.

19. Robert P. Jones, Daniel Cox, and Juhem Navarro-Rivera, "What Americans (Still) Want from Immigration Reform," Public Religion Research Institute, November 25, 2013, http://publicreligion.org/research/2013/11/2013-immigration-ii/#.VT2KFPBmrpI.

20. Bob Smietana, "Evangelicals Say It Is Time for Congress to Tackle Immigration," LifeWay Research, March 11, 2015, http://www.lifewayresearch.com/2015/03/11/evangelicals-say-it-is-time-for-congress-to-tackle-immigration/.

In November 2013, the frustration with the lack of action by Congress led some of us to participate in something that was at once radical, spiritual, and necessary: the Fast for Families.

We felt that was the only thing left to do—fast and pray. Fasting has long been a way for people—both biblical figures and social movement leaders—to focus their spiritual energy, power, and prayer. Daniel fasted to cleanse himself from the ways of the empire. Nehemiah fasted to discern the spiritual causes of the destruction of his people. Mordecai fasted at the entrance of the king's gate in protest of the conspiracy to destroy his people. Jesus himself fasted for forty days before announcing his mission in Luke 4: "to bring good news to the poor" and "to let the oppressed go free" (v. 18).

Fast for Families began with a small and brave group of immigrants, some of them undocumented, who started their fast on November 12, 2013, on the National Mall, right across from the Capitol. Led by inspirational leader Eliseo Medina, a veteran organizer and disciple of Cesar Chavez, the fasters vowed to take only water. I was grateful to be at the official start of the fast and honored to be asked to "commission" the core fasters, who included Medina and my Sojourners colleague Lisa Sharon Harper, by placing crosses around their necks as they began abstaining entirely from food.

Over the course of the fast, its public and prophetic witness grew each day, attracting a growing number of people, including faith and community leaders and then some Democratic and Republican members of Congress who came to visit.

Eventually, President Barack Obama, First Lady Michelle Obama, and Vice President Joe Biden all came to see the fasters. During his visit, the president "held the shoe of an immigrant who perished in the desert trying to seek a better life, which the fasters [held] in reverence as a symbol of why they are fasting to underscore the plight and suffering of immigrants."[21] He made it clear that the fast was receiving a great deal of attention, and that he heard the fasters' message.

After twenty-two days, the first group of core fasters had grown weak, nearing the point of medical danger. When they decided to pass the fast

21. Beatriz Lopez, "President and First Lady Visit 'Fast for Families' on the National Mall," SEIU.org, November 29, 2013, http://www.seiu.org/2013/11/president-and-first-lady-visit-fast-for-families-o.php.

to a new group, I was humbled to join the effort this way. On December 3, in the shadow of the US Capitol, I received the cross from Medina that I had given to him three weeks before. At that ceremony, each of us shared why we were committing to this discipline and willing to subsist only on water.

Personally, this was an invitation to go deeper. This was a prayerful, spiritual fast. The Fast for Families kept alive the national conversation on immigration reform, gaining national momentum and demonstrating real moral authority. It was not a hunger strike or a threat, but a witness to the urgency of immigration reform and offering aspiring Americans a way to earn citizenship.

Faith leaders and "Dreamers"—young people who came to this country as children with their parents, and for whom the United States is the only country they have ever truly called home despite their undocumented status—joined this historic fast on behalf of immigrant families who suffer because our leaders refused to address a glaring problem. It is politics, and politics only, that stands in the way of progress.

This fast revealed a spiritual movement around families and children who are suffering. This was about people, not politics. But the fast and the prayer that came with it had the potential to change our politics. So many people—11 million immigrants, who are our families, friends, and neighbors—are stuck in an untenable situation. And our broken political system can't fix it. Our politics are stuck. And stuck politics hurt people. So in the tent near the Capitol, we prayed and fasted for them.

The scene at the fasting tent was powerful and revealing, and the national attention to the fast seemed to grow every day. There were two kinds of power represented on the National Mall, so close to each other. On one side of the street, at the US Capitol, was political power. But across the street, in this tent, which had become a chapel, even a holy place, was spiritual power—and it was growing every day across the country and in the media. This fast was begun by immigrants themselves, but on December 3, 2013, it was passed on to the nation, with thousands joining all across the country.

So how does the spiritual power of a prayerful fast change the political power of a broken system? Prayer and fasting change those who pray and fast and also those who watch and listen. It draws us—including our lawmakers—to go deeper into our hearts, our souls, and our faith.

Over the course of the thirty-one days, from when the immigrants began the fast until we officially ended it on December 12, many people came to the fasting tent at the Capitol, including members of Congress, faith leaders, celebrities, heads of organizations, the president and the first lady, a famous chef who offered us a great meal when the fast ended, and so many "ordinary" people and undocumented immigrants themselves, with stories that were changing people's minds and hearts.

The people who came to visit us would sit in a circle with the fasters and hear the stories. Then we would hear the stories of our guests and why they had come. The visitors were asked for four things: to join us in fasting, even for a day or a meal to be in solidarity together, to act in the ways they could to bring about immigration reform, to pray with us, and then to take a picture together! Every leader who came to visit was asked to lead us in prayer, which came easily for the faith leaders but was new for some of our other guests. One of my favorite prayers came from a member of Congress who had been very supportive of comprehensive immigration reform. A public figure not usually short for words, he said, "Well, I have never led a public prayer before but here goes: Dear God, please do whatever you have to do to change those knuckleheads up on the Hill." There were hundreds of visits where we saw and felt people going deeper—as we all fasted and prayed. Overall more than five thousand people joined the fast for a period of time, and hundreds did so in our tent.

One of the most powerful moments came when Rep. Debbie Wasserman Schultz connected mother-to-mother, on a very emotional level, with an undocumented immigrant woman who was weeping over being separated from her daughter who was the same age as the congresswoman's own daughter. United by the bond of both having teenage daughters, these two women held each other and cried together. I asked the congresswoman how experiences like these could change the hearts of her colleagues up on the Hill. But she lamented how many "layers" there were between that tent and the Capitol across the street. This fast was intended to help break through those layers with prayer, sacrifice, and real people's stories. We hoped to connect beyond and beneath politics by going deeper into our own hearts as parents, fellow human beings, and people of faith.

The fast was an example of what both Martin Luther King and Mohandas Gandhi called "soul force." Our hope and prayer was that this soul force would ultimately change the political forces across the street—spiritual power changing political power. We knew the usual politics of Washington wouldn't fundamentally change, but we hoped those politics could make an "exception" with the urgent need for immigration reform. And we hoped that members of Congress would recognize this matter as different from business as usual in Washington—that it was about people more than politics, about parents and children, and about our faith and deepest values.

Fast for Families ended on December 12, when the Congress closed down in Washington and its members went back home to their districts for the holidays. A large crowd marched to the Capitol to deliver our final message, with many members of Congress present with us on the Capitol steps. Then we went back to the tent to end the fast, but we took its energy back home with us. The marches to and from the Capitol were led by the eight core fasters who had carried on the fast in the tent—including those in both the first group and the second group. After more than two weeks without food, it is difficult to walk very far, so the first core fasters, who had now taken food again, pushed the second core group in wheelchairs at the front of the procession. At the closing of the fast, all eight of the fast leaders shared personal words of reflection and the call to continue this spiritual *and* political process until immigration reform ultimately passed. Again, the power was in the *picture* of the eight core fasters together on the stage. We were Latino, Asian, African American, and white—all standing together for the benediction.

Going Forward

More than two years after our fast, the immigration system has yet to be comprehensively reformed.

But as Rev. Gabriel Salguero, one of my fellow fasters and leaders on the Evangelical Immigration Table, said in an article in New York City's *Observer News* that appeared Easter weekend in 2015, "Immigration is inevitable. . . . You can slow it down, but you can't stop it." Reverend Salguero went on to say, "I am the son of a homeless man . . . my father was a homeless junkie." While still a boy, Gabe witnessed the "transformative power of the gospel"[22] change his father and make him into a pastor. Gabe

22. Roja Heydarpour, "Higher Power: New York's Most Influential Religious Leaders," *Observer*, April 3, 2015, http://observer.com/2015/04/higher-power-new-yorks-most-influential-religious-leaders/.

and his wife, Jeanette, have continued in the family business of hope and now copastor the Lamb's Church of the Nazarene in New York City, a multiracial church where services are held in English, Spanish, and Mandarin.

After the election in 2014 and the failure of the Republican Congress to allow a vote on immigration reform, the president announced courageous executive orders that could at least relieve some of the suffering undocumented immigrant families were enduring until the necessary legislation to really reform the system could one day pass. The executive actions would replace the current threat of deportation for several million previously undocumented people with papers that would allow them to work. But those executive actions are being held up in courts as I write.

Urgent and Unfinished

Washington moves slowly, as we are told by people on the inside. Some say that we should wait longer to work on the immigration system, do it slowly, over time, down the road, piece by piece, and not act now.

But it's the lives of the people on the outside that give us our time frame for fixing this broken immigration system, and we call that *moral urgency*.

The urgency of protecting families and keeping children with their parents. Defending and reuniting families that have been shattered is an urgent issue for people of faith.

The urgency of bringing peaceful and productive people out of the shadows of fear and insecurity. In religious language, it is time to cast out fear and have people live unafraid.

The urgency of protecting vulnerable people who must live without critical health care and even legal protection. We've heard so many heartbreaking stories from pastors of immigrants regularly robbed and women raped who can't seek the protection of the police, and injured people unable to seek medical care or even go to the emergency room, so instead they curl up alone with their wounds and hope they don't die.

The urgency of young people who came to this country as children, doing what their parents told them to. They have gone to school and made this their home. They have almost no relationship to their countries of origin. These "Dreamers"—so named because they could eventually qualify for permanent status under the DREAM Act if Congress were to pass it—are Americans now and should be regarded as such.

The urgency for Christians to be faithful to Christ, who tells us that how we treat "the stranger" is how we treat him. As Rev. Gabriel Salguero preached in the shadow of the Capitol, "Tell the Congress that we are here to welcome Jesus."[23] To not welcome the immigrants among us is to not welcome Christ, and we will be held accountable for that.

The urgency of our unity as the body of Christ, which is so dramatically on display in our congregations. Immigrant believers, including the undocumented, are now part of our churches, and when one part of our body suffers, we all suffer. When one part of our body rejoices, we all rejoice.

It's time for Congress to feel the urgency—to make immigration reform an exception from its polarization and gridlock and finally show the nation that it can lead, govern, and actually solve a problem in a bipartisan way. It's time for Republicans and Democrats to do something positive together for the good of the nation. We have told our members of Congress that we can no longer wait to fix this broken system, and they will keep hearing from us until we as a nation have finally achieved comprehensive immigration reform.

Fear of the New America

I know and respect a number of Republicans who believe in an inclusive party for their future, but their congressional leaders have yet to reject the politics of racial fear that informs so much of the fierce opposition to reform. The face of that racial fear expresses itself in ugly ways across the country. A 2014 case in California is a good example.

On July 1, 2014, in Murrieta, California, three buses full of women and children who had fled violence in Central America were being taken by Homeland Security to a US Border Patrol station for processing and eventual deportation. But the buses were blocked by adults yelling that they weren't wanted here in the United States.[24] Big angry white men,

23. Wallis, "Moral Urgency."
24. Michael Martinez and Holly Yan, "Showdown: California Town Turns Away Buses of Detained Immigrants," CNN.com, July 3, 2014, http://www.cnn.com/2014/07/02/us/california-immigrant-transfers/.

holding signs the children couldn't read, with angry faces screaming at them in a language they didn't understand—when they were already in a strange place, facing an unknown future—would certainly make children feel very afraid.

The town mayor, Alan Long, said the women and children posed a threat to his community and that he was "proud" of the demonstrators.[25] Nearly 150 protesters waved American flags, chanted "USA! USA!," and shouted to the scared children, "Go home—we don't want you here."[26] Totally blocked from reaching the processing center, the buses turned around and left for another Border Patrol station, where some of the children were reportedly taken to a hospital for unspecified treatment.[27]

More than 68,000 unaccompanied children, primarily from Guatemala, El Salvador, and Honduras, walked across the US border between October 2013 and October 2014—some, unfortunately, by way of human trafficking networks through Mexico.[28] Some of these kids are reportedly as young as six years old.[29] Thousands more, like those in Murrieta, came with their mothers or other relatives. The surge overwhelmed the system and became a very serious humanitarian crisis to which US officials scrambled to respond. And, of course, it was politicized in Washington.

Incredibly, some Republicans used this tragic situation as an excuse for derailing immigration reform—when having a smart, fair, and humane immigration system in place would have helped avoid this crisis.

Reforming our immigration system is still a task that is urgent and unfinished. And it has become a powerful metaphor for the great challenge that lies ahead to build a bridge to a new America. But what is the new America, and how can we build that bridge?

25. Raul A. Reyes, "Murrieta Immigration Protests Were Unfortunate, Unnecessary," *Huffington Post*, July 9, 2014, http://www.huffingtonpost.com/raul-a-reyes/murrieta-immigration-prot_b_5569351.html.

26. Marty Graham, "Anti-immigration Protestors Block Undocumented Migrants in California," Reuters, July 2, 2014, http://www.reuters.com/article/2014/07/02/us-usa-immigration-california-protesters-idUSKBN0F65L720140702.

27. Martinez and Yan, "Showdown."

28. Rachel Roubein, "Far Fewer Unaccompanied Minors Are Now Crossing the U.S. Border," *National Journal*, October 10, 2014, http://www.nationaljournal.com/congress/far-fewer-unaccompanied-minors-are-now-crossing-the-u-s-border-20141010.

29. Jens Manuel Krogstad, Ana Gonzalez-Barrera, and Mark Hugo Lopez, "Children 12 and Under Are Fastest Growing Group of Unaccompanied Minors at U.S. Border," Pew Research Center, July 22, 2014, http://www.pewresearch.org/fact-tank/2014/07/22/children-12-and-under-are-fastest-growing-group-of-unaccompanied-minors-at-u-s-border/.

10 | Crossing the Bridge to a New America

The most important immigration talk I've given was to my son's fifth-grade elementary school class in the fall of 2013. They were studying the subject of immigration and invited me to speak about it. First, we went through the long history of immigration in this country. All the children in my son's class learned that they were part of our national history—of people who had chosen to come to America (or were forced to by the chains of slavery). So they all heard the history of their own ancestries.

Then I told the students about our current problem of 11 million undocumented people living in uncertainty and fear for years and even decades; being unable to safely obtain medical care and police protection; being exploited without protection by unscrupulous employers; and, most painfully, being separated from family members, with fathers and mothers being torn away from their children. Hardworking and law-abiding people were being deported every day—at that time about 1,100 per day.

Looking very surprised, these students asked the obvious question, "Why don't we fix that? Why doesn't Congress change the system?"

I answered, "They say they're afraid."

The students looked even more confused and asked, "What are they afraid of?"

I paused to consider their honest question and looked around the room—the classroom of a public-school fifth-grade class in Washington, DC. I looked at their quizzical and concerned faces, a group of African American, Latino, Asian American, Native American, and European American children. Then it hit me.

"They are afraid of you," I replied.

"Why would they be afraid of us?" the shocked students asked, totally perplexed. I had to tell them.

"They are afraid you are the future of America. They're afraid their country will someday look like this class—that you represent what our nation is becoming."

This multiracial, multicultural, and multinational group of eleven-year-olds now looked more confused than ever.

"They are afraid this won't work," I said. "Does it work?"

The children looked at one another, then responded with many voices, saying, "Yeah . . . Sure . . . Of course it works . . . It works great . . . It's really cool!"

Together we decided that our job was to show the rest of the country that this new America coming into being is, in fact, really cool.

Where Do We Go from Here?

In his final book, Martin Luther King Jr. asked the pivotal question with the book title, *Where Do We Go from Here: Chaos or Community?*

That is exactly the right question for us today. King's last volume was published in 1967, and he was assassinated in Memphis, Tennessee, on April 4, 1968.

So where do we go from here?

In the next few decades, a fundamental change will occur in the United States. By the year 2045, the majority of US citizens will be descended from African, Asian, and Latin American ancestors, according to the US Census Bureau projections.[1] For the first time in its 240-year history since 1776, America will no longer be a white majority nation. Rather, we will have become a majority of minorities—with no one race being

1. Marcie Bianco, "The Year White People Will Become a Minority in America Has Been Declared," Mic.com, December 11, 2014, http://mic.com/articles/106252/the-year-white-people-will-become-a-minority-in-america-has-been-declared.

in the majority. The United States will be no longer a dominant white nation but a multiracial nation, which will make the assumptions of white privilege that we discussed in chapter 5 increasingly *less assumed*. That multiracial reality is already the case in many major cities around the country such as Los Angeles, New York, San Francisco, Dallas, Chicago, Boston, and Milwaukee, among others.[2] It's also true for several whole states, including California, Texas, New Mexico, Hawaii, and the District of Columbia.[3]

This is a historical milestone, a fundamental demographic shift. Demographic changes are already impacting our nation's elections in many states and especially at the national level. But demographic shifts don't automatically or easily make shifts in wealth, power, or governance, and the white "minority" will still retain economic and political dominance for a long time to come.

Nonetheless, the demographic shift in America, with a majority of its citizens being people of color, is both significant and dramatic for the culture, ethos, and politics of a new America. And the truth needs to be told that many if not most white Americans are simply not ready for that demographic change—especially older white Americans.

The question becomes, who will help navigate this fundamental demographic change? Who will provide the moral compass for such a transformation? It's an important question to ask, because demographic shifts do not make positive change inevitable or easy. On the contrary, these great demographic shifts could simply lead to more and more confrontations and conflicts. For real and positive change to occur, choices must be made, and somebody has to provide leadership. The choices are between *collisions* or *community* or, as Dr. King's final book put it, between "chaos or community."

For me, the most powerful metaphor for where we are going is *crossing a bridge*. Will we be willing and able to cross the bridge to a new America, from a majority white culture with minorities, to a *majority of minorities* society, with white people as one of the minorities? Can we find our way to

2. "The Most and Least Diverse Cities in America," Priceonomics.com, December 15, 2014, http://priceonomics.com/the-most-and-least-diverse-cities-in-america/.
3. Karen R. Humes, Nicholas A. Jones, and Roberto R. Ramirez, "Overview of Race and Hispanic Origin: 2010" (Washington, DC: US Census Bureau, March 2011), https://www.census .gov/prod/cen2010/briefs/c2010br-02.pdf, 18.

a genuinely diverse society, racially and culturally, where diversity is seen as a strength rather than as a threat? Or are we headed for a conflictual future where minorities, including whites, just have one collision after another with one another? Are we ready to cross that bridge, and how can we best do it? These are the questions we address here in the final chapter.

Selma and Our Next Bridge to Cross

The Edmund Pettus Bridge was named after a Confederate general who became a Grand Dragon in the Ku Klux Klan. His name, still emblazoned over the top of that now-infamous bridge, was a powerful and threatening symbol of white power and supremacy in Selma, Alabama. The Student Non-Violent Coordinating Committee (SNCC) had at one time removed Selma from its list of places to organize because "the white folks were too mean, and black folks were too afraid."[4] But that didn't deter a group of courageous African Americans from marching across that bridge a half-century ago, risking their lives for the right to vote in America. They were attacked and beaten by fierce forces, led by the notorious sheriff Jim Clark, for their resistance to the frightening violence of white power.

On Saturday, March 7, 2015, I was in Selma for the fiftieth anniversary of that "Bloody Sunday." My ride to Selma from Birmingham turned out to be a powerful beginning to these extraordinary days of celebration and reflection. The woman who drove me to Selma was from Birmingham, and she helped frame the day for me. Her grandmother was a black housekeeper in a house of wealthy white people. "Did you see the movie *The Help*?" she asked me. I had and remembered the powerful story. "That was my grandmother, one of those women who made 25 cents per day" (and it cost her a nickel for the round-trip bus ride). Her grandfather was a miner and a minister in a local church. Nonetheless, despite their low wages, her grandparents had raised all their children to go to college, including my traveling companion, who was a college graduate and an experienced welder.

I asked her about the famous days of Martin Luther King Jr.'s campaign in Birmingham. She was in high school at the time, and when King

4. Debbie Elliott, "50 Years Ago, Selma's Bloody Sunday Sparked Voting Rights Act," NPR .org, March 2, 2015, http://www.npr.org/2015/03/02/390119321/50-years-ago-selmas-bloody -sunday-sparked-voting-rights-act.

and the movement called for school children to join in a march, many of the parents and school principals were against it—and they locked down the schools. But my new friend, and many of her friends, climbed out of their school windows and joined King in the streets. "We got fire hosed by Sheriff Bull Connor's water cannons and chased by his dogs." She told me all about how that felt on our long drive to Selma. "But we were ready and proud to be there."

Of course, it turned out to be the presence of children in the streets of Birmingham that finally made the difference and won the Birmingham campaign. What a story to hear again, from one of the children who was there; what a way to begin that day, on my way to the fiftieth anniversary of the Selma march.

When we arrived in Selma, I was led to a section of seats for civil rights and faith leaders who have been part of the struggle for a long time. President Obama was still en route to Selma, so we all enjoyed the precious time together at that very special place. We spent many hours just looking at that bridge and reflecting together. The words that kept coming to me were "courage" and "resistance." My question became: What bridge will we now have to cross?

Representative John Lewis, whose skull was cracked by the police that day as a young man, opened the main event. "On that day, 600 people marched into history, walking two by two, down this sidewalk. . . . We were so peaceful, so quiet, no one saying a word. We were beaten, tear gassed, some of us [were] left bloody right here on this bridge. Seventeen of us were hospitalized that day. But we never became bitter or hostile. We kept believing that the truth we stood for would have the final say."[5]

Then Lewis introduced the president: "If someone had told me, when we were crossing this bridge, that one day I would be back here introducing the first African-American president, I would have said you're crazy."[6]

President Barack Obama began his remarks with a tribute to Lewis, "It is a rare honor in this life to follow one of your heroes. And John Lewis is one of my heroes." Then he put the bridge in the context of history. "There are places and moments in America where this nation's destiny has been decided. . . . Selma is such a place. In one afternoon 50 years ago, so

5. "Rep. John Lewis (D-GA) at Selma 50th Anniversary," C-SPAN.org, March 9, 2015, http://www.c-span.org/video/?c4530609/rep-john-lewis-selma-50th-anniversary.

6. Ibid.

much of our turbulent history—the stain of slavery and anguish of civil war; the yoke of segregation and tyranny of Jim Crow; the death of four little girls in Birmingham; and the dream of a Baptist preacher—all that history met on this bridge."[7]

During Obama's remarks, the emotion from long-time civil rights leaders and young activists was palpable. What happened on this bridge, the president said, was "a contest to determine the true meaning of America," and where "the idea of a just America and a fair America, an inclusive America, and a generous America . . . ultimately triumphed."[8] But after celebrating the heroes of that generation, Obama did an important thing: he turned from the past to the future, highlighting the ongoing struggle going forward. Three short paragraphs summed up what the first black president of the United States believes that vision of the future should be. Obama challenged those who suggest that nothing has changed, or that American racism can't be changed, or that we now live in an essentially postracial America.

> We do a disservice to the cause of justice by intimating that bias and discrimination are immutable, that racial division is inherent to America. If you think nothing's changed in the past 50 years, ask somebody who lived through the Selma or Chicago or Los Angeles of the 1950s. . . . To deny this progress—our progress—would be to rob us of our own agency . . . our responsibility to do what we can to make America better.
>
> Of course, a more common mistake is to suggest that Ferguson is an isolated incident; that racism is banished; that the work that drew men and women to Selma is now complete, and that whatever racial tensions remain are a consequence of those seeking to play the "race card" for their own purposes. We don't need the Ferguson report to know that's not true. We just need to open our eyes, and our ears, and our hearts to know that this nation's racial history still casts its long shadow upon us.
>
> We know the march is not yet over. We know the race is not yet won. We know that reaching that blessed destination where we are judged, all of us, by the content of our character requires admitting as much, facing up to the truth.[9]

7. Barack Obama, "Remarks by the President at the 50th Anniversary of the Selma to Montgomery Marches," White House Office of the Press Secretary, March 7, 2015, https://www.whitehouse.gov/the-press-office/2015/03/07/remarks-president-50th-anniversary-selma-montgomery-marches.

8. Ibid.

9. Ibid.

When the president said, "The march is not yet over," I could feel my mind and heart asking, "What is next?"

Obama's moving remarks were among the very best of his presidency. Of course, Barack Obama's own "patriotism" has been attacked from America's white right; it happened again in the weeks just before his Selma address by former New York City mayor Rudy Giuliani, who questioned whether Barack Obama really loved our country.[10] So it was appropriate and significant for the first black president to define, at Selma, what patriotism really means.

> What greater expression of faith in the American experiment than this, what greater form of patriotism is there than the belief that America is not yet finished, that we are strong enough to be self-critical, that each successive generation can look upon our imperfections and decide that it is in our power to remake this nation to more closely align with our highest ideals? . . . It's the idea held by generations of citizens who believed that America is a constant work in progress; who believed that loving this country requires more than singing its praises or avoiding uncomfortable truths. It requires the occasional disruption, the willingness to speak out for what is right, to shake up the status quo. That's America.[11]

When I heard the words "America is not yet finished," I looked around at the incredibly diverse crowd of the thousands gathered together at the Edmund Pettus Bridge with their eyes on our first black president. I especially noted all the local young people who were there and thought of my own teenage boys, Luke and Jack. What would it take to keep finishing America, this "constant work in progress," and how would they, the next generation, do that?

After the president spoke, some of us were graciously invited to join him and his family in walking up the bridge with the "foot soldiers"— those who marched on the bridge that historic day fifty years before. The feelings I had as I marched behind those humble and courageous heroes of that first march were very deep and almost overwhelming. All of them were, of course, quite elderly now, but all were still marching, some in wheelchairs.

10. Darren Samuelsohn, "Rudy Giuliani: President Obama Doesn't Love America," *Politico*, February 18, 2015, http://www.politico.com/story/2015/02/rudy-giuliani-president-obama-doesnt-love-america-115309.html.

11. Obama, "50th Anniversary of the Selma to Montgomery Marches."

Walking alongside people such as C. T. Vivian, with his characteristically bright smile and incredible humility, and next to a woman over a hundred years old being pushed along by her daughter, I felt so honored and blessed to *just be in the presence* of these men and women whose march literally changed the world. And hugging my friend John Lewis at the top of the Edmund Pettus Bridge brought joyful tears to my eyes.

On the bridge, I asked myself: What bridge must the next generation now cross? What bridge must we all cross now that these old foot soldiers won't be able to? They crossed their bridge, but what bridge must we and our children cross now? What is our bridge?

Then it struck me, standing there at the top of the Edmund Pettus Bridge with my tears and my friends: *the next bridge to cross is America's transition from a majority white nation to a majority of racial minorities.* That will be ours and our children's bridge to cross.

The historic demographic shift that will occur in the next few decades, and the very prospect of it, is what now lies beneath the current racial tensions in America: the racial divisions over policing issues that have so visibly erupted, the opposition to immigration reform, the battle over voting rights, and even the personal animosity to President Obama, who symbolizes this enormous demographic transition.

Although it is possible that the demographic changes could just lead to greater collisions and increasing racial tensions and conflicts, it is also possible that we could cross the bridge together, willingly and hopefully, to a new American future, a new America.

Seeking, finding, learning, welcoming, embracing, and creating new relationships and frameworks for a richly multiracial culture, with economics and politics that reflect our diversity, is *the great task before us now*. I believe that will be the mission of the next generation, and I believe many will claim it. As the president said, "It is you, the young and fearless at heart, the most diverse and educated generation in our history, who the nation is waiting to follow."[12]

My ride back to Birmingham the next day reminded me again of "courage." Ironically and blessedly, my new driver also had a story to tell. Again, he was from Birmingham and was one of the children who marched in the streets. I asked him how old he was then. "I was eight years old! I was

12. Ibid.

the youngest and littlest one around me; so they called me 'the runt.'" We talked about how it is often "the runts" who change history. He remembered staying home from school in order to march. He also remembers being hit by the water cannons and chased by the dogs, "But I was fast!" Today he is retired, but still a Church of God in Christ minister when he can serve. His story of courage, even as a child, was the perfect ending to my memorable days in Birmingham and Selma.

Let's look at what it will mean to walk the bridge to a "new America." Perhaps the first and most important thing to learn is how to listen, really listen to one another, as we are walking together to a new America.

Believing the Stories

When it comes to criminal justice, immigration, economic fairness, voting rights, or educational equity, we clearly need to change national habits, policies, structures, and directions. But what changes our attitudes in ways that lead us to want to make those big changes? What changes our hearts and minds? Usually it's when the issues become personal—when we meet the people, see the faces, and hear the human stories that show us something is very wrong and we need to help change it. *Stories* are what change us.

In 1992, Los Angeles police officers who had been filmed severely beating a black man named Rodney King were acquitted of all charges. After the riots that followed that verdict, I joined a delegation of international church leaders in Los Angeles, where the unrest had exploded. We were there to conduct hearings and listen to community groups around the city about the causes of the angry violence.

Simi Valley had been the site of the Rodney King trial, the place where an overwhelmingly white jury had acquitted the police officers seen brutally beating King on an infamous video. Overnight, this sleepy, affluent suburb became famous as a bastion of upper-middle-class white racism. It was a notoriety not welcomed by the citizens of Simi Valley.

Several of our delegation traveled to the embattled suburb one night to participate in a dialogue that had been set up between a black church and a white church in Simi Valley. Yes, despite the public perception, there were also black people in Simi Valley, mostly middle-class professionals like most of their neighbors. These two churches, while inhabiting the same community, had never before met or spoken together. The atmosphere was tense, perhaps made more so by the presence of outside "church leaders." Nonetheless, a substantial and fascinating conversation followed.

The pivotal moment in the discussion came when a black mother spoke. "My son is a member of the Los Angeles Police Department," she said, "and I become deeply concerned for his safety when he goes undercover." Across the room, a white woman responded with great sympathy. "I am a mother too, and I know how you must feel. If my son were a police officer and worked undercover, I'd be frightened to death if he had to work with those gangs."

"No, you don't understand," replied the first woman. "When my son takes off that police uniform, he looks like any other young black man in Los Angeles. I'm not afraid of the gangs, I'm afraid of what white Los Angeles police officers might do to my son." You could see the stunned look on the face of the white mother. It was an absolute shock to her to think that this mother would fear her son's fellow police officers more than gang members. Nothing in her experience prepared her to hear something like that.

All eyes in the room were on the two women. To her great credit, the white woman *believed* the testimony of the black woman. She was clearly amazed at the story, but she was convinced the black mother was telling the truth.

That was the turning point in the conversation. More stories followed. Other black mothers expressed their fears about the safety of their children, especially their sons. African American businesspeople told stories of being dragged out of their expensive cars, accused of being drug dealers, and spread-eagled across their car hoods by white police officers. And then white suburbanites shared their fears about driving through black neighborhoods, of being terrified by the riots, and of feeling defensive when the media portrayed Simi Valley as a racist enclave.

Real conversation took place that night. People listened to one another and took their neighbors seriously. Even without great class differences in Simi Valley, the utterly different life experiences across the racial divide were evident to everyone in the room. Many expressed regret that such conversations hadn't occurred before and were especially embarrassed because they were all Christians. Both sides stated how much they valued this opportunity, and people from each church were appointed to set up more meetings.

Ever since that night in 1992, I have watched for that response from white people when hearing the stories of people of color. Do they believe what they are hearing? Can mothers trust other mothers, parents trust other parents, students trust other students, Christians trust other Christians—across racial lines? It is precisely that kind of conversation we need now in local communities across the nation since the parable of Ferguson.

America's successful future depends upon honest cultural exchanges between different racial communities. We need focused, honest, serious, and disciplined conversations on race between white people and people of color. And people on all sides need to find the freedom and safe space to share their very different experiences, to voice both their fears and their hopes.

I remember doing that at my own college, Michigan State University, when racial tensions were strong in the late 1960s. MSU was a land-grant institution that attracted many students from Michigan's rural areas, which were not much different from rural areas in the American South. But the university also attracted students from inner-city Detroit whose lives couldn't have been more different from their new classmates and dorm mates who were raised on farms. I was a resident assistant in my dormitory, and I watched the interactions on my floor between young urban black men with music boxes or big radios on their shoulders and other big white guys on hockey scholarships from rural Canadian and Michigan towns.

It was clear that some conversation needed to take place. So I offered my room, one night each week, for an honest conversation that I moderated. People were invited to share their feelings, experiences, and opinions across racial lines, but not to attack one another, and instead *listen* to one another's perspectives. We created a safe space to talk, where all the guys had to respect one another, where they learned to listen to one another. The numbers grew and before long spilled into the hallway; the meeting became packed each week. I saw students from starkly different cultural backgrounds become quite good at listening and even drawing one another out as we went deeper into the discussions. The following spring, racial tensions broke out on campus, but our housing complex was peacefully quiet, because students had been talking and listening to one another. We were even able to send some of our black and white students into places on campus where the tensions were the strongest—to help calm things down.

Over the last fifty years, I have seen those same successful conversations taking place many times across racial lines when people really sit down and commit themselves to an honest and respectful discussion, with good and effective moderation. It is critical to understand how racism has impoverished us all if we hope to dismantle the racial structures and attitudes that still shape American life and block our greatest potential as a nation. And rather than waiting for the politicians to act, local leaders and communities should begin to convene those conversations themselves.

Together, we will get to the place where our racial and cultural diversity is understood not as America's biggest problem but as our greatest gift. If we can do that, it will also be our best contribution to a world threatened as much by ethnic, racial, and religious conflict as by economic confrontation and environmental catastrophe. The consequences of not talking are too great to risk, while the rewards and potential of racial justice and healing are too important to miss.

The Geography of Race

Fifty years after the great victories of the civil rights movement, and Dr. King's dramatic reminder that Sunday morning at eleven o'clock was the nation's most segregated hour, most Americans still live most of their lives segregated from other races. It is the *geography of race* that continues to separate us, keeping us in different neighborhoods, schools, and churches and keeping us from talking more deeply together and developing the *empathy* and *relationships* that bring understanding, friendships, common citizenship, and even spiritual fellowship.

When you are not with other people, you simply don't know what their lives are like, what they are most concerned about, what their core values or top priorities are, what they are currently going through, and what they most want for their children. You learn about other people when they are your neighbors, or parents of your children's classmates or teammates, or the fellow members of your religious congregation. Being coworkers in the same workplace can certainly help, but often work is not the most interactive or personal place, nor does it offer time to more deeply connect to people.

I want to encourage you to check out a remarkable interactive map released in 2013 by the University of Virginia's Weldon Cooper Center for Public Service. Called the Racial Dot Map, it uses 2010 census data to create a map of the United States with more than 308 million dots (one for each person in the United States), color-coded by race.[13] You can look at the racial distribution of our population at the national level or zoom in to look at particular states, cities, or even neighborhoods. This map reveals how racially segregated we still are as a nation in terms of where we live. Looking at the wide, national-level zoom, you can clearly see how we are racially separated by region, with whites overwhelmingly in the Midwest, African Americans in the Deep South, Latinos in the Southwest, and Asian Americans in California, to give a few very broad examples.

What's considerably more instructive is what happens when you start to zoom in on specific counties, towns, and large cities. It quickly becomes apparent that the cities with the most racial diversity, in terms of having significant black, white, Latino, and/or Asian populations, also seem to be the most racially segregated. Whether it's big cities, such as Los Angeles, New York, Chicago, Houston, or Washington, DC, or less racially diverse smaller cities, such as Holland, Michigan, or Iowa City, Iowa, it's immediately apparent from this color-coded map where the black and Latino neighborhoods are, where a city's Asian enclaves are located, and where the white people live.

As we pointed out in chapter 3, 75 percent of white Americans have *entirely* white social networks.[14] That means that, except for perhaps the workplace, they have no meaningful interactions with people of color. I believe that is a very important statistic to explain where we are today, especially with the nation's deep history of racism and the clear data about the implicit racial biases we have been discussing. The lack of direct, regular, and personal connection makes it very difficult to get beyond the racial biases and stereotypes that are still so very strong in white American society. And the media is still absolutely full of racial bias and stereotypes,

13. Dustin Cable, "The Racial Dot Map," Weldon Cooper Center for Public Service at the University of Virginia, July 2013, http://www.coopercenter.org/demographics/Racial-Dot -Map.

14. Robert P. Jones, "Self-Segregation: Why It's So Hard for Whites to Understand Ferguson," *Atlantic Monthly*, August 21, 2014, http://www.theatlantic.com/national/archive/2014/08 /self-segregation-why-its-hard-for-whites-to-understand-ferguson/378928/.

with some cable and radio shows demonstrating outright racism.[15] The data and polling also show that people who do have regular, sustained, and personal contact with people and families of other races have much more positive, respectful, and reciprocal relationships.[16] So how do we change our racial geography?

Changing Our Geography

The geography of racism must be deliberately changed. Proximity is the key to understanding. Where we live, where we spend our time, where we work or volunteer, who we know, and where we become involved can all change the geography of racism. Because it is about relationships—the personal and family contact that breaks down bias and stereotypes.

There are many ways to break up and transform the geography of racism. Perhaps a most dramatic way is when white people actually move into neighborhoods of color. That's what our Sojourners community did when we began in Chicago and then moved to Washington, DC, in 1975. Those decades were certainly a transforming experience for the hundreds of people who were part of our community and the thousands who came to visit us over the years. Civil rights activist Stokely Carmichael reportedly said, "Your view of the world depends on what you see when you get out of bed in the morning." I don't know if the quote is accurate, but the point certainly is. From the days we moved into poor neighborhoods of color, our views of the world began to change and kept changing. We always hoped our presence and work in those neighborhoods would help make them better places, but one thing I do know is how much our living and being present in places like that changed our worldviews and life experience and shaped everything else we had to say to the world through *Sojourners* magazine.

We started by settling in with our new neighbors and doing a lot of listening. What was happening in the neighborhood? Who were the natural leaders already there? What did people want or need, and what didn't

15. For a long list of recent examples, see the "Diversity & Discrimination" section of the Media Matters for America website, http://mediamatters.org/issues/diversity-discrimination.

16. Frances E. Aboud and Morton J. Mendelson, "Cross-Race Peer Relations and Friendship Quality," *International Journal of Behavioral Development* 27, no. 2 (March 2003): 165–73, doi: 10.1080/01650250244000164.

they want? How could we begin to join in with the good things going on and help change the things that everyone thought were bad? The more we listened, the more we learned; and the more we paid attention, the more our old ideas and assumptions fell away.

I will never forget the day we pulled up in our moving truck to the two houses we had rented in Washington, DC. There was a whole group of young people out on the street who offered to help us move in if we would give them all the old mattresses they knew would be in our rental houses. Of course we agreed, and when we saw all the nasty mattresses that were left in those rented houses, we were very glad to be rid of them but wondered why the kids wanted them so badly.

A few days later we were invited by the kids to come down the street, and we saw why the mattresses were so popular. In the alley behind the houses, the kids had assembled dozens of old mattresses, placing them end to end. Then we witnessed some of the best gymnastics we had ever seen, with these inner-city kids bouncing high off the mattresses instead of traditional gymnastic mats. They proudly called themselves "the Afrobats," and many of these urban gymnasts went on to win city tournaments. Following their careers, we learned how talented young urban athletes seldom get the schooling they need.

With our neighbors and at the request of several families, we began tutoring in our homes each day after school. Then we started a daycare center for children, which was a big felt need because good, safe, and affordable child care was so necessary and hard for poor working families to find. We eventually established a neighborhood center, providing "safe space," a visible presence in the community, a food bank, and basic foods distribution for hungry people, and, ultimately, an afterschool program for children and young adults focused on tutoring, computer learning, and self-help. Sojourners Neighborhood Center became our base in the community, with a picture of African American hero Sojourner Truth inside the front door. In the summertime, we pioneered a new model for a "Freedom School," with an all-day program centered on developing math and reading skills, teaching critically needed conflict resolution and self-esteem formation to counteract drugs and early sexual activity, and every day immersing young people in African American and global black history. We ended up joining our freedom school with a national effort to create such places started by Marian Wright Edelman and the Children's

Defense Fund. My sister, Barb Tamialis, developed and led the center for many years and became an expert in child development, which she now teaches in a California community college after she and her husband, Jim, moved out there to be close to their grandchildren.

The center became a place for leadership development. Many volunteers came to join us from Howard University, one of the nation's leading historically black colleges. A typical story for us was a young African American Howard student tutoring and mentoring a young black girl from the neighborhood. The college student would end up feeling that the time spent with the young kid was the best time in *her* week—the college student's. She felt like she was making a difference in somebody's life, which is rare these days. It helped shape her vocation as a student, changing what she wanted to do and be when she graduated from college. Meanwhile, the young girl being mentored gained in her self-confidence. She was being shaped and empowered by the young Howard student: "She's really smart; she thinks I'm smart, and she thinks I could go to college too. Maybe I will!"

At the same time, people from the neighborhood (not Howard students) became the leaders of efforts such as the food program. One who became a dear friend was James Starks. He had been an alcoholic for many years, but when he came to the food program, he decided that he could help. He became one of our key leaders and, with lots of support, overcame his addictions. I will never forget a terrible, snowy day in Washington, DC, when the schools and federal government both closed; but James insisted on picking up the food that would be needed for the next day. Somehow, he got the neighborhood center van through the snow and brought back the food, so we had a full line of groceries for all the families who needed them. We were even able to help James save his eyesight, after years of drinking, with access to successful cornea surgery. When he finally died of old age, I spoke at the funeral service for James Starks at the Sojourners Neighborhood Center. Family and friends of James came up from his home state of North Carolina to witness a house full of people in Washington, DC, who had come to love, respect, and depend upon the leadership of James Starks—an alcoholic whom most people had written off years before.

We also organized the young people who came to the center every day around political issues that impacted their lives and our neighborhoods, which got the attention of our city council members and our congressional representative, Eleanor Holmes Norton, who came to the center to have discussions with our young leaders. Sojourners also ran shelters for the city's growing homeless population in church parish halls in nearby congregations that eventually took over the leadership themselves and developed some of the most creative and successful housing programs for homeless people in our city.

One thing always led to another. The tutoring led to relationships with families. The Williams family had nine kids all under the age of fourteen involved with the tutoring programs in our living rooms. One day ten-year-old Ronnie said his mother had told the children they were leaving because they were being evicted from their apartment. We knew little about low-income housing in those days, but Ms. Williams shared the eviction documents with us. We discovered they were illegal and just a way for lawyers to scare low-income people into leaving their homes, which could then be renovated and rented or sold at higher rates to the new "urban pioneers" who wanted to come in. When we appeared with Ms. Williams in court, the case was dropped without any discussion.

But Ronnie came back with the same message a few months later—they were leaving, this time because of rats in the house; older sister Theresa had just snatched baby Isaac out of his crib after a rat had got into it. I remember going into the house with boots and baseball bats and encountering the biggest rats I had ever seen. We couldn't get the rats out, so the Williams family moved in with us for almost a year. Sharing a house with the family taught me more about generational urban poverty than had all my college courses in social science. And that's how we kept learning.

Another woman from across the street came by one day to say that she was also being evicted and heard we helped people in that situation. She wanted to stay and fight, and asked for our help. When the owner laughed at our offer to help make the apartment building a cooperative for those living there and predicted he would make a "hundred percent profit" in his housing "flip," we decided to move in to the building ourselves and fight the eviction. The next morning, a federal marshal, backed up by many DC police, came to the building, arrested us, and took us to jail; the story was told in *The Washington Post*, describing the growing trend in the city toward "gentrification" that was moving poor black residents out of their homes and moving higher-paying white people in.

After dealing with the realities of gentrification that led to the evictions of low-income people, taking some of those homeless families into our homes, and getting arrested for blocking evictions, we started community organizing! With local neighborhood leaders we created the Southern Columbia Heights Tenants Union (SCHTU), which eventually turned a dozen properties into tenant-owned cooperatives, for which we got the financing outside the neighborhood, and SCHTU effectively influenced housing policy in the DC City Council, including rent control in the District of Columbia. Perry (Perk) Perkins was our chief organizer, and when he went back home to the South, he became a lead organizer for the Industrial Areas Foundation (IAF), where he now leads all their organizing work in Louisiana.

It is likely true that a number of young people from Columbia Heights might not be alive today without the protection and formation of the Sojourners Neighborhood Center, since at that time ours was one of the most violent neighborhoods in Washington, DC. But those decades in the black community mostly changed those of us who were white people, teaching us to see the world in a completely different way—from the point of view of our neighbors, friends, housemates, and coworkers in food programs, alternative schools for youth, and neighborhood organizing. Only our direct and daily involvement in the communities and the people there could change our minds, hearts, and worldviews. Just reading and studying and thinking wouldn't have done the same thing. Not until issues impact people who are your friends do they become personal for you.

We learned to live in neighborhoods that most said were too dangerous to live in, where cab drivers didn't want to take us or our visiting families and friends, and where gunfire was common on most nights. But that neighborhood became our home, and our neighbors turned it into our neighborhood too. Yes, we did have some break-ins and some robberies and a few scary incidents. One of the most dramatic happened to me.

Street Blessing

After two decades of living and working in many of America's meanest streets, I was mugged. As a veteran urban pastor and organizer, I'm embarrassed to say that I was taken by surprise. It was only six o'clock in the evening, but already dark, when I headed out to my pickup truck parked at

Thirteenth and Fairmont Streets NW, right around the corner from where I lived in DC's Fourteenth Street corridor, which was then quite violent.

Looking over my shoulder in response to the sound of running feet, I saw four young men bearing down on me. The first one hit my slightly turned head with something sharp enough to open a cut below my left eye. The force of the blow and a push from two others sent me to the pavement. One of them yelled, "Keep him down! Get his wallet!" It finally registered. These guys were trying to roll me over.

Still under forty at that time, I popped up quickly, which seemed to surprise them. Seeing no weapons flashed, I squared to face my attackers. This was the first chance we had to really see one another face-to-face. They were just kids—three about fourteen or fifteen, and one smaller boy who couldn't have been more than thirteen. The boys backed up a little when they saw I was bigger than they had expected. The one who had hit me moved into a boxing stance while the others circled. It's good to make eye contact with a group's leader, so I did. The little guy began attempting some ineffectual karate kicks, which I assumed he had seen on television.

Intending not to hurt them, only to fend them off, I instinctively began to scold these lost young souls. I knew lots of kids like them, but didn't recognize these boys as being from our neighborhood. So I told them just to stop it, to stop terrorizing people, to stop such violent behavior in our neighborhood. "Who are you guys anyway?" I asked them. Finally I shouted at them, "I'm a pastor!" And I told them if they wanted to try to beat up and rob a pastor, they should come ahead. Maybe it was my desire to confront these kids with what they were doing and give a personal identity to their potential victim. But invoking the authority of the church in the street is hardly a sure thing these days, when our churches often have such little involvement in those streets.

Whatever it was that changed their minds, my assailants turned and ran. "Get back here," I shouted after them—then instantly realized it probably wasn't a good thing to say at that point. But then something unusual happened. The littlest kid, who couldn't have been more than four and a half feet tall, turned back to look at me as he ran. With a sad face and voice, the young karate kicker said, "Pastor, ask God for a blessing for me." He and his friends had just assaulted me. The little kid had tried so hard to be one of the big tough guys. Yet he knew he needed a blessing. The young boy knew he was in trouble.

Here were young people demonstrating social pathologies that make them a very real threat. Yet they are themselves also vulnerable and feel very alone. Their dangerousness should not be underestimated, as some socially concerned individuals who live at a safe distance sometimes do. On the other hand, these young perpetrators are much more than just social pathologies, as some politicians in Washington, DC, seem to imply.

Driving to the doctor to get stitched up, I was especially conscious of other people out walking, many just coming home from work and being more vulnerable than I am on the street—so many potential victims for my gang of four. All these people deserve to be safe on the streets of their own neighborhoods. That must be a bottom line to which we commit ourselves. But we must also commit ourselves to those kids. They too must become our bottom line. What they need most is nurture, discipline, and a real opportunity. Many of them have none of those right now. And as long as they don't, our streets will get more dangerous.

How do we rebuild the relationships, structures, and environments that provide these essentials for our young people? The rhetoric of "being tough on crime" and "locking them up" won't do it. And it's certain that what's needed is beyond what the government can do, though it does need to really *invest* in these children. But bringing about change will take all of us—our families, churches, our businesses, and all the organizations in our communities. It will test our moral resolve and political will and require both the private and the public sector to become involved in new and creative ways. No one gets to opt out. The violent behavior of street criminals must be stopped. But the four young men who attacked me are more than just criminals. They are also children—our children—and they are in a great deal of trouble. And getting to know them personally makes all the difference. The violence will only be turned around when the young people who now roam wild are included in our future. Young people who feel like they are part of society's future will not be attacking the rest of us on the streets. If we can find the ways to include them, we will all receive a blessing.

Relocation

Perhaps the best part of those early Sojourners years was our Sunday worship service in our little neighborhood center, which became a multiracial place of faith—a worship I still dearly miss. We had both good preaching and a wonderful liturgy every week, coming right out of our experience in the neighborhood and the world around it. A local gardener was one of our most faithful attendees and liked to tell others, "People from around the world come to my church every Sunday!" And he was always very happy to greet all the visitors to Sojourners Community. The people you share life and faith with end up changing and shaping your own world-view, and that's what happened to us. We began to work with several faith communities like our own around the country—an effort we called "the Community of Communities"—which were mostly in poor neighbor-hoods across America.

At the same time, John Perkins from Mississippi was starting the Chris-tian Community Development Association (CCDA) based on the "three R's—relocation, redistribution, and reconciliation." John was a dear friend and strong Sojourners ally with whom I often traveled to conferences and places where people were trying to build communities in new and multi-racial ways. CCDA is now a vibrant and powerful network of nearly one thousand wonderfully diverse community organizations, parachurches, and local congregations in every state in America; and their annual multi-racial conference attracts three thousand people every year. CCDA makes a difference on the ground in many places, doing community economic development, building new institutions that serve neighborhoods, and taking on national issues such as immigration reform and mass incarcera-tion—from the bottom up with the people who are most impacted by those problems. Read the stories of CCDA, and you too will be inspired and instructed in how to change the geography of racism. You can visit CCDA's website at http://www.ccda.org/.

One of the reasons Sojourners came to Washington, DC, was to be close to the Church of the Saviour, founded by Gordon Cosby, who became a mentor and spiritual director for me until he died in 2013 at the age of ninety-five. When the Church of the Saviour started in the late 1940s, it was one of the first interracial churches in the still-segregated District of Columbia. Gordon Cosby shaped the vocations of so many that it made him one of the most influential pastors of his generation with one of the smallest churches. "C of S," as it is called, was a small church in a megachurch world, and eventually became several small churches, but with more social ministries than I had ever seen in any church—even the biggest ones. People lived in different places but all joined small "mission groups" that took on big visions and issues. They relocated Christian mission in the city of Washington, DC. Church of the Saviour started the first Christian coffeehouse in the nation, the Potter's House, in the midst of the city, to dream about how the city could be changed. They established Jubilee Jobs and Housing, Columbia Road Health Center for poor immigrants, the Christ House clinic for homeless men, Joseph House for dying people, and a legion of other projects that grew directly out of the church's commitment to both an "inward and outward journey." Dr. Janelle Goetcheus, who began Christ House and still lives there, has helped to quietly create a whole network of health care services for the most vulnerable people in the city of the most powerful. A very small group of Christians has made a very large difference in Washington, DC, while influencing many other churches around the nation and even the world.

Now there are many more stories of such "relocation," including the wonderful saga of the Simple Way Community in Philadelphia, where Shane Claiborne and other young Christians moved in to live and work in one of their city's poorest and most violent neighborhoods—three decades after Sojourners began. Their network also began to grow and was named another "community of communities"!

We would all probably say that what most changed us was *proximity to the poor*. We were all engaged in "simple living," and although voluntary poverty is nothing like forced poverty, it put us in direct and daily relationship with some of the poorest people in the country, which became a school for us—a very formative school—that enabled us to experiment with the gospel when it came to both race and poverty.

All these communities lived in a multiracial world because of where we chose to go. And while most of us began with a lot of talking about the visions we were called to and very excited about, we ended up doing a lot of listening to the people we came to meet and share our lives with. And that is what changes us in the end—who we see, who we meet, who we know, who we hang out with, whose families become like our families, whose joys and pains we come to understand and even begin to share. Relocation leads to listening and a very new kind of conversation.

But while not everyone moves into new neighborhoods, many people repeatedly visit the work and ministries they have been drawn into or the inner-city multiracial churches they now attend. The "new talk" we need to have between our racial communities can only come out of some kind of relocation—of time, energy, resources, faith, and friendship.

The New Talk

It's time for a new conversation on race in America, and this time it will also be a new generational discussion. The *old talk* is the one that black and brown parents still have with their children about how to behave in the presence of police—to protect themselves from them—an almost universal conversation that white parents know little about, as we discussed in chapter 1. The *new talk* is to make that old talk known to white parents and to together have a new conversation about the kind of country we want for all our children. Again, the issue is proximity. Our separated racial geography prevents those new talks from ever happening, so the changing of our geography has to be deliberate. Let's look at three places that can happen: schools, sports, and congregations.

Schools

One place we can start is with *parents*: parents of students at the same school with children of different races. Nearly all parents care deeply about the education of their kids, and they want the schools their children are in to be good for them and for all their children's classmates, too. My wife, Joy Carroll, served for many years at John Eaton Elementary School in Washington, DC, the most racially integrated of any public elementary school in the District of Columbia. As president of the Home School Association, a group like the PTA, she was always dealing with diversity—not just what the numbers were, but with the reality and depth of the relationships between children and parents across racial lines. I asked her to describe how diversity had to be deliberately worked for in our kids' school. Joy said, "Diversity doesn't just happen." Here is what she and some of her team say about it.

> What we have learned over the years is that diversity doesn't "just happen." Even in a healthy diverse environment like John Eaton we know that we must always be aware, thinking, consciously considering our life together as set in a historic culture of racism and white privilege.

I shared the role of PTA president at John Eaton with my copresident Mark Boss, an African American dad who says, "The diversity at John Eaton works because the adults value the global representative reality for their children that they had or did not have as children. In order for Eaton to thrive as it does, the conscious intention of inclusive diversity that permeates the environment must be continually reinforced by the adults. And we must understand that diversity is more than ethnicity. It includes culture, family structure, socioeconomics, physical differences, LGBTQ [identity] and religion."

At one of our meetings, another board member—a mom and a DC judge, Yvonne Williams—made the following observation, "At the 'Footloose' school dance a few weeks ago, I realized something. I picked up my pizza and drink and went to sit at a table with my friends to watch our kids dance. I turned around to hug my white friends [at] the table behind me and noted that my table was full of African American moms and dads and the table behind me was full of white moms and dads. I looked out at our kids who do a much better job than us when it comes to 'mixing it up' and sharing our lives. We like each other, but we need to work harder at 'mixing it up' as adults."

This was the start of a fresh commitment on behalf of the parent leadership to keep working on being intentional about our diversity and keeping it healthy. This is not a new work. It's been part of life at Eaton for years, and for Eaton to continue to be healthy in its diversity, the conversations must continue. Open, honest and sometimes painful or uncomfortable conversations need to be "scheduled" in some way. This is intentional diversity. If diversity is left to "just happen" it will eventually succumb to the sickness that is in the air we breathe in America.[17]

I especially see the difference that multiracial schools make in the lives of kids for whom that is "normal." Our children's experiences and assumptions about who teaches them is a very important issue. I recall when my fifth-grade son, Jack, came home on his first day of school to tell me about his new teacher and how much he liked her. My wife was also very pleased with the teacher Jack had for his last year of elementary school. But I didn't get to meet Jack's teacher until the first parent-teacher night several weeks later. When I walked into the class, I saw that Jack's teacher was an African American woman, as many other teachers at John Eaton are, and I realized that her race had never come up in any conversation at home. Neither Jack nor Joy had ever thought to mention it. One of Jack's classmates, a white kid whom I have coached on my Little League baseball team, once told me about a visit he made to a cousin's home in

17. Joy Carroll, email to the author, April 28, 2015.

another city. "It was really weird, coach; all the kids in the school were white."

Often, in the liberal white world, comments like this are made: "My son's teacher is African American, and she is really good!" The "and" is often a code word for "but" and implies levels of expectation. Recall how many times you have heard admired blacks talked about as "articulate," implying that most blacks aren't, or as "clean" and "smart," as Barack Obama was described by some when he was first running for president.

Our sons' middle school, Alice Deal, and high school, Woodrow Wilson, are also the most diverse public schools in the city at each of their levels. Of course, the teachers and principals at our boys' elementary, middle, and high schools are also very multiracial. Out of parental and student choices, strong and lasting relationships develop across racial lines, certainly for the students, but also for the parents. When national discussions erupted over the Trayvon Martin tragedy, Ferguson, and other incidents, those relationships can bear the conversations.

This is what makes segregated schools such a devastating part of the nation's racial geography. In cities such as Washington, DC, most young people of color go to public schools that are almost entirely made up of students of color. When it comes to resources, the most talented teachers and principals, parental involvement, size of classes, and attention to students, most of those schools suffer in comparison to the public schools in the suburbs that are mostly white. Honestly, do you think we as a nation would accept the low quality of our urban public schools if their students were mostly white, instead of mostly black and brown? I believe we all know the answer to that question.

Many of the schools in the poor black neighborhoods I have lived in are literally unsafe, with children being injured or even shot *during* their school days. Painfully, many have become more like prisons than schools, where we send our poorest students of color. Yet, as exemplary programs such as the Harlem Children's Zone, started by Geoffrey Canada in New York City, have shown, it is very possible to create transformative and successful educational environments, even in the nation's poorest neighborhoods. But that takes focused and strategic attention, dynamic leadership, disciplined commitment, and sustained resources. It really is a choice between cradle to college, as Geoff puts it, or school to prison (as we discussed in chap. 7).

Sports

Another place where those new discussions can occur is around sports and the sports teams on which our children play. We are a baseball family, with our two boys playing on many teams over the years with multiracial teammates, coaches, and leadership in the organizations shaping those programs. I have always been a Little League baseball coach, and Joy has been the commissioner at every level too. In baseball, talent and teamwork are the metrics and measuring sticks, not the race of one's teammates. For both of my boys, their teammates are their closest friends.

Both our boys were drawn early in their lives to the story of Jackie Robinson, the first black player in Major League Baseball, and each did elementary school projects on him. Luke's first travel team was named the Grays, after the Negro League team in Washington, DC, and it gave him and us his favorite uniform so far! Jack's Little League team was called the Eagles, named after a Negro National League team that played in Newark. Choosing names from the historic Negro Leagues gave us as Northwest Little League Baseball the chance to teach a little racial history to the kids and the parents on our Little League teams about what those black players had to go through during the decades they played and were not allowed to join the all-white big league teams, even though many of the Negro League stars were some of the very best players in the country.

It's not a coincidence that two of the very best white US senators on race were Bill Bradley, a Democrat from New Jersey who was once a professional basketball player for the New York Knicks, and Jack Kemp, a Republican who played football for the Buffalo Bills. Both said it was their experience of having black teammates who became such close friends that opened their eyes, helped them to understand the experience of black people and families, and motivated them to challenge the racism they saw and experienced all around them as white Americans.[18] Again, the issue is proximity.

When Dean Smith, the great basketball coach for the University of North Carolina, died, I wrote a piece about him called "Amazing Grace."[19] At his

18. John Blake, "When You're the Only White Person in the Room," CNN.com, September 11, 2014, http://www.cnn.com/2014/09/11/us/white-minority/; Michael Weisskopf, "Jack Kemp: Running a Very Different Republican Race," *Time*, May 8, 2009, http://content.time.com/time /politics/article/0,8599,1896881,00.html.

19. Jim Wallis, "Dean Smith: Amazing Grace," *God's Politics* (blog), *Sojourners*, February 12, 2015, http://sojo.net/blogs/2015/02/12/dean-smith-amazing-grace.

pastor's urging, Coach Smith recruited the first black basketball player in the Atlantic Coast Conference, Charlie Scott.[20] After Congress passed the Civil Rights Act of 1964—at the beginning of Smith's UNC career—he, his pastor, and a black theology student walked into the best restaurant in town, which had been adamantly segregated, and asked to be served. "When they saw Dean, they realized they had no choice," his pastor, Robert Seymour, told me. The opening of a historically segregated restaurant signaled a significant change in the public accommodations history of Chapel Hill, North Carolina. Seymour said of his dear friend, "He was willing to take controversial stands on a number of things as a member of our church—being against the death penalty, affirming gays and lesbians, protesting nuclear proliferation."[21] Of course, we were thrilled when we learned years ago that Dean Smith was a subscriber to *Sojourners* and a contributor to Sojourners Neighborhood Center! When he would order twelve copies of every new book I wrote, I dreamed it was for the UNC basketball team, but it turned out to be for the Sunday school class that Smith taught in his church. Dean Smith did, however, take his players to visit prisoners and even death row—where he lobbied his state's governor for clemencies. Sports and sports figures can make a difference.

Being a Little League baseball coach (for eleven years and twenty-two seasons!) has given me a place to reflect on our nation's racial issues. Playing baseball brings you closer together. My son Luke often says his high school teammates are the best friends he's ever had, and in every level of Little League, my players always testify in our last team meeting of the season how they have all become such close friends. Being teammates really does overcome racial bias and prejudice, because it is the issue of proximity that finally helps human beings to understand one another and learn empathy.

On Little League teams we are all cheering for one another, looking out for one another, picking one another up when we fall down or make a mistake, and learning to be positive as we work together for our common goals. More affluent families with two parents and multiple cars are more easily able to take players to and from games and practices, while less-affluent families with one parent and one car, at most, have work schedules

20. "Dean Smith Dies at Age of 83," ESPN.com, February 12, 2015, http://espn.go.com/mens -college-basketball/story/_/id/12296176/dean-smith-former-north-carolina-tar-heels-coach -dies-age-83.
21. Robert Seymour, interview with the author, February 10, 2015.

that cause their players to need help with rides. And the kids see all that. But white players also see the black parents of their teammates who are lawyers and successful professionals—all serving to break up stereotypes.

Perhaps the best thing to watch is how the parents of players begin to talk and, over the course of a season or many seasons, become friends as well, across racial lines. It is especially interesting to see how conversations develop over time, moving from just baseball talk to school and future talk, to work and family talk, to sharing of life experiences talk, to national events talk—even sometimes having to do with race.

It's a great opportunity for white dads and moms to hear from black and brown dads and moms what they say to their sons and their daughters about how to behave around police. White parents can ask, "How did you feel when you had to tell your son he couldn't trust the law enforcement officials who are supposed to protect him, and that he had to protect himself from them?" Then the white parents can ask themselves, "How would I feel if I had to have that 'talk' with my children?"

These are both great places to begin those conversations—schools and sports.

Congregations

Another place for the needed interracial talks to occur is in and between religious congregations. We have already discussed how segregated religious congregations in America have been, and how that is beginning to change. Faith communities that are becoming more multiracial are some of the best places to have the difficult, painful, and personal conversations Americans need to have about our racial future. If we understand that we are all children of God together, created in the image of God, that's a good starting point to patiently explain to one another how different our racial experiences have been right here in our own country—and even in our churches. If we worship together, hear God's Word together, and confess our sins together, while our children are in Sunday school together, we may be in the best position of any group to have the new talks that Americans need to have for the sake of a more multiracial future.

Even here in the United States, it is the multiracial faith communities that reflect what the church was meant to be from its founding. Creating new relationships, "sister churches" between white and black and Latino and Asian American churches, across our own cities' racial dividing lines, is often a first and necessary step. Visiting one another's churches, hearing one another's preachers, singing with one another's choirs all can be perspective- and life-changing experiences. Pastors must make racial reconciliation and justice a *regular pulpit topic* in their own churches. But all this is more than just creating "Kumbaya" moments of emotional fellowship. It's also about setting the stage for the new talks we need to have together about the changes in policy and practices we need in our country. Only with deliberate efforts and energy to build cross-racial relationships between churches can we create the "safe spaces" we need for the hard but necessary conversations we must have in order to build a bridge to a new America.

Churches can also play a crucial role in convening and hosting public conversations and problem solving in the community—gathering together believers and nonbelievers alike. I vividly remember one such conversation I attended in Spokane, Washington.

I had been invited to go to Spokane for two days, first to speak at a Christian college, Whitworth University, and the next day to help moderate an event hosted by a local church with young people from the streets of Spokane—where there had been growing crime. The increasing violence in the city had made the whole community fearful, and some of the churches in the area were trying to respond by focusing on how to help the young people involved. Several youth workers from the church had made connections on the street and persuaded many of the street youth to show up for the day at the church.

Because of the crime crisis, many leaders from the Spokane community also showed up: educational leaders, business leaders, the police chief, the chief official charged with drug policies and enforcement, several other local pastors, and many concerned citizens.

The final session of the day was dramatic. In the front of the sanctuary, a whole row of young people from the streets sat facing the crowd and were invited to *tell their stories*. And they did. One young man, who was a clear leader, spoke of how his mother was a drug addict and her welfare check was gone each month after a few days, so he had to support all his siblings. McDonald's didn't pay enough for that, he told us, so he began dealing drugs himself and now was supporting dozens of people, including his whole extended family. Another said that he always wanted to attend college but had no money, so he joined a gang and kept studying on his own. A young woman spoke of being sexually abused at home by her stepfather, so she ran away and went to a gang for protection, but then had to become a gang girl. I listened to the stories, one after another, and watched the audience as community fears turned into community tears. Both the young street youth and gang members up front, and the audience listening to them, were multiracial—black, Hispanic, Asian, and white.

During an emotional question-and answer period, one pastor asked what those in the meeting could do to help. A young man replied with his version of what the pastors in the room knew was really an "altar call." He said, "I don't know, man, why don't you just do what you do best, and throw that in here!" Then, in a succession of responses, I saw the community respond to the altar call given by the young man. The president of Whitworth stood up. "After Jim Wallis spoke in our chapel yesterday I felt I needed to come today. Now I know why. I heard many of you say you always wanted to go to college. Well, if you can meet me next week, I will give you a personal tour of our university and, if you just pass your GED [high school equivalency], and we will help with that, you can come to Whitworth for free." A business owner was next. "Clearly some of you have some extraordinary entrepreneurial skills; I may just disagree with your personnel policies! But I have got some jobs for talented young people like you." The new pastor of a big downtown mainline church was next. He said, "I have just arrived in town to a big church with no people inside. I heard many of you say you had no safe place to go after school and even do your homework. Well, starting tomorrow, our church will be open to you." My favorite response came from a middle-aged woman who said, "I am not a university president, don't own a business, or pastor a church. But I work at the McDonald's right downtown and get a fifteen-minute break in the morning and one again in the afternoon. Some of you said you don't ever have anybody to talk to. Well, come by McDonald's and I will talk to you and even buy you a Big Mac."

Time and time again, in communities around the country, I have seen congregations become gathering places for "town meetings" about things that have to be solved in their cities or regions. At our best, congregations can become "safe spaces" for those vital discussions, not about religious doctrine but about the *common good*.

The young man on the panel of urban kids asked for the right thing: "Just do what you do best, and throw that in here!" Just offer what you have. And that is the right question to ask in every neighborhood with the problems we have examined in this book. What do you have to offer and how can you offer it? That is an "altar call" for all of us.

What makes for a genuine multiracial life experience is what happens in the most personal places in one's life. Who are our friends, neighbors, and coworkers? Who comes over for dinner? Whose homes do we go to for dinner? Which kids are over at our house, and what houses do our kids go to? Who is at our kids' birthday parties, and whom do they have play-dates with?

Who do we have long talks with—parent to parent—about our plans and hopes for our children's futures? Whose pictures are up in our houses, and what public figures are honored and admired in our homes and in our dinner-time conversations? What kind of art is on the walls of our homes, and what music is heard and discussed? What shows do we watch on television, and who are the role models our children see? What sports do we play and watch, and which athletes do we most talk about? What movies or plays do we see, and who are some of our favorite actors, musicians, and cultural performers? What congregations do we go to: are they mostly people of our own race, or are they as diverse as the children of God? And, very important, what is the talk in our households about race and the public events happening around the country over issues of race?

Walking While We Talk

But of course, talking isn't enough. We need to *talk while we walk over the bridge to a new America*. That means *doing and not just talking*. What I would like to suggest is that we "talk" while we are "doing." There are some very critical racial justice issues that we have already discussed that require real action as well as better talking.

We have laid out what is wrong with our policing and criminal justice systems and made some clear recommendations for how to repair them. This should be a bipartisan issue and a cause around which people of different views on other issues could unite. Community policing, fair and unbiased procedures in arrests and prosecutions, commonsense sentencing laws, and the protection of criminal offenders from being stripped of their basic democratic rights as citizens after they are released from prison are all concrete goals that could be achieved. It's time to overturn the "new Jim Crow." And, on an even deeper moral and spiritual level, it is time to move from a retributive justice system, which is clearly not working, to a legal system based on restorative justice.

We spoke about the fundamental issues of voting rights. Political campaigns aimed at the suppression of minority votes are now in play in many states around the country. Those regressive campaigns are designed to slow, delay, and even veto the more diverse political future that America's new demographics will create. Both Democrats and Republicans should have a stake in reaching out to the racial minorities that will soon become the new majority, instead of trying to deny them their voting rights and power. This is a core issue for democracy and should not be politicized; even more deeply, this is a philosophical and moral issue about denying people their human citizenry and moral identity, rooted in our dignity of being made in the image of God.

We have revealed how broken and brutal our immigration system has become. Leaders from business, law enforcement, and the faith community have come together to say how bad the current immigration system is for a healthy economy, a safe and secure society, and a positive human environment where families and communities can be protected and even flourish. This, too, should be a bipartisan issue, and both Republicans and Democrats should serve the common good here and compete for the votes of the new Americans who come to our country hoping for a better life. That new demographic should be embraced with a reasonable, fair, and lawful immigration system.

We have discussed how societal acceptance of such massive economic inequality between whites and people of color is a continuing proof of our "original sin" of racism. Equal education, good jobs, and strong families are goals to which all of us—across racial lines—must not only aspire but commit to, a commitment that requires doing the creative and hard work that will make these realities possible. Racial justice will be a necessary part of racial healing.

As we walk across the bridge to a new America, we will *make justice more possible* with the changes we have outlined above, and we will grow stronger with the rich diversity of the many cultures we can all embrace.

We can go deeper to understand ourselves not as members of one race against another but as fellow citizens with common dreams for our future, hopes for our children, and commitments to a better nation. In the end, we can and must shed ourselves of our racial idols and divisions that have bound and separated us, and find our dignity together as the children of God all made in the image of the One who loves us all.

It is time to take the dramatic events we have experienced around immigration, voting rights, and the need for criminal justice reform and *turn those moments into movements*.

In his last book, Martin Luther King wrote, "We are faced with the fact that tomorrow is today. We are confronted with the fierce urgency of *now*."[22]

The time has come to cross the bridge to a new America.

---

22. Martin Luther King Jr., *Where Do We Go from Here: Chaos or Community?* (Boston: Beacon Press, 2010), Google eBook edition, conclusion.

Afterword

This book is dedicated to Vincent Harding, who died in 2014. One of my most important and dearest mentors is gone; there are countless other people across America—indeed, around the world—who felt the same as I did.

"Uncle Vincent has died and passed on," I told fifteen-year-old Luke and eleven-year-old Jack. I could see the sadness in their faces.

My boys have vivid memories, which we talked about on the night of Vincent's death, of a bitterly cold January day in early 2009 when the country inaugurated its first African American president. Barack Obama represented the dramatic changes occurring in American life regarding who would constitute the new America—a majority of minorities. In his late seventies, Vincent had come from his home in Denver to be present for the inauguration, which drew nearly 2 million people. I remember his health wasn't so good at the time, and the weather was unbelievably cold. But I had helped get Vincent tickets to attend President Obama's inauguration, and he was determined to accompany our family on that cold day. Vincent had a warmth in his heart and face that lifted the temperatures of all those around him.

What an amazing gift, to have your two boys watching the celebration—more than just the inauguration—of the first black president, accompanied by the whispered commentary of Vincent Harding. Vincent was a leading historian of the civil rights movement and a participant in those extraordinary events—and someone who could tell my children how Martin Luther King Jr. might have felt about this day.

At the Iliff School of Theology in Denver—the last place he worked and taught—Vincent's title was "Professor of Religion and Social Transformation." That was apt for someone who spent his life teaching and showing how faith was meant to transform the world, beginning with our own lives.

But the good news is that although he may have passed away, Vincent isn't really gone. His memory and presence will continue on with us in a "cloud of witnesses," which is the most important thing Vincent ever taught me.

The first time I met Vincent Harding was at a talk he gave at Eastern Mennonite University titled "The People around Martin Luther King Jr." We expected to hear about all the famous civil rights leaders from the movement. Instead, he spoke of those who had gone before, often many years before King, who had shaped, inspired, and sustained him like a family tree, a community of faith, or "a cloud of witnesses."

Vincent was not only a historian of the civil rights movement and a respected author, he was a professor who was also a practitioner, and a friend of Martin Luther King Jr. Vincent and his wife, Rosemarie, were part of the inner circle of the southern freedom movement. Vincent was also a speechwriter, and he wrote the historic speech that King delivered at Riverside Church in New York City on April 4, 1967, where he came out against the war in Vietnam and identified the "giant triplets" of racism, materialism, and militarism. Vincent Harding was a teacher, encourager, spiritual director, and chief cheerleader—in the deepest sense of that word—for many people.

Vincent became a contributing editor for *Sojourners* and came to our community many times, often to lead retreats. The two of us met often, when we were together in the same places around the country, or whenever I visited Denver. In February 1985, he preached a sermon at Sojourners Community worship on Hebrews 10, 11, and 12 called "In the Company of the Faithful,"[1] which became one of the best articles ever published in *Sojourners* magazine.

1. Vincent Harding, "In the Company of the Faithful," *Sojourners*, May 1985, http://sojo .net/magazine/1985/05/company-faithful.

This marvelous text from the book of Hebrews describes our "heroes of faith," the men and women who have gone before us, suffered incredible things, often died without seeing success, and yet remained faithful.

Harding says:

> Here are the people. Here are the beautiful, suffering, overcoming people . . . faithful ones tortured, refusing to accept release; the people suffering mocking, scourging, chains, imprisonment; and some stoned, some cut in two, some going around in caves and in deserts.
>
> What a wild company we belong to! I mean, do you understand? These are our fore-parents. Do you understand? These are the founders of our faith. Do you understand? These are the old alumni. These are the ones who established the "institution"—these wild people, persecuted people, afflicted people, impractical people, going-out-not-knowing-where-they're-going people.[2]

The grand conclusion to the famous recitation of faith leaders in Hebrews 11 begins like this:

> Therefore, since we are surrounded by so great a cloud of witnesses, let us also lay aside every weight and the sin that clings so closely, and let us run with perseverance the race that is set before us, looking to Jesus the pioneer and perfecter of our faith, who for the sake of the joy that was set before him endured the cross, disregarding its shame, and has taken his seat at the right hand of the throne of God. (Heb. 12:1–2)

Harding always recounted the names of our more recent cloud of witnesses, such as Dorothy Day, Martin Luther King Jr., Rosa Parks, Fannie Lou Hamer, Sojourner Truth, Dietrich Bonhoeffer, Clarence Jordon, Thomas Merton, Howard Thurman, Oscar Romero, Malcolm X, Gandhi, and others. All their pictures, along with others, are on a wall in my home office, where I am writing this afterword. My own "cloud of witnesses," my "family tree," hovers over me as I think, write, and decide what I am going to next say or do to live out my own faith.

Vincent focuses, in particular, on the powerful meaning of Hebrews 11:39–40: "Yet all these, though they were commended for their faith, did not receive what was promised, since God had provided something better so that they would not, apart from us, be made perfect." Harding says this great cloud of witnesses in the book of Hebrews and those who have

2. Ibid.

come after them are heroes "whose fulfillment cannot take place without our own." Because, "apart from us, they should not be made perfect." Therefore, Vincent thought, they are "like a *great cheering squad* for us." Vincent would lift up for me a vivid picture of our battling in the dirt and mud of the field, while King, Fannie Lou Hamer, Sojourner Truth, Gandhi, Dorothy Day, and all our friends were now sitting in the bleachers, on the sidelines, enthusiastically *cheering* for us. He said, "In the midst of everything that seems so difficult, that seems so powerful, that seems so overwhelming, they are saying to us: 'We are with you,' and, 'There is a way through; there is a way to stand; there is a way to move; there is a way to hope; there is a way to believe. Don't give up!'"[3]

And this is not only about the "heroes" but also about all of us as people of faith and conscience. Vincent always reminded us: "Living in faith is knowing that even though our little work, our little seed, our little brick, our little block may not make the whole thing, the whole thing exists in the mind of God, and that whether or not we are there to see the whole thing is not the most important matter. The most important thing is whether we have entered into the process."[4] And he always invited us to add more names to the cloud of witnesses, especially those for each of us—parents, uncles and aunts, teachers, coaches, role models, and elders—who helped shape our lives and are now cheering up in the stands for us. Remembering them was always very moving for us.

Vincent Harding taught me about the company of the faithful as a living reality, a community of those who have gone before but now care about us because we are part of them and they are a part of us, "citizens of a country that does not yet exist—and yet does."[5] The Letter to the Hebrews is about the visionaries and leaders who "died in faith, not having received what was promised, but having seen it and greeted it from afar" (Heb. 11:13).

"To know them, to know that they are present," said Vincent Harding, "is to know that regardless of how alone we feel sometimes, we are never alone. We are never alone: nowhere, no how, in nothing. Never."[6]

Vincent's picture went up on my "wall of faith." And my vivid memories of him will help me remember that I am never alone. His spirit will

3. Ibid.
4. Ibid.
5. Ibid.
6. Ibid.

always endure with my family and with the many people he brought into the family of the faithful. Vincent Harding will *still* be one of the best cheerleaders I've ever had. And it is so good and comforting to know that as we cross the bridge to a "new America," we have such cheerleaders calling us forward.

Vincent Harding always was calling for and helping to create the new multiracial "beloved community" and the "more perfect union" that we must become. Today, he would understand, more than most, what it will mean to cross that bridge, and, I believe, he will always be there alongside me and all of us, encouraging us all to keep moving forward.

Thank you, Vincent.

Acknowledgments

I have a great many people to thank for this book. You really can't write a book alone; so many people and voices influence you, shape you, inspire you, and help expand your worldview and personal perspectives. And, of course, many people also help with the actual work. This is especially true for an author of European descent trying to write about America's original sin of racism.

So to the many people of color, over so many years, whom I have listened to, worked with and lived with, partnered and allied with, and who have been patient with me as I have learned—I owe you an enormous debt of gratitude. Graciousness is not the expected human response to the oppression of racism that all persons of color in the United States have experienced, but it is what I have consistently experienced in communities of color in America, especially in the places where people worship and exercise their faith. Being trusted with hearing the honesty, hurt, and anger that come from being so unjustly mistreated is also a gift that I will always treasure. Being able to glimpse the blessings and power of the multiracial beloved community that our Christian faith calls for—and that our nation, at its best, seeks to aspire to—has perhaps been the greatest gift to my life and family from the many people of color who have graced us with their presence and friendship. This book comes out of all of those relationships and experiences, which have taught me the incredible promise and potential of human diversity. This diversity is the intention of God and the best vision for our own country to become a "more perfect union."

To all the activists, academics, public servants, artists, preachers, pastors, grassroots organizers, and friends and neighbors from across the entire cultural and racial spectrum in America and around the world whose own experience, research, writings, speeches, and reflections provided a foundation for this book, I want to thank you deeply for the thoughts and insights that I cite in these pages.

In particular, I want to thank Dr. Gail Christopher and the Kellogg Foundation for their work on implicit bias, for speaking to those issues at the Sojourners Summit, and for their support of the important work of racial equity and reconciliation. I would also like to thank Eric Ward of the Ford Foundation for supporting our work in addressing the larger national dialogue on race and criminal justice, drawing on lessons being learned in Ferguson.

I want to especially thank a new and diverse generation of faith leaders, some of whom belong to an "emerging voices" group that I try to encourage, support, and mentor. Racial justice, reconciliation, and healing are a regular part of our conversations and work together. Conversations about the issues covered in this volume with many of them and discussions about the book itself were very helpful to me. Included in that group are people such as Adam Taylor, a rising national NGO leader who is also the new Chair of the Sojourners Board of Directors; Lisa Sharon Harper, who is our Sojourners Chief Church Engagement Officer and another of the public voices of our organization; Peggy Flanagan, who is an extraordinary community organizer, an Indigenous spokesperson, and a new state representative in Minnesota; Soong-Chan Rah, who is a brilliant theologian, author, and professor at North Park Theological Seminary; and Paul Alexander, the president of Evangelicals for Social Action and Sider Professor of Religion, Ethics, and Public Policy at Palmer Seminary of Eastern University (Soong-Chan, Peggy, and Paul are also Sojourners board members). Longtime conversations on race with other emerging voices have also been very helpful for me. These conversation partners include Leroy Barber, Alexie Torres Fleming, Onleilove Alston (who is also a former Sojourners intern and current board member), Kathy Khan, Mark Charles, Troy Jackson, Lindsay Mosely, Phil Jackson, Aaron Graham, Tim King, and Chris La-Tondresse (the latter three also former staff at Sojourners). All of these young leaders have influenced this book, with both Adam and Lisa giving it a good read with specific and very helpful feedback.

Many conversations with Gabriel Salguero, president of the National Latino Evangelical Coalition, and Noel Castellanos, president of the Christian Community Development Association, two dear friends and influential voices in America, have also been important to me in refining the message of this book.

The voices of allies in organizations such as PICO, including the Reverends Michael McBride, Alvin Herring, and Michael Ray Matthews, and leaders of the Samuel DeWitt Proctor Conference such as Dr. Iva Carruthers—whose organizations do important work on issues like policing and criminal justice—have also influenced this book. Watching and listening to the best African American preachers in the country has shaped my life and work, and there are too many to thank here, but they are well represented by prophets/preachers such as Rev. Dr. Otis Moss Jr., Rev. Dr. Otis Moss III, Rev. Dr. Frederick Haynes, Rev. Dr. Cynthia Hale, and Bishop Vashti Murphy McKenzie of the African Methodist Episcopal Church. Getting arrested and into trouble with many black pastors and leaders on a regular basis, such as Rev. Timothy MacDonald, Dr. Cornel West, and Dr. Obery Hendricks, has been a blessing! My admired colleague and friend Rev. Dr. William Barber II, of the Moral Mondays movement, now is offering that ministry of prophetic nonviolent civil disobedience to many church members today.

I was blessed to be at the fiftieth anniversary of the original crossing of the Edmund Pettus Bridge on "Bloody Sunday" a half century ago—a march that led to the Voting Rights Act in 1965. On Saturday, March 7, 2015, I was able to march over that bridge with the "foot soldiers" who risked their lives by marching fifty years ago, and I was especially blessed to walk beside two of my heroes, Rev. Dr. C. T. Vivian and Congressman John Lewis. I want to thank them both for their courage and inspiration.

The young leaders in Ferguson have also inspired me in the writing of this book. Some of them joined us for the faith leaders retreat Sojourners held in Ferguson in December 2014, which I describe in chapter 4. We also honored many of them at our annual leadership summit in June 2015. Specifically, I want to thank Johnetta ("Netta") Elzie, Brittany Ferrell, Brittini Gray, DeRay McKesson, Brittany Packnett, Tef Poe, Montague Simmons, Alexis Templeton, and Ashley Yates. I also want to lift up the clergy who joined these young people in the streets of Ferguson, especially exemplary leaders such as Rev. Traci Blackmon and Rev. Starsky Wilson.

From the beginning of Sojourners, racial justice has been central to our mission, and many of our board chairs and members have shaped, honed, and held us accountable to that message and mission. Some of those early board leaders who helped us lead on race were the Reverends Yvonne Delk, Calvin Morris, and Wallace Charles Smith. Many other board members have helped us lead on this issue over the years, including Leah Gaskin Fitchue, Art Cribbs, Ray East, Angela Glover Blackwell, Ivy George, Bill Watanabe, Staccato Powell, Robert Franklin, Wyvetta Bullock, and Michael Battle—and more recently key leaders such as Barbara Williams-Skinner, Mary Nelson, Wes Granberg-Michaelson, Joe Daniels, and Derrick Harkins. A new group of diverse board members will now help us move forward.

One of our earliest board members was Bill Pannell, the now-retired Dean of Chapel at Fuller Theological Seminary, who is also from my hometown of Detroit. He was the first black church leader to ever speak to me as a young teenager, full of questions, who sojourned into the city. His book *My Friend, the Enemy* was one of the first books I read about race. Bill was one of the most important black evangelical leaders and became a life-long mentor to me. Thanks also to Brenda Salter McNeil, who has been a consultant to Sojourners on our own practice of racial diversity as an organization.

Special thanks go to Rev. Jeffery Haggray, who was my pastor at First Baptist Church in Washington, DC, and his family, which became close to ours, for the many conversations we had about the process of trying to transform the church into a more multiracial "beloved community." We also shared the painful experience of seeing the established white leaders of that church reject this vision. Both the hope and the failures of churches seeking to become more racially diverse have influenced this book.

For the producing of this book I want to thank the good folks at Brazos Press for believing in me and in this book and wanting it to reach the many people who want or need to be part of new conversations and actions on race. In particular, let me thank President Dwight Baker, who persuaded me to come to the publishing house he leads because he believes in my message. I am grateful to Executive Editor Robert Hosack, who helped enlist me for Brazos and has been a creative editorial partner. Tim West and his editorial team were invaluable in making sure the message of the book was communicated with clarity and focus. I enjoyed working with Bryan Dyer, who oversaw the marketing and publicity with Executive Vice President of Sales and Marketing David Lewis. Great thanks go to Kathryn Helmers, my literary agent, with whom I had extensive, creative, and fruitful conversations about the message and mission of this book.

I want to thank Rob Wilson-Black, my CEO at Sojourners who manages the organization, which allows me time to write books like this, as well as Jim Simpson, my Executive Assistant, who manages my schedule and found ways to set aside specific blocks of time for me to write. Jim Rice, the editor of *Sojourners* magazine and the best editor of my writing over the years, somehow found the time to do a great edit of this book. Karen Lattea, our Vice President of Human Resources, tries to help us walk our talk in how we do our work, including our commitment to diversity. The whole staff of Sojourners was supportive of my writing this book and helped protect my space to do so.

Most of all, I want to thank J. K. Granberg-Michaelson, Research Assistant to the President, who was my primary partner in this book project—doing excellent research, providing vital information, material, and resources, helping with overall editing and content decisions, consistently offering good editorial judgment, and being a liaison with the publisher. J. K. is an extraordinary young man who did extraordinary work in helping me complete this book.

Mary Ann Richardson often provides hospitality for me in Daytona, Florida, for getting a book started, and did so again with this one. Her editorial insights are an extra gift!

Finally, I want to thank my family. My wife, Joy Carroll, has shown her commitment to diversity throughout her career as a priest in the Anglican Communion and now in her vocation as the "village priest" in all the school, sports, and community activities she now leads with our family. Our boys—Luke, 16, and Jack, 12—live in a diverse cultural world with their schools, sports, and friends. For them, multicultural living has become not only their experience but also their expectation. So many of our conversations around the house have contributed to this book.

This book is dedicated to Dr. Vincent Harding, who was an elder, mentor, and friend to me, to Sojourners since its beginnings, and to my family, where he is fondly remembered as "Uncle Vincent." Harding and his wife,

Rosemarie, were part of the inner circle of the southern freedom movement with Dr. Martin Luther King Jr., and he became an eminent and unique historian of the civil rights movement, having been both a courageous participant and a keen observer. Vincent passed in 2014. The afterword of this book suggests what Vincent might have to say to us today and how he would inspire us to cross the bridge to a new America.

Index

233